Reading Mastery Plus

SRA

Plus

Textbook B

Level 5

Siegfried Engelmann
Jean Osborn
Steve Osborn
Leslie Zoref

A Division of The McGraw-Hill Companies

Columbus, Ohio

Illustration Credits

Meg Aubrey, Jan Benham, Antonio Castro, John Edwards
and Associates, Doris Eltinger, Kate Flanagan, Anni
Matsick

www.sra4kids.com

SRA/McGraw-Hill

A Division of The McGraw·Hill Companies

Copyright © 2002 by SRA/McGraw-Hill.

Send all inquiries to:
SRA/McGraw-Hill
4400 Easton Commons
Columbus, OH 43219

Printed in the United States of America.

ISBN 0-07-569160-4

9 10 11 12 13 RRW 10 09 08 07

Table of Contents

Unit 3

Helping Others

Some people think only of themselves. They don't care about anybody else, and they rarely lend a helping hand.

Luckily, other people act differently. Instead of thinking only of themselves, they help others. The world is a better place because of their kindness.

In this unit, you will read biographies, myths, and folktales about people who help others. Each story is unique, but they all remind us of a common truth: It is better to give than to receive.

Jackie Robinson
The Golden Touch
The Miraculous Pitcher
Beauty and the Beast
Jane Addams

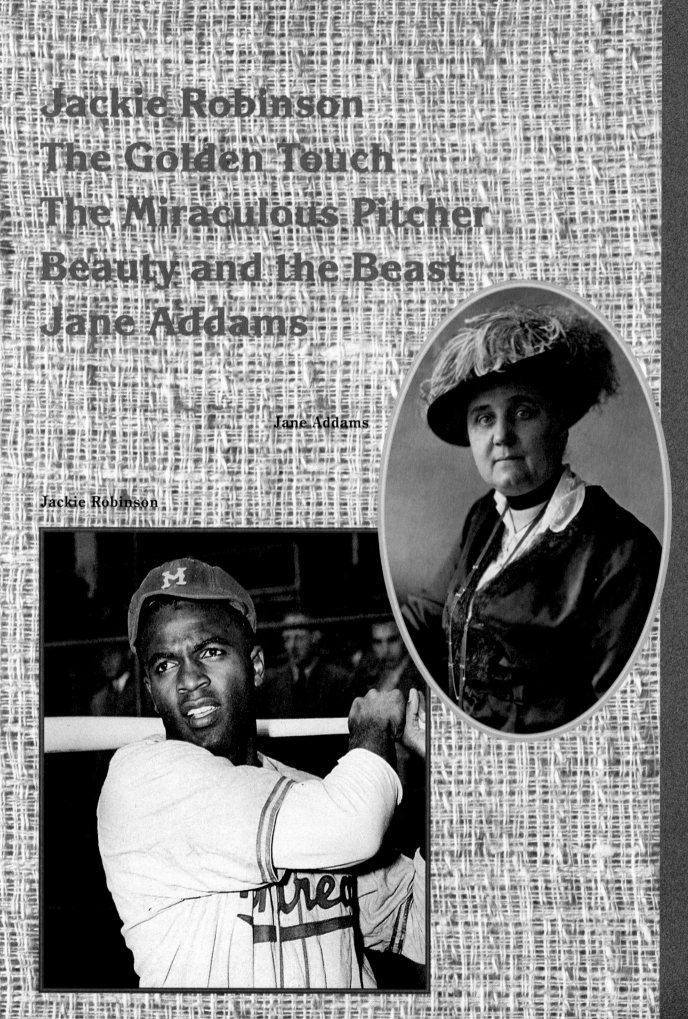

Jane Addams

Jackie Robinson

61

A WORD LISTS

1	2	3
Hard Words	*Word Practice*	*New Vocabulary*
1. Ebbets Field	1. Jackie Robinson	1. major leagues
2. Brooklyn	2. athlete	2. plant
3. entrance	3. Dodgers	3. bold
4. resent	4. umpire	4. daring
5. Phillies	5. league	5. athlete
		6. dugout
		7. biography
		8. narrator

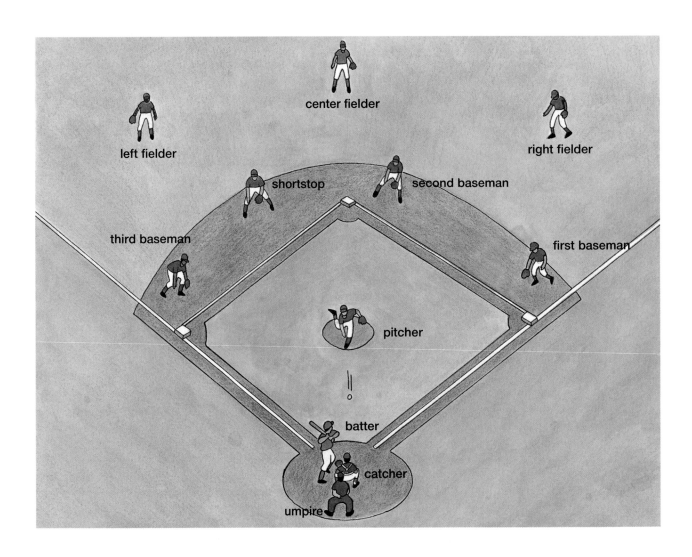

Facts about Baseball

The picture on the opposite page shows a game between two baseball teams, the Reds and the Blues. There are nine players on each team. All nine Blues are in the field. One player from the Reds is standing at home plate. That player is called the batter. The other Reds players are in the dugout, waiting for their turn at bat.

The pitcher on the blue team throws the ball toward the catcher, who plays behind home plate. There are players at first base, second base, and third base. Between second and third base is another player called the shortstop. In the outfield, there are three more players: the left fielder, the center fielder, and the right fielder.

When the pitcher throws the ball, the batter tries to hit the ball to a spot where nobody on the blue team can catch it. Then the batter runs as far as possible around the bases, starting with first base. If the batter can run all the way around the bases and come back to home plate, the batter scores a run.

The picture also shows an umpire right behind the catcher. The umpire calls out "Strike!" for good pitches and "Ball!" for bad pitches.

In this lesson, you will begin reading a biography of a famous baseball player, Jackie Robinson. Jackie's story is told by a fictional person. The narrator is fictional, but he tells facts about Jackie Robinson.

C READING

Jackie Robinson
by Duane Jefferson
Chapter 1

The year 1947 was a long time ago, but I can remember some things about that year as if they had happened yesterday. At that time, I worked in a meat-packing plant. The work was hard, and I didn't like it very much. But I had one great interest that made the days more exciting: I was a sports fan.

I didn't just enjoy watching good athletes compete in sporting events—I loved it! Every chance I had, I'd go to a football game or a basketball game or a boxing match. But my favorite team played right here in Brooklyn, New York. They played baseball.

That team is no longer in Brooklyn. They moved to Los Angeles in 1958, and now they're called the Los Angeles Dodgers. But back in 1947, they were the Brooklyn Dodgers. People used to call the Dodgers "the bums," but they sure weren't bums. They were rough, and they were good.

I never missed a game on the weekends. The Dodgers used to play in Ebbets Field. And when the Dodgers played on Saturday or Sunday, I'd be there in the stands. I'd be yelling at the umpire. I'd be booing the players from the other teams. And I'd be cheering like mad for the Dodgers.

For me, the games wouldn't end when they were over on the field. At work the next Monday, we'd talk about the weekend games, and we'd go over every play. I couldn't even begin to count the hours we spent talking about the Dodgers. We'd argue about who was the best hitter, who was the best first baseman, or who was the best pitcher. But we'd always agree on one thing—the Dodgers were the greatest. Even if they didn't win, they were the best team to watch. They were bold and daring. They were tough. And when they played baseball, they played the real thing. ♦

The other day I went to the place where Ebbets Field used to stand. It's not there anymore. There's nothing but city there now. But when I stood on the corner where the entrance used to be, I had a strange feeling. It was almost as if the clock had turned back to 1947. I could almost see

Ebbets Field, with a line of fans waiting to get in. I could almost hear the great roar that came from the stands when a Dodger hit a home run.

I must have stood on that corner for ten minutes, thinking back to 1947. A lot of games went through my mind, and I remembered a lot of great players. But as I stood there, the one player that my mind kept going back to was Jackie Robinson. It's amazing, but I can remember a game when the man sitting next to me said, "Why is that player wearing a Dodger uniform?"

I remember I turned to him and said, "Don't you read the papers? That's Jackie Robinson."

I'd read about Jackie Robinson. He was the first African American to play major league baseball, the very first one. And that day in April 1947 was the first time anybody ever saw an African American playing in a major league baseball game.

If I'd known then what I know now, I would have stood up and yelled, "Yea for Jackie!" I would have said, "He's the greatest! We should be shouting for joy that he's in a Dodger uniform!" But many Dodger fans were not cheering. They were asking each other why a black man was dressed in a Brooklyn Dodgers uniform.

Robinson was in a tight spot. He knew how some of the white fans and players felt about him. He knew they were looking for the slightest excuse to throw him out of the major leagues. When he walked out there on the first day at Ebbets Field, he looked like the loneliest person in the world. He was the only black man on the team—the only black man in the major leagues.

Some of the other players on the Dodgers wouldn't even talk to Robinson. They wouldn't joke with him or help him

out or stick up for him. Can you imagine what that's like—when the men on your team aren't with you? And the team's fans don't cheer for you?

Can you imagine how lonely Robinson must have felt each time he walked up to the plate with his bat? Sometimes, when I think about that day and realize what a fine, gentle person Robinson was, I get kind of choked up. But as I said, I didn't know much about Jackie Robinson back then.

D COMPREHENSION

Write the answers.
1. Why was the narrator so interested in sports?
2. Why didn't the games end for the narrator when they were over on the field?
3. Why did many of the fans not cheer for Jackie Robinson during the first game he played for the Dodgers?
4. Why did some of the other Dodgers not talk to Robinson?
5. How did Robinson feel during that first game? Why did he feel that way?

E WRITING

What is your favorite sport?
• Write an essay that explains your answer. Tell why you like your favorite sport better than other sports. Tell what experiences you've had playing or watching your favorite sport. Tell what you think of other sports.

A WORD LISTS

1	2	3	4
Place Names	*Word Practice*	*Vocabulary Review*	*New Vocabulary*
1. Pearl Harbor	1. Branch Rickey	1. bold	1. steal a base
2. Kansas City	2. Eddie Stanky	2. plant	2. National League pennant
3. Georgia	3. lousy	3. daring	3. talented
4. Hawaii	4. fault	4. athlete	4. insult
5. Germany	5. articles		5. rookie
6. Montreal	6. addition		
7. Kentucky	7. additional		

B STORY BACKGROUND

More Facts about Baseball

In the last lesson, you learned facts about the players on a baseball team. Here are more facts about how baseball is played.

The game lasts nine innings unless there is a tie. The number of innings is easy to remember because it's the same as the number of players on the team that's on the field—nine.

During each inning, both teams have a turn at batting. A team can continue to bat until it makes three outs. After the team makes three outs, it goes onto the field, and the other team takes a turn at batting.

If a game is tied at the end of nine innings, the teams play additional innings. They continue to play until one team is ahead of the other at the end of an inning.

The scoreboard on the next page shows the results of a game between the Dodgers and the Phillies. The number at the top of each column is the inning number. The number in each box below the inning number shows how many runs the team scored during that inning.

	1	2	3	4	5	6	7	8	9	10	11
Dodgers	1	5	0	0	0	0	0	0	0	0	3
Phillies	0	0	2	2	0	0	2	0	0	0	0

C READING

Jackie Robinson
Chapter 2

After Jackie Robinson's first game with the Dodgers, we had a lot of arguments at work. Some of the workers thought Robinson had every right to be in the majors, but others didn't agree. One man kept saying, "If you're a Dodger fan, you've got to be behind the whole team. That means you've got to be behind every player. When you're against one player, you're against the whole team." What he said kept running around in my head, and later on, I admitted to myself that he had a good point. But I still wasn't a big fan of Jackie Robinson.

I began to change my mind after the third game of the season, when Robinson hit his first major league home run. But what really changed my mind was a game between the Dodgers and the Phillies. During that game, the Phillies players yelled at

Robinson from the dugout and called him names. Instead of yelling back, Robinson just ignored them.

At first, we thought Robinson had no fight in him, but then we began to learn the true story. Robinson had made a deal with Branch Rickey, the general manager of the Dodgers. Rickey wanted to give black players a chance to compete in major league baseball. He didn't like the idea that talented black athletes could not play in the major leagues. So he picked Robinson to be the first black player in the majors. Rickey knew that if Robinson failed, other black players would have a tough time getting into the majors.

Rickey also knew that other major league teams didn't want black players. A couple of teams even said they wouldn't play the Dodgers if a black player was on

the team. Rickey knew there would be problems—big problems. So he selected a player who was strong enough to take insults without fighting back. That player was Jackie Robinson.

Before Robinson put on a Dodger uniform, he promised Rickey he wouldn't fight or argue or cause any kind of trouble. Rickey knew that if anything happened, some white people wouldn't even consider who was really at fault. Instead, they would just say, "Jackie Robinson is a troublemaker. Throw him out of the majors."

Can you imagine how much courage it took not to fight back and argue? Can you imagine what it would be like to know that you're as good as any other player on the field and listen to people call you names? ♦

During that game with the Phillies, every player on the Dodgers knew that Robinson had made a bargain with Rickey. They could see he had a lot of courage because he was keeping the bargain. So when the Phillies kept calling Robinson names, the second baseman for the Dodgers, Eddie Stanky, told the Phillies, "Why don't you yell at somebody who can answer back?" Then the Dodger shortstop, Pee Wee Reese, went over and put his arm around Robinson's shoulder. He was showing everybody he was on Robinson's side.

I started to get on Robinson's side, too. There was no way the Phillies could call him names. Robinson was a Dodger, and as far as I was concerned, I was going to stick up for him against the whole Phillies team.

After that game, I became one of Robinson's biggest fans. He was something to watch. He seemed to stir up the whole team and make all the players play better.

Sure, he could hit the ball. But when he got on base, that's when the action really started. He could steal a base as fast as you can blink your eye. He'd drive the pitchers on the other teams crazy. One pitcher said that when he pitched to Robinson, he would rather have him hit a home run than get a base hit. He said that with Robinson on the bases, he'd get so nervous he could hardly pitch for the rest of the inning. ★

The Dodgers really started to play great ball in 1947, and the player most responsible for the team's success was Jackie Robinson. It wasn't just his batting and his base stealing that fired up the team. It was the man. He was a fierce competitor, and he played baseball as if his life depended on it. The other Dodger players seemed to pick up this fierce way of playing. They were daring and confident. You never saw anybody loafing on that team.

Robinson played so well and became such a leader that the Dodgers won the National League pennant in 1947. Near the end of the season they had a Jackie Robinson Day at Ebbets Field. Before the game, people made speeches about Robinson and how they admired him. When it was Robinson's turn to talk, the crowd cheered long and loud.

After winning the National League pennant, the Dodgers played the New York Yankees in the World Series. I don't want to talk much about that series, because the Yankees won it. But the Dodgers still had a great year. Best of all, they had a new star—Jackie Robinson.

When the 1947 season was over, the National League gave Robinson the Rookie of the Year award. That winter, I did a lot of reading about Jackie Robinson. I read just about everything I could find. And the more I read, the more I realized how much courage that man had.

D COMPREHENSION

Write the answers.
1. How did Branch Rickey want to change major league baseball?
2. What agreement did Jackie Robinson make with Rickey before the 1947 season?
3. Explain how Robinson kept that agreement during the game with the Phillies.
4. Why did pitchers get so nervous when Robinson got on base?
5. What qualities did Robinson have that inspired the Dodgers to play great baseball?

E WRITING

Do you think it's harder to keep quiet or to fight back?
• Write an essay that explains your answer. Give an example of when you would have to choose between keeping quiet or fighting back. Explain what would happen if you kept quiet; then explain what would happen if you fought back. Which choice would be better? Why would it be better?

A WORD LISTS

1 *Hard Words*	2 *Vocabulary Review*	3 *New Vocabulary*
1. complain	1. insult	1. long jump
2. Edgar	2. rookie	2. complain
3. mechanic	3. resent	3. quarterback
4. Olympic	4. talented	4. mechanic
5. schedule		5. schedule

B READING

Jackie Robinson
Chapter 3

I began to read everything I could find about Jackie Robinson, and I learned a lot. I learned he was born in a small town in Georgia. When Robinson was still a baby, his mother moved the family to California. Robinson had three older brothers and an older sister. There was a lot of love in that family, but there was little money. The Robinsons were so poor that they sometimes did not have enough to eat.

Even though there was a lot of love in the family, you still wonder how Robinson ever made it. If you looked at Robinson a few years later, you'd have even more doubts that he'd ever be able to climb out of the world he lived in. When he was a young teenager, he became a member of a street gang—the Pepper Street Gang. They'd throw things at cars on the street. They'd knock out street lights at night. They'd go into nearby orchards and pick fruit from the trees. And sometimes they'd get caught by the police.

Robinson's mother didn't like what was happening to her son, but Robinson wanted to belong to a group. He wanted to be like some of the other kids in the neighborhood.

An auto mechanic named Carl Anderson helped Robinson look at the world in a different way. Anderson worked near Robinson's house. One day, he heard Robinson complaining to his mother that all the other kids were in the gang, so why shouldn't he be? Anderson told Robinson, "You're behaving just like a sheep." Anderson explained that sheep are stupid animals because they all follow one sheep without even thinking. Then he told Robinson, "You've got a good head, so use it—unless you want to be like a stupid sheep."

Robinson remembered what Anderson had said, so he started playing sports. One of Robinson's older brothers, Mack, was already a talented athlete. When Mack went to junior college, he set a record by jumping twenty-five feet. Later, Mack went to the Olympics and won a silver medal in the two hundred-meter dash. Let me tell you, that young man had talent. ◆

Robinson imitated everything his brothers did. He ran; he jumped; he practiced. In high school, he played football, basketball, and baseball. He was a star in all these sports.

After high school, Robinson went to a junior college. By now, sports were his whole life. He was a quarterback on the football team. In basketball, he was also a star. During one game, he scored a record number of points. In baseball, he was named the most valuable player in his junior college league. As you might guess, he was also a star in track.

One day showed just what a fierce competitor Robinson was. There was a baseball game scheduled in one city and a track meet in a city forty miles away. These events were scheduled at the same time, and Robinson was on both the baseball team and the track team. The track coach asked Robinson which sporting event he wanted to compete in. Robinson said, "Both." And he did compete in both.

The track coach arranged for Robinson to compete in the long jump early, before the other events. The idea was for Robinson to compete in the long jump, get into a waiting car, be driven forty miles, and play in the baseball game, which would already be under way. So Robinson did his first long jump. It was a good jump, a little over twenty-three feet. That was enough to win the event.

But Robinson wasn't satisfied. He said, "I can do better than that." So he jumped again. The second jump was more than a foot farther than the first.

The driver who was taking Jackie to the baseball game said, "Fantastic. Now let's get out of here."

Robinson shook his head and said, "I can do better than that." So he went for his third try. And what do you think? He jumped twenty-five feet, six and a half inches—more than half a foot farther than the record set by his brother Mack. ★

Finally, Robinson darted off the field, jumped into the car, and changed into his baseball uniform on the way to the game. There were only five innings left by the time they got there, but Robinson still managed to get two hits and help his team to a victory.

When Robinson finished junior college, he decided to go on to the University of California at Los Angeles (UCLA), which was close to his family's home. Robinson had a lot of reasons for going to UCLA, but the main reason was his brother Frank.

Unlike Jackie and Mack, Frank wasn't a star athlete. But he could coach, and he spent a lot of time working with Jackie, particularly when Jackie was getting started in high school and junior college. So Jackie chose UCLA because it was close to Frank.

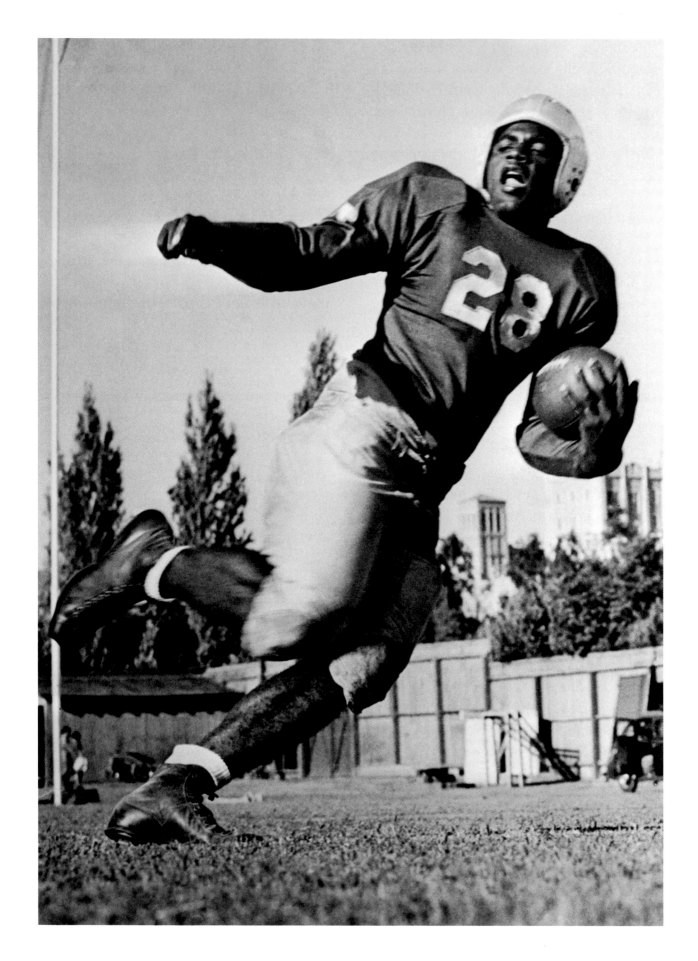

This part of Robinson's story has a sad ending. While Robinson was at UCLA, Frank was killed in an accident. That made Robinson feel terrible, but he turned his sadness into strength, and he played football, basketball, and baseball and ran track better than ever.

In football, Robinson set a college record for returning punts, and he led the team in scoring. In basketball, he was the top scorer in UCLA's league, even though he didn't get to play in all the games. In track, he was the best long jumper. Strangely enough, the sport he did the worst in was baseball. He was great when he got on base, but he didn't bat well.

Robinson was the first athlete in the history of UCLA to play on four teams—football, basketball, baseball, and track. In 1941, he was considered the best all-round college athlete in the United States. He could do anything. If any person ever deserved a chance to play professional baseball with the best players in the world, it was Jackie Robinson.

But Robinson was black, and in 1941, black athletes weren't allowed to play in the major leagues. Those leagues were only for white players.

C COMPREHENSION

Write the answers.
1. When he was in the Pepper Street Gang, how was Robinson like a sheep?
2. One day, Robinson competed in both a track meet and a baseball game. What did that show about his character?
3. Explain why Robinson's choice of going to UCLA had a sad ending.
4. The biography says that when Robinson was at UCLA, "Strangely enough, the sport he did the worst in was baseball." Why is that so strange?
5. Why couldn't Robinson play in the major leagues in 1941?

D WRITING

Write a conversation between Jackie Robinson and the mechanic Carl Anderson. In the conversation, Anderson is trying to convince Robinson to quit the Pepper Street Gang and play sports instead. Have Robinson give his reasons for wanting to stay in the gang. Have Anderson give reasons why Robinson should leave the gang. Also have Anderson explain what else Robinson could do.

A WORD LISTS

1
Hard Words
1. decent
2. promote
3. accuse
4. graduated
5. career
6. Monarchs
7. Rae

2
Word Practice
1. strict
2. restrict
3. Japanese
4. practice
5. sizzle
6. organize
7. organization

3
Vocabulary Review
1. complain
2. schedule
3. mechanic

4
New Vocabulary
1. promoted
2. officer
3. scout
4. organization

5
Vocabulary Preview
1. restricted to
2. decent
3. career
4. rattled

B VOCABULARY FROM CONTEXT

1. The hotels were **restricted to** white people, so no other people could go into them.
2. Jobs were so hard to find that he couldn't earn a **decent** living.
3. He was so interested in working as a coach that he decided to make coaching his **career**.
4. The pitcher became so **rattled** that he couldn't even hold the ball.

Jackie Robinson
Chapter 4

In 1941, Jackie Robinson was a big college star, but his family was still poor. His brother Mack could only find odd jobs, like cleaning up yards. A couple of years before, Mack had been the pride of the United States, winner of a medal in the Olympics. But now he couldn't even get a decent job. Why? Because he was black, and there weren't many good jobs for black people.

Robinson thought about his family and said to himself, "There is no point in continuing with this sports career." What would he get for the hours he put into practicing? What difference would it make that he had more sports talent than just about anybody in the world? He was black, and black players didn't play major league baseball, major league football, or any other major league sport. They could only play in the Negro leagues. The players in those leagues didn't earn much money, and they led a tough life.

So Robinson quit school and took a job, and then another job. Then, on Sunday, December 7, 1941, something terrible happened. The Japanese attacked Pearl Harbor, which is in Hawaii. On the same day, the United States declared war against Japan and Germany. The United States was now fighting in World War Two.

The day the United States entered World War Two was a sad day. I remember sitting by the radio all day long, listening to the news. At first, we figured that the war would be over in a couple of months, but it lasted until 1945.

In the spring of 1942, Robinson joined the United States Army. He was such a strong leader that he became an officer at an Army camp in Kansas. Black soldiers at the camp weren't allowed to sit next to white soldiers in the snack bar. Instead, the black soldiers had to eat in a small section that didn't have enough seats.

Robinson complained to the Army about the way black soldiers were treated at the camp. Finally, the Army increased the number of seats for black soldiers, but they still had to eat in their own section. ♦

When Robinson got out of the Army in 1944, he wanted to marry a young woman named Rae. She was studying to be a nurse, and she had known Robinson since he'd been at UCLA.

Rae lived in California, and Robinson wanted to be near her, but he couldn't get a good sports job in California. So in 1945, he went to Kansas City and took a job with the most famous Negro League team—the Kansas City Monarchs. For the first time in his life, Robinson earned good money—four hundred dollars a month. That was more money than Robinson had ever seen.

But when the Monarchs went from city

to city, it was the same old story. The team could not stay in the same hotels white people stayed in. Often the players had to sleep in the team bus. In some cities, the players couldn't even eat in restaurants because the restaurants were restricted to white people. So the players ate sandwiches on the bus.

After a while, Robinson got tired of traveling with the Monarchs. He didn't get to see Rae very often because he was moving around all the time. So he finally decided to quit the Monarchs, go back to California, and try to get a job there. In the back of his mind, he had a great desire to play major league baseball. But that didn't seem possible. To Robinson, it seemed that as long as he stayed in baseball, he would go from city to city in the Monarchs' bus and feel like somebody who didn't really belong.

Just when Robinson made up his mind to quit the Monarchs, something happened that changed his whole life. The Monarchs were playing in Chicago. One of the scouts from the Brooklyn Dodgers told Robinson that Branch Rickey, the general manager of the Dodgers, was thinking of starting a new league for black players. The scout told Robinson that this league would pay the players more money and offer better living conditions. Robinson was interested, so he agreed to meet with Rickey.

Rickey wasn't really thinking of forming a new league. Instead, he wanted his scouts to find one outstanding black baseball player. This player had to have enough courage to stand up against the trouble he would experience as the first black player in the major leagues. Rickey wanted a player who could thrill the crowd with his

skill. He wanted a player who would be a leader and who wouldn't quit.

Rickey had been looking at many black players. But when he met with Jackie Robinson, he knew he had found the right man. He already knew a lot about Robinson from his scouts' reports. He knew Robinson was smart, that he was brave, and that his coaches admired him.

Imagine how Robinson felt on that day in Brooklyn when he walked into Rickey's office. Robinson had almost accepted the idea that he would never play in the major leagues. Imagine how he felt when he heard Rickey say, "I'll tell you the real reason you're here. You were brought here to play for the Dodger organization. I want you to start with our top minor league team, the Montreal Royals. If you do well, you'll get to play for the Brooklyn Dodgers."

Robinson sat there shocked, trying to make sense out of what Rickey had told him. The Montreal Royals were the best minor league team in the whole Dodger organization. Every year, the best players from the Royals and other minor league teams would move up to the major leagues.

Then Rickey and Robinson talked about how hard it would be for Robinson to be the first black player in the major leagues. Rickey said, "I need someone who is strong enough to take insults without fighting back." He told Robinson that white people would be watching him. If Robinson got into the slightest trouble, many of them would blame him, regardless of whose fault the trouble really was.

"It's not going to be easy," Rickey said. And it certainly wasn't.

D COMPREHENSION

Write the answers.
1. When Robinson was at UCLA, why did he think there was no point in continuing his sports career?
2. When Robinson was in the Army, how did he improve conditions for black soldiers?
3. How were players on the Monarchs treated differently from white players?
4. Why did Branch Rickey want to meet with Robinson?
5. Why did Rickey want Robinson to take insults without fighting back?

E WRITING

Write a conversation between Branch Rickey and Jackie Robinson. During the conversation, Rickey should offer Robinson a chance to play baseball with the Dodgers. Have Rickey explain why he wants Robinson to play with the Dodgers and what challenges Robinson will face. Have Robinson explain how he feels about the offer. Have them agree on a plan for making the offer work.

65

A WORD LISTS

1 *Hard Words*	**2** *Word Practice*	**3** *Vocabulary Review*	**4** *New Vocabulary*
1. balk	1. lease	1. restricted to	1. contract
2. cousin	2. release	2. organization	2. cousin
3. honor	3. field	3. promoted	3. balk
	4. fielding	4. officer	
		5. rattled	
		6. decent	
		7. career	

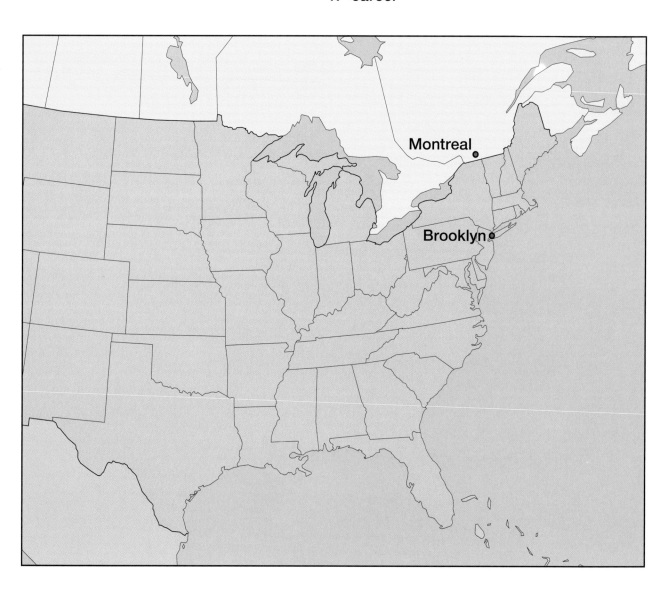

Jackie Robinson
Chapter 5

Branch Rickey made it very plain to Robinson that Robinson would have a tough time playing for the Montreal Royals. He said Robinson would be all alone and the other players would resent him. The last thing he said was that Robinson should marry Rae. Then he added, "You're going to need her with you from now on."

When word got out that Robinson had signed a contract with Montreal, all the papers carried the story. In March 1946, Robinson joined the Royals for spring training in Florida. Then Rae and Jackie got married. For a while, Rae was just about the only friend Jackie had.

The first time Robinson walked into the locker room with the other Montreal players, he tried to be friendly, but they didn't talk to him. The coaches and trainers talked to him, but not the other players.

Each day Robinson got dressed in his new uniform and went onto the field. He saw the wives of the players sitting in the stands and watching the practice. Then he saw Rae sitting all by herself. Robinson was hurt and angry. There she was, the person he loved more than anybody in the world, and the other wives wouldn't even talk to her.

Rae would smile at Jackie and wave. He would smile and wave back. Robinson knew he wasn't the only one who had to be brave. One day Jackie told Rae he hated to see her treated that way. But she smiled, shook her head, and said, "Don't worry. Things will soon be better for us. And thanks to you, they'll soon be better for all black athletes." ♦

That is what Robinson had to keep reminding himself—that he would make things better for other black athletes. Every time he wanted to fight, and every time he didn't think he could take it anymore, he tried to remember he was doing something important. He told himself that even though he had to suffer, he was doing something that could help other black players. So he worked and worked, and he worked even harder.

One day, the Royals played a practice game with the Dodgers. At first, the fans yelled at Robinson. He was scared, but he was also determined.

Robinson was in the field, playing second base. A Dodger batter smashed a fast ground ball that looked like a hit. Robinson raced for the ball, scooped it up, and in one quick motion, fired it to the first baseman. The batter was out, and people in the stands started to say things like, "Did you see that man move?" and "What speed!" Robinson made a lot of dazzling plays in that game, and the fans were impressed.

The first game Montreal played after spring training in Florida was held across

the river from New York City. The place was crowded with people who had come to see Jackie. The first time Robinson was up to bat, these people didn't have much to cheer about. He tapped a little ground ball that dribbled toward the shortstop. Out!

But the next time Robinson was up, he brought all the fans to their feet. Two Montreal players were on base. The pitcher threw Robinson a sizzling fast ball. Crack! By the sound of the bat, the fans knew the ball was gone. There it went, a shot over the left field fence. It was a home run, with three players scoring. When Robinson crossed home plate, both players who had just scored shook his hand and slapped him on the back. ★

The next time Robinson was up, he got on first base with a hit. Before the pitcher settled down, Robinson stole second base, and the crowd went wild. Suddenly, Robinson stole third base. The pitcher got so rattled with Robinson dancing around on third base that he threw the ball to third after he had wound up for the pitch. That's a balk, which meant that Robinson could walk to home plate and score.

The crowd cheered and shouted. That game showed the kind of baseball that Robinson could play. He was daring and al-ways ready to take a chance. He was so good at stealing bases that the other team couldn't throw the ball fast enough to get him out.

When Robinson arrived in Montreal after the Royals had won three games on the road, the fans loved him, and he loved the city.

There were still rough times ahead for Robinson. During one game, one of the players in the other team's dugout threw a black cat onto the field. The player yelled, "Hey, Robinson, there's your cousin!"

Robinson looked over at the cat and said nothing. But a few moments later, he was at bat, and he made his bat do all his talking for him. He smashed the ball and ran like a streak to second base. When one of the Montreal players hit a single, Robinson scored. As he went past the dugout of the other team, he said in a very pleasant tone, "Well, I guess my cousin is pretty happy now."

By the end of the season, Robinson had answered every player on the other teams who insulted him. He answered in a language they all understood. The Montreal Royals won their minor league pennant, and Jackie Robinson was the top batter in the league.

C COMPREHENSION

Write the answers.

1. How was the treatment Rae received during spring training like the treatment Robinson received?
2. What did Robinson remind himself of every time he wanted to fight?
3. What made Robinson such a great base runner?
4. When another player threw a cat onto the field, what did the player mean by saying the cat was Robinson's cousin?
5. The biography says that Robinson answered the players who insulted him "in a language they all understood." What does that mean?

D WRITING

Pretend you are a sports reporter.

• Write a newspaper article about one of the games Robinson played with the Royals. Tell what happened in the game. Tell who made the hits, who scored the runs, and what the final score was. Tell which players made outstanding plays. Also tell about any other events that occurred during the game.

66

A WORD LISTS

1
Vocabulary Review
1. balk
2. contract
3. cousin

2
New Vocabulary
1. oppose
2. honor
3. retire
4. defeat

Jackie Robinson
Chapter 6

After the Montreal Royals won their minor league pennant, they played a team from Kentucky in the minor league World Series. The first team to win four games would win the series, which began with three games in Kentucky. In those three games, Robinson got only one hit, and the Royals lost twice.

Robinson was worried about how the fans in Montreal would respond to him now that the Royals were behind in the series two games to one. He was in for a pleasant surprise when the Kentucky team came to Montreal. The Royals won three games in Montreal and won the series. And I'll bet you can figure out who scored the winning run of the last game.

Robinson had changed the minds of many people in Montreal. The manager of the Royals had been strongly opposed to having a black player on the team. That was before the beginning of the season. At the end of the season, the manager told Robinson, "You're a great baseball player and a fine gentleman. It's been wonderful having you on the team."

The next year was 1947, which was when I began watching Robinson. For me, it was all new. Sure, I had read some of the reports about Robinson before I saw him play. But he was just so many numbers on a piece of paper. The numbers told me that the man could bat, steal bases, play the field, and win. But still, when I saw him for the first time, I had my doubts.

By the end of Robinson's first season, I was singing a different tune, along with the rest of the Brooklyn fans. We were behind Robinson all the way as he led the Dodgers to a National League pennant. And we stayed behind him for ten years. I remember how proud I was of him each time he earned a new honor, particularly in 1949. In that year, the Dodgers won the National League pennant again, and Robinson was the league's batting champion. He was also named the league's most valuable player.

By 1949, other teams were bringing black players into the major leagues, and that made Robinson feel good. Also during that year, Branch Rickey released Robinson from his promise not to fight back. Rickey said, "You've proved that you're a great player. So now you can do what you want." ♦

During the years that followed, Robinson received honor after honor. And he earned every one of them. He was named to the All-Star Team year after year, and during many of those years, the Dodgers won the National League pennant. But after winning the pennant, they'd play the New York Yankees in the World Series and lose.

By 1955, people were saying that Robinson was getting too old for the game. He didn't play much during that year, but the Dodgers still made it to the World Series with the Yankees.

The Yankees took the first two games. In the third game, Robinson came to bat with the score tied at two. Most fans cheered encouragement to him, but a few said, "What's Old Man Robinson doing out there?"

They found out. He hit a single. Now he was on base, and now the old magic started. Robinson danced around so much that the pitcher hit the next batter with a pitch.

Now Robinson was on second base. The next batter got a hit and Robinson shot to third. The bases were now loaded. Robinson kept running toward home plate and stopping. The pitcher became so rattled that he walked the next batter.

Robinson walked home, and the crowd went wild.

The next time Robinson got up to bat, he slugged a clean double, but he stretched it into a three-base hit. He scored when the next batter got a hit. The Dodgers won that game and the next two games. Finally, in the seventh and last game of the Series, Brooklyn won. I couldn't believe it. I never thought I'd see Brooklyn win the World Series, but they did, for the first and only time. ★

People celebrated all over Brooklyn. For a week, every time I'd look at one of the guys at work, we'd smile at each other. We didn't have to say anything. Thanks to Robinson, Brooklyn had won the World Series.

After the 1956 season, Robinson retired from baseball. He was thirty-seven years old, and he had slowed down a lot. I wrote him a letter after he retired. I told him I thought he was the greatest and that I'd miss him. He wrote back and thanked me for my letter.

I still have Robinson's letter, and I have a lot of pictures of Robinson and a lot of books about him. But, most of all, I have memories. I've got happy memories, like the memory of Robinson being elected to the Baseball Hall of Fame. I've got sad memories, like the memory of Robinson's son being killed in a car accident in 1971.

The saddest memory of all is of Robinson's death in 1972, just a few days after the Dodgers retired the number he wore on his uniform—42. He was only fifty-three years old when he died. One of the men I worked with came over and said, "A brave man is dead."

That's what he was, a brave man who could teach all of us about the meaning of the word *courage*. You can search the world over for a person who has more strength, courage, and talent than Jackie Robinson. You're not going to find one. One sports writer did a good job of describing Robinson in one sentence. He wrote, "He would not be defeated, not by the other team and not by life."

C COMPREHENSION

Write the answers.

1. The narrator describes several of Jackie Robinson's seasons with the Royals and Dodgers, including 1946, 1947, 1949, and 1955. Which season do you think was Robinson's best? Explain your answer.

2. In 1949, Branch Rickey released Robinson from his promise not to fight back. Why had Robinson made that promise in the first place?

3. What do you think Robinson proved to the fans by his plays in the 1955 World Series?

4. One of the narrator's friends said that Robinson was a brave man. Give some examples of Robinson's bravery.

5. One sports writer said, "Robinson would not be defeated, not by the other team and not by life." What do you think that statement means?

D MAIN IDEA

For each passage, write the main idea.

1. Trucks use the freeway.
   Cars use the freeway.
   Buses use the freeway.

2. Hubert put on his pants.
   Hubert put on his shirt.
   Hubert put on his shoes and socks.

3. Francesca sat on her bike.
   Francesca turned the pedals.
   Francesca went down the street.

4. People love to watch baseball.
   People love to watch hockey.
   People love to watch football.

E WRITING

Pretend you are a Brooklyn Dodger fan who has watched Jackie Robinson play from 1947 through 1956. You have just found out Robinson is retiring from baseball.

• Write a letter to Robinson and tell him what he meant to you.

67

A WORD LISTS

1
Compound Words
1. Marygold
2. buttercup
3. farewell
4. bedside
5. handrail
6. staircase
7. hallway

2
Word Practice
1. petal
2. fragrant
3. conclude
4. perfume
5. concluded

3
Vocabulary Preview
1. inhale
2. calculate
3. sift
4. gleam

B VOCABULARY FROM CONTEXT

1. The athlete controlled his breathing by first breathing out, then **inhaling**.
2. He was always figuring things out. So when he looked at the gifts, he **calculated** what they must have cost.
3. The little girl poured sand into her hand and watched it **sift** through her fingers.
4. The bowl was so bright and shiny that it **gleamed** in the sunlight.

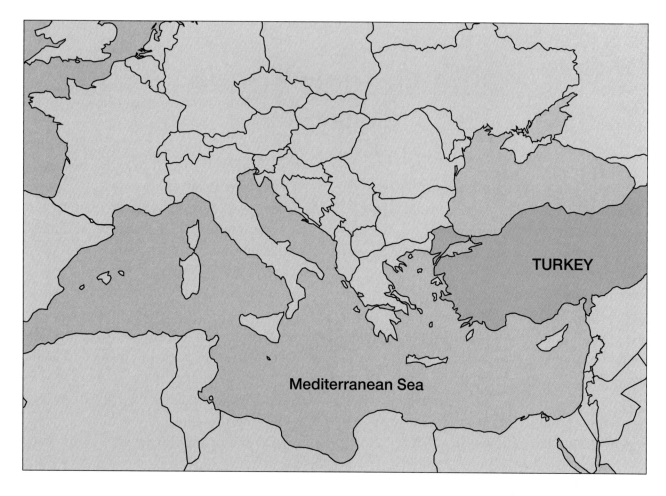

Today you will begin reading "The Golden Touch," a myth that takes place thousands of years ago in Turkey, a country on the Mediterranean Sea.

A myth is an old, old story that often includes gods or goddesses. Many myths try to explain how the world began or where people came from. Other myths describe the adventures of ancient heroes or teach us lessons about how to behave.

"The Golden Touch" teaches us a lesson about gold. As you read the myth, think about what it means and if its lesson is still true today.

The Golden Touch
Chapter 1

Once upon a time in ancient Turkey there lived a rich king named Midas, who had a daughter named Marygold.

King Midas was very fond of gold. The only thing he loved more was his daughter. But the more Midas loved his daughter, the more he desired gold. He thought the best thing he could possibly do for his child would be to give her the largest pile of yellow, glistening coins that had ever been heaped together since the world began. So Midas gave all his thoughts and all his time to collecting gold.

When Midas gazed at the gold-tinted clouds of sunset, he wished they were real gold and that they could be herded into his strong box. When little Marygold ran to meet him with a bunch of buttercups and dandelions, he used to say, "Pooh, pooh, child. If these flowers were as golden as they look, they would be worth picking."

And yet, in his earlier days, before he had this insane desire for gold, Midas had shown a great love for flowers. He had planted a garden with the biggest and sweetest roses any person ever saw or smelled. These roses were still growing in the garden, as large, as lovely, and as fragrant as they were when Midas used to pass whole hours looking at them and inhaling their perfume. But now, if he looked at the flowers at all, it was only to calculate how much the garden would be worth if each of the rose petals was a thin plate of gold. ♦

After a while, Midas became so unreasonable that he could scarcely bear to see or touch any object that was not gold. Therefore, he passed a large part of every day in a dark and dreary room underground, in the basement of his palace. It was here that he kept his wealth. Midas went to this dismal hole whenever he wanted to be particularly happy. After carefully locking the door, he would take a bag of gold coins or a golden bowl as big as a hat or a heavy golden bar or a bag of gold dust. He would bring his precious gold objects from the corners of the room into the one bright and narrow sunbeam that came from the window. He only liked the sunbeam because it made his treasure shine.

Midas would then count the coins in the bag or toss up the bar and catch it as it came down or sift the gold dust through his fingers. He would often look at the funny reflection of his own face in the polished surface of a golden bowl. At those times, he would whisper to himself, "Oh, Midas, rich King Midas, what a happy man you are."

But it was strange to see how the reflection of his face kept grinning at him out of the polished surface of the bowl. It seemed to be aware of his foolish behavior and to make fun of him. ★

Midas called himself a happy man, but he felt he was not as happy as he might be. His peak of enjoyment would never be reached unless the whole world became his treasure room, filled with his own gold.

One day, Midas was enjoying himself in his treasure room as usual when he saw a shadow fall over the heaps of gold. He looked up and saw a stranger standing in the bright and narrow sunbeam. It was a young man with a cheerful face. King Midas thought the smile on the stranger's face had a kind of golden glow. And even though the stranger blocked the sunshine, the gleam upon all the piled-up treasures was brighter than before. Even the corners were lit up when the stranger smiled.

Midas knew he had carefully turned the key in the lock and that no human being could possibly break into his treasure room. So Midas concluded that his visitor must be a god. In those days, gods interested themselves in the joys and sorrows of men, women, and children. Midas had met gods before, and he was happy to meet another. The stranger's face was so kind that it seemed as if he had come to do Midas a favor.

E COMPREHENSION

Write the answers.

1. Why did Midas give all his thoughts and time to collecting gold?
2. When Midas looked at roses now, what would he calculate?
3. What was the only reason Midas liked the sunbeam in his treasure room?
4. Why did Midas think the stranger must be a god?
5. What kind of favor do you think the stranger might do for Midas? Explain your answer.

F WRITING

Would you like to be Midas?

• Write an essay that explains your answer. Tell which parts of Midas's life you like and which parts you don't like. Then explain why you would or wouldn't want to be Midas.

A WORD LISTS

1
Hard Words
1. linen
2. frenzy
3. appetite
4. credit
5. woven
6. despair
7. pity
8. secure

2
Word Endings
1. precious
2. delicious
3. anxious
4. spacious

3
Word Practice
1. flexible
2. convenient
3. inconvenient
4. accompany
5. accompanied

4
New Vocabulary
1. deserve
2. linen
3. frenzy
4. occupied
5. envy
6. despair

5
Vocabulary Preview
1. discontent
2. appetite
3. secure
4. pity

B VOCABULARY FROM CONTEXT

1. She was unhappy about many things, but she was most **discontented** about the mess in the basement.
2. When he started eating he had a huge **appetite**, but when he had finished the main part of the meal, he had no room for dessert.
3. He didn't want anybody to steal his treasure, so he looked for a **secure** place to keep it.
4. The little boy was so poor, sad, and cold that I felt great **pity** for him.

The Golden Touch
Chapter 2

The stranger gazed about the room, and when his glowing smile had shone on all the golden objects, he turned again to Midas.

"You are a wealthy man, friend Midas," he observed. "I doubt whether any other four walls on earth contain so much gold as this room contains."

"I have done pretty well—pretty well," answered Midas in a discontented tone. "But after all, it is a very small amount when you consider that it has taken me my whole life to gather this much gold. If one could live a thousand years, he might have time to grow rich."

"What?" exclaimed the stranger. "Then you are not satisfied?"

Midas shook his head.

"And what would satisfy you?" asked the stranger. "I would like to know."

Midas paused. He felt this stranger had the power to grant any wish. He had only to speak and obtain whatever he might want. So he thought and thought and thought. His imagination heaped up one golden mountain after another. But he was unable to imagine mountains that were big enough. At last, a bright idea occurred to King Midas. It seemed really as bright as the glistening metal he loved so much.

Raising his head, he looked the stranger in the face.

The visitor observed, "Well, Midas, I see you have at last hit on something that will satisfy you. Tell me your wish."

"It is only this," replied Midas. "I am weary of collecting my treasures with so much trouble and seeing the heap so small after I have done my best. I wish everything I touch could be changed into gold!"

"The Golden Touch!" exclaimed the stranger. "You certainly deserve credit, friend Midas, for having such a brilliant idea. But are you quite sure this will satisfy you?"

"How could it fail?" said Midas.

"And you will never regret having it?"

"What could make me regret it?" asked Midas. "I need nothing else to make me perfectly happy."

"You shall have your wish," replied the stranger, waving his hand in farewell. "To-morrow at sunrise, you will find yourself gifted with the Golden Touch." ♦

The stranger then became so terribly bright that Midas closed his eyes. When he opened them again, he saw only one yellow sunbeam in the room. All around him was the glistening of the precious metal he had spent his life collecting.

Midas did not sleep well that night. His mind was like the mind of a child who has been promised a new plaything in the morning. Day had hardly peeped over the hills when King Midas was wide awake. He

stretched his arms out of bed and began to touch objects that were within reach. He was anxious to prove whether the Golden Touch had really come, according to the stranger's promise.

Midas laid his finger on a chair by the bedside, and on other things, but he was disappointed to find they remained exactly the same as before. He was afraid he had only dreamed about the stranger or that the stranger had been making fun of him. And how miserable it would be if Midas had to be content with the little gold he could scrape together by ordinary means, instead of creating gold by a touch.

All this happened while it was only the gray of the morning, with only a streak of brightness along the edge of the sky. Midas was in a very bad mood. He kept growing sadder and sadder until the earliest sunbeam shone through the window and lit up the ceiling over his head. It seemed to Midas that this bright yellow sunbeam reflected in an unusual way on the white covering of the bed. Looking more closely, he was astonished and delighted to find that this linen cloth had been changed into woven gold, the purest and brightest he had ever seen! The Golden Touch had come to him with the first sunbeam!

Midas started up in a joyful frenzy and ran about the room grasping at everything that happened to be in his way. He seized one of the bedposts, and it immediately became a golden pillar. He pulled open a window curtain, and the cord grew heavy in his hand—a mass of gold. Midas took up a book from the table. At his first touch, the cover became solid gold. And when he ran his fingers through the pages, the book became a bundle of thin gold plates, and all the wise words in the book disappeared. ★

Midas quickly put on his clothes and was overjoyed to see himself in a magnificent suit of gold cloth. The cloth was flexible and soft, but it was heavy. Then Midas drew out his handkerchief, which little Marygold had made for him. That was also gold.

Somehow or other this last change did not quite please King Midas. He would have rather had his little daughter's handkerchief remain just as it was when she climbed upon his knee and put it into his hand.

But it was not worthwhile to worry about a handkerchief. Midas now took his spectacles from his pocket and put them on his nose to see more clearly. But he discovered that he could not possibly see through them, for the glass had turned into a plate of yellow metal. They were worthless as spectacles, but valuable as gold. It seemed rather inconvenient to Midas that, with all his wealth, he could never again be rich enough to own a pair of usable spectacles.

"It is no great problem," he said to himself. "Every great good is accompanied by some small inconvenience. The Golden Touch is worth the loss of a pair of spectacles. My own eyes will serve for ordinary purposes, and little Marygold will soon be old enough to read to me."

Wise King Midas was so excited by his good fortune that the palace did not seem large enough for him. He therefore went downstairs, and he smiled when the handrail of the staircase became a bar of gold as his hand passed over it. He lifted the door latch. It was brass only a moment ago, but it became golden when his fingers left it. He went into the garden, where he found a great number of beautiful roses in full bloom and others in all the stages of lovely bud and blossom. Their fragrance was delicious in the morning breeze.

But Midas knew a way to make them far more precious, to his way of thinking. So he went from bush to bush and used his magic touch until every flower and bud was changed to gold. By the time this work was completed, King Midas was called to breakfast. The morning air had given him an excellent appetite, and he quickly returned to the palace.

D COMPREHENSION

Write the answers.
1. Why did Midas decide to ask for the golden touch?
2. How do you think the stranger feels about Midas? Explain your answer.
3. How can you tell that the stranger is a god?
4. Why do you think Midas wasn't pleased when his handkerchief turned to gold?
5. What problems do you think Midas will have when he eats breakfast?

E WRITING

Midas has already turned several objects into gold.
- Write an essay that compares what those objects were like before they were turned into gold and what they are like now. Tell how Midas used those objects before they turned to gold and how he might use them now. Describe how valuable those objects were before and how valuable they are now. Finally, give your opinion about whether those objects should have been changed to gold.

69

A WORD LISTS

1	2	3	4
Hard Words	*Word Practice*	*Vocabulary Review*	*Vocabulary Review*
1. occupy	1. experiment	1. deserve	1. appetite
2. ornaments	2. breakfast	2. pity	2. occupied
3. terrify	3. potato	3. secure	3. linen
	4. appearance	4. discontented	4. frenzy
	5. woven	5. envy	5. despair

B READING

The Golden Touch
Chapter 3

On this particular morning, King Midas's breakfast consisted of hotcakes, some nice little fish, roasted potatoes, fresh boiled eggs, and tea. There was also a bowl of bread and milk for his daughter, Marygold. This was a breakfast fit for a king!

Little Marygold had not yet made her appearance, so her father ordered her to be called. Then Midas seated himself at the table and waited for his daughter to arrive before beginning his own breakfast. Midas really loved his daughter, and he loved her even more this morning because of his good fortune. It was not long before he heard her coming along the hallway, crying bitterly.

Her crying surprised him because Marygold was almost always cheerful and hardly shed a spoonful of tears in a year. When Midas heard her sobs, he decided to put the girl into better spirits by giving her a surprise. So he leaned across the table and touched her pretty bowl. The bowl was instantly changed to gleaming gold, but because Midas did not touch the bread and milk, they did not change.

Meanwhile, Marygold slowly and sadly opened the door. She held her apron at her eyes and sobbed as if her heart would break.

Midas asked, "What is the matter with you this bright morning?"

Marygold, without taking the apron from her eyes, held out her hand and showed Midas one of the roses that had recently changed to gold.

"Beautiful!" exclaimed her father. "And what is there in that magnificent golden rose to make you cry?"

"Ah, dear Father," answered the child through her sobs. "It is not beautiful, but the ugliest flower that ever grew. As soon as I was dressed, I ran into the garden to gather some roses for you because I know you like them. But all the beautiful roses that smelled so sweet and had so many lovely colors are spoiled! They have become quite yellow, just like this one, and they no longer have any fragrance. What is the matter with them?" ♦

Midas said, "Pooh, my dear little girl. Please don't cry about it." Midas was ashamed to admit that he had brought about the change which saddened her. "Sit down and eat your bread and milk. But don't be sad. You can easily exchange the golden rose for an ordinary one that would wither in a day."

"I don't care for such roses as this!"

cried Marygold, tossing it away. "It has no smell, and the hard petals stab my nose!"

The child now sat down at the table, but she was so occupied with her grief that she did not even notice the wonderful change in her bowl. Perhaps this was for the best. Marygold usually took pleasure in looking at the odd figures that were painted on the bowl, yet these ornaments were now entirely lost in the yellow metal.

Midas, meanwhile, had poured out a cup of tea, and the teapot, which had been brass, was gold when he set it down. He thought to himself that it was unusual to eat off golden plates, and he began to worry about keeping his treasures safe. The cupboard and the kitchen would no longer be a secure place to keep articles so valuable as golden bowls and teapots.

As he was thinking these thoughts, he lifted a spoonful of tea to his lips and, sipping it, was astonished to notice that the instant his lips touched the liquid, the tea became liquid gold, and the next moment, it hardened into a lump.

"Ugh!" Midas exclaimed.

"What is the matter, Father?" little Marygold asked, gazing at him with the tears still in her eyes.

"Nothing, child, nothing," said Midas. "Eat your bread and milk before they get cold."

He looked at one of the nice little fish on his plate and touched it with his golden fork and then experimented by touching its tail with his finger. To his horror, it immediately changed from a fried fish into a gold fish. But it was not like a goldfish that people often keep in fish bowls. It was a metal fish that looked as if it had been made by a goldsmith. Its little bones were now golden wires; its fins and tail were thin plates of gold; and there were the marks of the fork in it. It was a very pretty piece of work—except King Midas would rather have had a real fish in his dish instead of this valuable imitation. ★

He thought to himself, "I don't quite see how I am to eat any breakfast."

He took one of the hotcakes and had scarcely broken it when it turned yellow. If it had been an ordinary white hotcake, Midas would have prized it a good deal more than he now did. Almost in despair, he helped himself to a boiled egg, which immediately changed the same way the fish and hotcake had changed.

"Well, this is a problem," he thought, leaning back in his chair and looking with envy at Marygold as she ate her bread and milk with great satisfaction. Midas said to himself, "My breakfast is quite valuable, but I cannot eat it."

Midas thought he might solve his problem by moving faster. He snatched a hot potato and attempted to cram it into his mouth and swallow it in a hurry. But the Golden Touch was too nimble for him. He found his mouth full of solid metal, which so burnt his tongue that he roared aloud. He jumped up from the table and began to dance and stamp about the room, feeling both pain and fright.

"Father, dear Father," cried Marygold. "What is the matter? Have you burnt your mouth?"

"Ah, dear child," groaned Midas sadly. "I don't know what is to become of your poor father."

And truly Midas was a person you should pity. Here was the richest breakfast that could be set before a king, but its richness was worth absolutely nothing to Midas. The poorest farmer, sitting down to his crust of bread and cup of water, was far better off than King Midas, although the fine food that Midas had before him was worth its weight in gold. And what was he to do? Already, Midas was extremely hungry. How would he feel by dinnertime? How many days could he survive on golden food?

Midas's hunger and despair were so great that he groaned aloud and very sadly, too. Marygold could endure it no longer. She gazed at her father a moment to discover what was the matter with him. Then with a sweet and sorrowful desire to comfort him, she started from her chair. She ran to Midas and threw her arms about him. He bent down and kissed her. At that moment, he felt that his little daughter's love was worth a thousand times more than the Golden Touch.

"My precious, precious Marygold!" he cried.

But Marygold made no answer.

C COMPREHENSION

Write the answers.

1. What reasons did Marygold have for not liking the golden rose?
2. The story says, "Midas was a person you should pity." Explain why you should pity him.
3. Why was the poorest farmer better off than Midas?
4. Why did Midas feel his daughter's love was worth more than the golden touch?
5. What do you think Midas will do in the next chapter? Why?

D WRITING

In the story, Midas learns that his daughter's love is worth much more than the golden touch. What things in your life are worth the most to you?

- Write an essay that explains your answer. Tell about the different things your have in your life, such as your parents, friends, toys, and activities. Then tell which of those things are worth the most to you and why. Explain what your life would be like if you didn't have those things.

A WORD LISTS

1	2	3	4
Hard Words	**Word Endings**	**Word Practice**	**New Vocabulary**
1. original	1. deadly	1. teardrops	1. insane
2. victim	2. faithfully	2. wring	2. dimple
3. desolate	3. seriously	3. moisten	3. greedy
	4. sincerely	4. stretched	4. glossy
	5. immediately	5. outstretched	5. original
	6. instantly	6. terrify	6. victim
		7. county	
		8. country	
		9. countries	

B READING

The Golden Touch
Chapter 4

What had Midas done? The moment his lips touched Marygold's forehead, a change had taken place. Her sweet, rose-colored face changed to a glittering yellow color, with yellow teardrops on her cheeks. Her beautiful brown hair took the same yellow color. Her soft and tender little form grew hard and rigid as she stood within her father's arms. She was the victim of her father's insane desire for wealth. Marygold was no longer a human child, but a golden statue.

Midas began to wring his hands. He could neither bear to look at Marygold, nor bear to look away from her. He could not believe she had changed to gold. But as he glanced at her, he saw the precious little figure, with a yellow teardrop on its yellow cheek. Her expression was so warm and tender that Midas hoped the expression would soften the gold and make it become flesh again. But she remained gold. So Midas could only wring his hands and wish he were the poorest man in the whole world. He would gladly have exchanged all his wealth to bring back the rose color to his dear child's face.

While Midas was feeling this terrible despair, he suddenly noticed somebody standing near the door. Midas bent down his head without speaking, for he recognized the figure as the stranger who had appeared the day before in the treasure room. The stranger's smile seemed to shed a yellow light all around the room. It gleamed on little Marygold's image and on the other objects that had been changed by the touch of Midas.

"Well, friend Midas," said the stranger, "how do you like the Golden Touch?"

Midas shook his head. "I am very miserable," he said.

"Very miserable? Indeed!" exclaimed the stranger. "And why is that? Have I not faithfully kept my promise to you? Didn't you get everything your heart desired?"

"Gold is not everything," answered Midas. "And I have lost all that my heart really cared for."

"Ah, so you have made a discovery since yesterday," observed the stranger. "Let us see, then. Which of these two things do you think is really worth the most—the gift of the Golden Touch or one cup of clear, cold water?" ◆

"The water!" exclaimed Midas. "I would love to have it moisten my throat."

The stranger continued, "Tell me which is worth more, the Golden Touch or a crust of bread?"

"A piece of bread," answered Midas, "is worth all the gold on Earth."

The stranger then asked, "And is the Golden Touch worth more than your own little Marygold as she was an hour ago?"

"Oh, my child, my dear child is worth a thousand Golden Touches," cried poor Midas, wringing his hands. "I would not have given one small dimple in her chin for the power to change the whole Earth into gold!"

"You are wiser than you were, King Midas," said the stranger, looking seriously at him. "I believe your heart has not been entirely changed from flesh to gold. You appear to understand that common things are more valuable than the riches so many people struggle for. Tell me now, do you sincerely desire to rid yourself of this Golden Touch?"

"Yes, yes!" Midas exclaimed. "The Golden Touch is hateful to me!"

"Go, then," said the stranger, "and plunge into the river that glides past your garden. Then take a vase of the river water and sprinkle it over any object you want to change from gold into its original material. If you do this sincerely, you may possibly repair the mischief your greed has caused."

King Midas bowed low, and when he lifted his head, the stranger had vanished.

Midas lost no time in snatching up a vase (which immediately turned to gold) and running to the riverside. As he scampered along and forced his way through the bushes, the leaves turned yellow behind him, as if autumn had come to one narrow strip of bushes. On reaching the riverbank, Midas plunged into the water without even pulling off his shoes.

"Poof, poof, poof," snorted King Midas as his head came out of the water. He was still holding the vase, and his eyes widened as he watched it change from gold into the

good, honest clay it had been before he had touched it. He was also aware of a change within himself. A cold, hard, and heavy weight seemed to have gone out of his chest, and his clothes felt lighter, although they were soaking wet. ★

King Midas charged back to the palace. The servants did not know what to make of it when they saw their royal master running around with a vase of water. They did not know all the evil that Midas had caused, and that the water was more precious to Midas than an ocean of liquid gold. The first thing he did was to sprinkle handfuls of that water over the golden figure of little Marygold.

As soon as the water fell on Marygold, the color came back to her cheeks, and she began to sneeze and sputter. She was astonished to find herself dripping wet and to see her father throwing still more water over her.

"Please stop, dear Father," she cried. "See how you have soaked my nice outfit."

Marygold did not know she had been a little golden statue; nor could she remember anything that had happened since the moment she ran with outstretched arms to comfort poor King Midas.

Her father did not think it necessary to tell his beloved child how very foolish he had been. Instead, he decided to show how much wiser he was now. He led little Marygold into the garden, where he sprinkled the remainder of the water over the rosebushes.

Two things, however, reminded King Midas of the Golden Touch for the rest of his life. One was that the sands of the riverbank sparkled like gold. The other was that little Marygold's hair now had a strange, golden tint. The change of color was really an improvement, and it made Marygold's hair more attractive than it had ever been.

When King Midas became an old man and sat with Marygold's children on his knees, he was fond of telling them this marvelous story. When he finished, he would say, "To tell you the truth, my dear children, ever since that morning I have hated the very sight of gold except for your mother's beautiful golden hair."

C COMPREHENSION

Write the answers.
1. At the beginning of the chapter, why was Midas ready to give up all his wealth?
2. How did Midas prove to the stranger that he had learned a lesson about gold?
3. The stranger said that common things are more valuable than the riches so many people struggle for. Give an example of what he means.
4. What were some of the lessons Midas learned about gold?
5. Do you think those lessons are still true today? Explain your answer.

D WRITING

Do you think people should spend all their time trying to get rich?
- Write an essay that explains your answer. Tell why people want to get rich and how they try to make money. Tell about the good things that can happen with money; then tell about the bad things. Finally, explain how you feel about people who try to get rich.

A WORD LISTS

1
Word Endings
1. Olympus
2. Olympics
3. Olympian

2
Compound Words
1. underworld
2. thunderbolt
3. earthquake

3
Greek Gods
1. Apollo
2. Ares
3. Hades
4. Hephaestus
5. Hermes
6. Poseidon
7. Zeus

4
Greek Goddesses
1. Aphrodite
2. Artemis
3. Athena
4. Demeter
5. Hera
6. Hestia

5
New Vocabulary
1. deity
2. conquer
3. in disguise
4. chariot

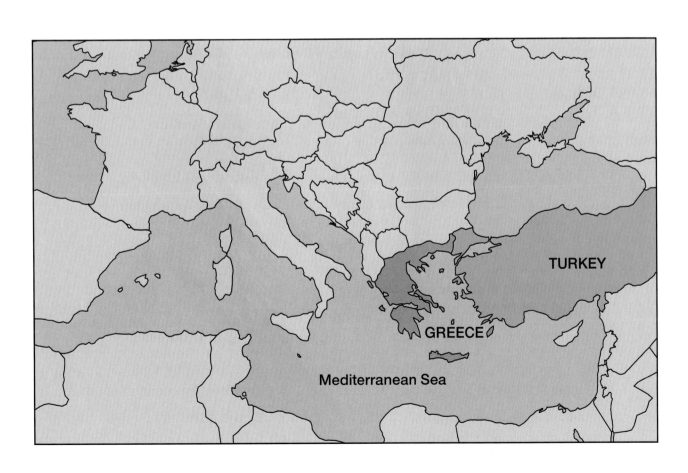

TURKEY

GREECE

Mediterranean Sea

Greek Gods and Goddesses

In the next lesson, you will begin reading a myth titled "The Miraculous Pitcher." Like "The Golden Touch," this myth includes gods and teaches us a lesson. The story takes place in Greece, a country that is just a little bit west of Turkey, where "The Golden Touch" took place. (See map on page 49).

About three thousand years ago, the people who lived in Greece (the Greeks) believed that the world was ruled by gods and goddesses, or deities. There were dozens of deities living all over Earth, but the twelve most important deities lived in a magic palace in the clouds on top of Mount Olympus, the tallest mountain in Greece. Because they lived on Mount Olympus, these gods and goddesses were called Olympian deities.

Each Olympian deity had special powers. Some controlled the sun or the ocean, while others had power over love, war, or fire. The list below shows the names and powers of the twelve Olympian deities. It also shows how to pronounce their names.

The Olympian Deities

Deity	Power
Aphrodite (af ruh DY tee)	goddess of love
Apollo (uh PAHL oh)	god of the sun
Artemis (AHR tuh miss)	goddess of hunting
Athena (uh THEE nuh)	goddess of wisdom
Ares (AIR eez)	god of war
Demeter (duh MEE tur)	goddess of farming
Hephaestus (hih FACE tuss)	god of fire
Hera (HAIR uh)	goddess of marriage
Hermes (HUR meez)	god of travelers
Hestia (HESS tee uh)	goddess of the home
Poseidon (puh SY dun)	god of the ocean
Zeus (zoose)	god of the sky

Although these twelve deities lived on Mount Olympus, they spent much of their time traveling around Earth trying to help people or to stir up trouble. They also argued with each other and fell in love. In many ways, they were just like people.

The rest of this article gives more details about some of these gods and goddesses. ♦

Zeus

Zeus was the king of all the Greek deities. When he was young, he conquered the world with the help of his brothers, Poseidon and Hades (HAY deez). The three of them then decided to rule over different parts of the world. Zeus ruled the sky, Poseidon ruled the ocean, and Hades ruled the underworld, where the Greeks believed dead people went.

As god of the sky, Zeus controlled thunder, lightning, rain, and wind. He sometimes carried a thunderbolt that he would throw in the air to create lightning and thunder. He had a thick beard and a booming voice.

The Greeks believed that Zeus saw and knew everything. He used his knowledge to punish evil people and reward good ones. He could take the form of any animal, and he often traveled in disguise. He was married to the goddess Hera.

Poseidon and Hades

Although Poseidon ruled the ocean, he lived on Mount Olympus and spent a lot of time on dry land. Besides making storms at sea, he could start earthquakes. Poseidon was also the god of horses, and he drove around in a chariot pulled by several of these powerful creatures. He carried a trident—a long spear with three prongs, like a fork. People were afraid of him, and he had many enemies.

Poseidon's brother Hades was the god of the dead. He did not live on Mount Olympus, so he was not an Olympian deity. Instead, he stayed in the underworld, a magic cave below the ground that was surrounded by strange rivers. The Greeks believed that

people went to the underworld after they died. Hades sometimes traveled above ground to capture people and bring them to his dark kingdom.

Aphrodite and Ares

Aphrodite and Ares were almost exact opposites, but that didn't stop them from falling in love with each other. Aphrodite was the goddess of love and beauty. Many gods and men were in love with her, and many goddesses and women envied her beauty. She had several love affairs, but the one with Ares is the most famous.

Ares was the god of war. The son of Zeus and Hera, he was quite handsome, with lots of muscles. He wore a helmet and carried a spear, and he was always fighting against other gods and people. Although Ares was more interested in blood than

beauty, he fell in love with Aphrodite. In some stories, the two of them get married, but in others she turns him down and marries ugly Hephaestus (the fire god) instead.

Hermes

Hermes was a fast runner who carried messages from Mount Olympus all over Earth. Because he had wings on his sandals, he could fly through the air and cover great distances in just a few seconds. He wore a round hat and carried a winged staff that had two snakes curled around it.

Hermes protected travelers and brought people good luck. He was also full of tricks. He loved playing jokes on the other deities, and sometimes he even stole things from them. He was tall, thin, and handsome, but he never got married. In his spare time, he played music.

C COMPREHENSION

Write the answers.
1. Why were the most important Greek deities called Olympian deities?
2. In what ways were the Olympian deities like people?
3. Why did Zeus know which people were evil and which ones were good?
4. Why were people afraid of Poseidon?
5. In what ways were Aphrodite and Ares different from each other?

D WRITING

Which Greek deity would you like to be? Why?
- Study the list of deities in this lesson. Read more about the deities that interest you. Then pick which one you would like to be.
- Write an essay that explains your choice. Describe your deity, and tell what powers he or she has. Explain why you would like to be that deity. Also explain which deities you would not like to be and why.

A WORD LISTS

1	2	3	4
Hard Words	*Compound Words*	*Word Practice*	*New Vocabulary*
1. Philemon	1. beehive	1. lodge	1. miraculous
2. Baucis	2. grapevine	2. lodging	2. hospitality
3. cultivate	3. neighborhood	3. vegetable	3. cultivate
4. fertile	4. nightfall	4. disagreeable	4. fertile
5. miraculous	5. mudball	5. light-footed	5. staff
6. hospitality		6. youth	6. toil
7. honey		7. fragrant	
8. olive			

B MAIN IDEA

Figure out a complete main-idea sentence for the following paragraph.
- Name the main character.
- Tell the main thing that character did.
- Tell when and where the character did that main thing.

In August, Clara went to the department store. She looked at clothing. She looked at sporting equipment. Then she recalled that she needed to fix her bike. So, she found a bike-repair kit and paid for it. Then she left the store.

The Miraculous Pitcher
Chapter 1

One evening, in times long ago, old Philemon and his old wife Baucis sat on a bench next to their cottage door enjoying the calm and beautiful sunset. They had already eaten their supper, and now intended to spend a quiet hour or two before bedtime. So they talked together about their garden, and their cow, and their bees, and their grapevine. But the rude shouts of children and the fierce barking of dogs in the nearby village grew louder and louder, until at last it was hardly possible for Baucis and Philemon to hear each other speak.

"Ah, wife," cried Philemon, "I fear some poor traveler is seeking hospitality in the village. But instead of giving him food and shelter, the villagers have set their dogs on him."

"I do wish the people in the village felt a little more kindness for their fellow human beings," Baucis said. "They bring up their children in this evil way and pat them on the head when they fling stones at strangers."

"Those children will never come to any good," said Philemon, shaking his white head. "To tell you the truth, wife, I would not be surprised if some terrible thing were to happen to all the people in the village, unless they mend their ways. But as for you and me, so long as we have a crust of bread, let us be ready to give half to any poor homeless stranger who may come along and need it."

"That's right, husband," said Baucis. "So we will."

Philemon and Baucis were quite poor, and they had to work hard for a living. Philemon toiled all day long in his garden, while Baucis was always making a little butter and cheese with their cow's milk, or doing something around the cottage. Their food was seldom anything but bread, milk, and vegetables, with sometimes a bit of honey from their beehive. But they were two of the kindest people in the world. They would cheerfully have gone without their dinners any day rather than refuse food to a weary traveler who might come to their door. They felt they should treat guests better and more thoughtfully than they treated themselves.

Their cottage stood on a hill a short distance from the village, which lay in a valley that was about half a mile wide. When the world was new, this valley had probably been the bed of a lake. There, fishes had glided back and forth in the water, and weeds had grown along the shore, and trees and hills had made reflections in the broad and peaceful water. But as the lake had dried up, men had cultivated the soil and built houses on it, so that it was now a fertile spot.

The valley bore no trace of the ancient lake except for a small brook that flowed through the village and supplied the villagers with water. The valley had been dry land so long that oaks had sprung up, and grown great and high, and died with old age, and been followed by other oaks as tall and stately as the first. Never was there a prettier or more fertile valley. The very sight of their rich surroundings should have made the villagers kind and gentle.

But the people of this lovely village were not worthy to dwell in such a beautiful place. They were selfish, hardhearted people and had neither pity for the poor, nor sympathy for the homeless. They would only laugh if anybody told them human beings should love one another.

These people taught their children to be like themselves. They clapped their hands when they saw their boys and girls run after strangers, shout at them, and pelt them with stones. They kept large, fierce dogs. Whenever a traveler came into the village, this pack of disagreeable creatures scampered to meet the traveler, barking, snarling, and showing their teeth.

This unfriendly greeting was hard on poor travelers, especially when they were sick, or feeble, or old. Some would go miles and miles out of their way rather than try to pass through the village. ♦

So now you can understand why Philemon spoke so sorrowfully when he heard the shouts of the children and the barking of the dogs. The noise lasted a long time and seemed to echo all the way through the valley.

"I never heard the dogs so loud," observed the good old man.

"Nor the children so rude," answered the good old wife.

They sat shaking their heads one to another, while the noise came nearer and nearer. At last, they saw two men approaching on foot. Close behind them came the fierce dogs, snarling at their heels. A little farther behind was a crowd of children, who cried shrilly and flung stones at the two strangers with all their might.

From time to time, the younger of the two men turned around and drove back the dogs with a staff he carried in his hand. His companion, who was a very tall person, walked calmly along, as if he didn't notice the fierce children or the pack of dogs. Both travelers were poorly dressed, and they looked as if they didn't have enough money in their pockets to pay for a meal.

"Come, wife," said Philemon to Baucis, "let us go and meet these poor travelers."

"You go and meet them," answered Baucis, "while I see if we can get them anything for supper. A bowl of bread and milk would raise their spirits."

Baucis hurried into the cottage. Meanwhile, Philemon went forward, extended his hand, and said in a hearty tone, "Welcome, strangers, welcome."

"Thank you," replied the younger of the two men. "This is quite a different greeting than we received in the village. Why do you live in such a bad neighborhood?" ★

"Ah," observed old Philemon with a quiet smile, "I live here so that I may make up for the rudeness of my neighbors."

"Well said, old father!" cried the younger traveler, laughing. "My companion and I need some help. Those children have splattered us with their mudballs, and one of the dogs has torn my cloak."

Philemon was glad to see the younger man in such good spirits. Indeed, the

traveler did not seem weary from his long journey, nor upset by the rough treatment he had received.

The younger traveler was dressed in an odd way. The edge of the round cap he wore stuck out over both ears. Although it was a summer evening, he wore a cloak, which he kept wrapped closely around him. Philemon also saw that he had an unusual pair of shoes. But because it was growing dark, the old man could not tell exactly what was strange about the shoes. One thing certainly seemed odd—the traveler was so wonderfully light-footed and active that it appeared as if his feet sometimes rose from the ground.

"I used to be light-footed in my youth," said Philemon to the traveler, "but my feet always became heavier toward nightfall."

"There is nothing like a good staff to help one along," answered the stranger, "and I happen to have an excellent one, as you can see."

The traveler's staff was the oddest looking staff that Philemon had ever seen. It was made of olive-wood, and it had something like a little pair of wings near the top. Two snakes, carved in the wood, curled themselves around the staff. The snakes were so skillfully carved that old Philemon almost thought they were alive, and that he could see them wriggling and twisting.

"A curious piece of work!" said Philemon. "I have never seen a staff with wings!"

D COMPREHENSION

Write the answers.
1. How did the villagers treat strangers?
2. How did Baucis and Philemon treat strangers?
3. Why were Baucis and Philemon having so much trouble carrying on a conversation?
4. Why did Baucis go inside the cottage when the strangers approached?
5. Who do you think the younger stranger is? Explain your answer.

E WRITING

Pretend you could have a cottage anywhere in the world.
• Write a description of your cottage and what you would do there. Tell where your cottage is located and what it looks like. Then tell what kinds of things you would do in and around your cottage.

A WORD LISTS

1	2	3	4
Hard Words	*Word Endings*	*Vocabulary Review*	*New Vocabulary*
1. sympathy	1. carelessly	1. fertile	1. shrewd
2. disguise	2. suddenly	2. miraculous	2. witty
3. shrewd	3. continually	3. staff	3. sympathy
4. Quicksilver	4. sorrowfully	4. hospitality	4. nimble
5. gesture	5. eagerly	5. cultivate	
		6. toil	

B MAIN IDEA

Figure out a complete main-idea sentence for the following paragraph.
- Name the main character.
- Tell the main thing that character did.
- Tell when and where the character did that main thing.

Rochelle went to her closet on the first day of April and took out her kite. Then she tied some string to the kite and went to the park. She held the string in her hand and started to run. The kite went into the air. Rochelle stopped running and let out more string. She watched the kite dart back and forth in the sky. After several hours, she pulled the kite back in and walked home.

The Miraculous Pitcher
Chapter 2

Philemon and the two travelers continued walking toward the cottage, and they soon reached the bench outside the door.

"Friends," said Philemon, "sit down and rest yourselves here on our bench. My good wife Baucis has gone to see what you can have for supper. We are poor folks, but you are welcome to whatever we have in the cupboard."

The young stranger sat down carelessly on the bench, and his staff fell to the ground. And then something marvelous happened. The staff seemed to get up from the ground by itself. It spread its little pair of wings and flew up to the wall of the cottage. Then it leaned against the wall and stood quite still, except that the snakes continued to wriggle.

Before Philemon could ask any questions, the older stranger drew Philemon's attention from the wonderful staff by speaking to him in a remarkably deep tone of voice. He asked, "In ancient times, wasn't there a lake covering the spot where the village now stands?"

"Not in my day, friend," answered Philemon, "and yet I am an old man, as you see. There were always the fields and meadows, just as they are now, and the old trees, and the little stream murmuring through the valley. My father and his father before him never saw it otherwise, so far as I know.

It will probably still be that way when old Philemon is gone and forgotten."

The older stranger observed, "Don't be too sure the valley will always be as it is now." There was something very stern in his deep voice. He shook his head, too, moving his dark and heavy curls. He continued, "Since the people of the village have forgotten affection and sympathy, it would be better if the lake rippled over their dwellings again!"

The older traveler looked so stern that Philemon was frightened. But that was not all, for when the traveler frowned, the twilight seemed suddenly to grow darker; and when he shook his head, there was a roll of thunder in the air.

But suddenly the older stranger's face became so kindly and mild that the old man quite forgot his terror. Still, he could not help feeling that this old traveler must be no ordinary person, even though he was poorly clothed and journeying on foot. Philemon did not think he was a prince in disguise but rather some very wise man, who went around the world in poor clothes, seeking to add to his wisdom.

When Philemon raised his eyes to the stranger's face, he seemed to see a lifetime of thought. ♦

While Baucis was getting supper, the travelers began to talk very sociably with

Philemon. The younger traveler was extremely talkative, and he made such shrewd and witty remarks that the good old man continually burst out laughing. Philemon thought the younger man was the merriest fellow he had ever seen.

"What is your name?" asked Philemon.

"Why, I am very nimble, as you see," answered the traveler. "So, if you call me Quicksilver, the name will fit well."

"Quicksilver? Quicksilver?" repeated Philemon, looking in the traveler's face to see if he was making fun of him. "It is a very odd name. And your companion there, has he as strange a name?"

"You must ask the thunder to tell you his name," replied Quicksilver, putting on a mysterious look. "No other voice is loud enough."

Philemon turned to look at the older traveler. He was probably the grandest figure that ever sat so humbly beside a cottage door. The older stranger talked in such a grave way that Philemon wanted to tell him everything he knew. This is often how people feel when they meet anyone wise enough to comprehend all their good and evil.

Simple and kindhearted Philemon did not have many secrets to tell. He talked about the events of his past life. He had never been more than ten miles from the very spot where he lived. Baucis and he had dwelt in the cottage since their youth, and they earned their bread by honest labor. They had always been poor but contented.

Philemon told what excellent butter and cheese Baucis made, and how nice the vegetables were that he raised in his garden. He said, too, that because he and his wife loved one another so very much, they both hoped that death might not separate them. They wanted to die together, just as they had lived together.

As the older stranger listened, a smile beamed over his face. "You are a good old man," he said to Philemon, "and you have a good old wife. Your wish will be granted."

And it seemed to Philemon just then as if the sunset clouds flashed brightly from the west and suddenly lit up the sky.

Baucis now had supper ready. She came to the cottage door and began to make apologies for the poor meal that she was forced to set before her guests.

"Had we known you were coming," she said, "my husband and I would have gone without a bite. But I took most of today's milk to make cheese; and our last loaf of bread is already half-eaten. Ah, me! I never feel the sorrow of being poor except when a traveler knocks at our door." ★

"All will be well; do not trouble yourself, my good woman," replied the older stranger kindly. "An honest, hearty welcome to a guest works miracles with any meal."

"A welcome you shall have," cried Baucis, "and likewise a little honey we happen to have left, and also a bunch of purple grapes."

"Why, Mother Baucis, it is a feast!" exclaimed Quicksilver, laughing, "An absolute feast! And you shall see how eagerly I will feast on it. I think I never felt hungrier in my life."

"Mercy on us!" whispered Baucis to her husband. "If the young man has such a hearty appetite, I am afraid there will not be half enough supper."

Before Philemon could reply, the travelers stood up from the bench and entered the cottage.

Quicksilver's staff, you will remember, had set itself up against the wall of the cottage. When Quicksilver entered the door, leaving his wonderful staff behind, it immediately spread its little wings and went hopping and fluttering up the doorstep. It did not rest until it had leaned itself against Quicksilver's chair. Baucis and Philemon, however, were attending so closely to their guests that they did not notice the staff.

As Baucis had said, the supper was quite small. In the middle of the table were the remains of a loaf of brown bread, with a piece of cheese on one side of it and a dish of honey on the other. There was a pretty good bunch of grapes for each of the guests. A medium-sized clay pitcher, nearly full of milk, stood at a corner of the table. But when Baucis had filled two cups and set them before the strangers, only a little milk remained in the bottom of the pitcher. Poor Baucis kept wishing she could provide these hungry folks with a hearty supper.

And, since the supper was so very small, she could not help wishing their appetites were smaller. But, right after they sat down, the travelers both drank all the milk in their cups in one gulp.

"A little more milk, kind Mother Baucis, if you please," said Quicksilver. "The day has been hot, and I am very thirsty."

"Now, my dear people," answered Baucis slowly, "I am so sorry and ashamed. But the truth is, there is hardly a drop more milk in the pitcher."

Quicksilver got up from the table and took the pitcher by the handle. Then he exclaimed, "Why, it appears to me that matters are not quite so bad as you think. There is much more milk in the pitcher."

And he proceeded to fill both cups from the pitcher that was supposed to be almost empty.

D COMPREHENSION

Write the answers.
1. Why was Quicksilver a good name for the younger traveler?
2. How do you know that Quicksilver's staff was magical?
3. Who do you think the older stranger is? Explain your answer.
4. Why was Baucis so worried when the strangers entered her cottage?
5. What was strange about the pitcher at the end of the chapter?

E WRITING

Philemon wanted to tell the older stranger everything he knew.
• Write a conversation between Philemon and the older stranger. Have Philemon tell the older stranger about his life: where he was born, what he does for a living, how he feels about his wife, and so forth. Also have the older stranger ask about the villagers and the lake.

A WORD LISTS

1

Hard Words
1. fragrance
2. abundant
3. spacious
4. inhabitant

2

Vocabulary Review
1. shrewd
2. witty
3. nimble
4. sympathy

3

New Vocabulary
1. astonishment
2. inhabitant
3. disagreeable
4. spacious
5. abundant
6. fragrance

B MAIN IDEA

Figure out a complete main-idea sentence for the following paragraph.
- Name the main characters.
- Tell the main thing those characters did.
- Tell when and where the characters did that main thing.

It was the Fourth of July. Mr. and Mrs. Dunbar woke up early and began to prepare for the day's big event. Mr. Dunbar made chicken sandwiches and a big potato salad. He put the sandwiches and salad in a large basket, then he woke up the children. Meanwhile, Mrs. Dunbar put gas in the car and checked the oil and tires. Then she picked up the family and the food and drove to Red Rock State Park. When they got to the park, the Dunbars got out of the car and put some blankets on the ground. Then they ate all the food.

The Miraculous Pitcher
Chapter 3

Baucis could scarcely believe her eyes. She had certainly poured out nearly all the milk, and she had seen the bottom of the pitcher as she set it on the table.

"But I am old," thought Baucis to herself, "and may be forgetful. I suppose I must have made a mistake. In any case, the pitcher must be empty now."

Quicksilver had turned the pitcher upside down and had poured every drop of milk into the last cup.

"What excellent milk!" observed Quicksilver after finishing his second cup. "Excuse me, my kind hostess, but I must really ask you for a little more."

Of course there could not possibly be

any milk left. Baucis lifted the pitcher anyway. To be polite, she went through the motion of pouring milk into Quicksilver's cup but without the slightest idea that any milk would come from the pitcher. She was very surprised, therefore, when so much milk fell bubbling into the cup that it was immediately filled to the brim and overflowed onto the table!

And she noticed what a delicious fragrance the milk had! It seemed as if Philemon's only cow must have eaten the richest grass in the world.

"And now a slice of your brown bread, Mother Baucis," said Quicksilver, "and a little of that honey."

Baucis cut him a slice. The bread, when she and her husband had eaten it, had been rather dry and crusty. But now it was light and moist. Baucis tasted a crumb that had fallen on the table, and found it more delicious than her bread ever was before. She could hardly believe that it was a loaf of her own. Yet, what other loaf could it possibly be?

Baucis began to think that something very unusual was going on. So, after helping the guests to bread and honey, she sat down by Philemon and whispered what she had seen.

"Did you ever hear of anything like it?" she asked Philemon.

"No, I never did," answered Philemon with a smile. "And I think, my dear old wife, that you have been walking about in a sort of dream. There happened to be a little more milk in the pitcher than you thought, my dear—that is the only possible explanation." ♦

"Ah, husband," said Baucis, "say what you will, but these are very unusual guests."

"Well, well," replied Philemon, still smiling, "perhaps they are. They certainly do look as if they had seen better days; and I am glad to see them having such a good supper."

Each of the guests now took a bunch of grapes. Baucis, who rubbed her eyes to see more clearly, thought the grapes had grown larger and richer. Each grape seemed to be nearly bursting with ripe juice. It was entirely a mystery to her how such grapes could ever have been produced from the old vine that climbed against the cottage wall.

"These are marvelous grapes," observed Quicksilver, as he swallowed one after another. "Where did you gather them?"

"From my own vine," answered Philemon. "You may see one of its branches twisting across the window. But my wife and I never thought the grapes were very fine ones."

"I never tasted better," said Quicksilver. "Another cup of that delicious milk, if you please, and I shall then have eaten better than a prince."

This time old Philemon got up himself and picked up the pitcher, for he was curious to discover whether there was any truth in what Baucis had whispered to him. He knew that his good old wife never lied, and that she was seldom mistaken. But this case was so unusual that he wanted to see into the pitcher with his own eyes.

As Philemon picked up the pitcher, he slyly glanced into it. He saw that it didn't contain a single drop. All at once, however, a little white fountain gushed up from the bottom of the pitcher and rapidly filled it to the brim with deliciously fragrant milk. It was lucky that Philemon, in his surprise, did not drop the miraculous pitcher from his hand.

"Who are you, you wonder-working

strangers?" he cried, even more confused than his wife had been.

"We are your guests and your friends," replied the older traveler in his mild, deep voice, which was both sweet and amazing. Then he added, "I would also like another cup of milk."

The older traveler seemed so solemn that Philemon did not ask him any questions. And when Philemon drew Quicksilver aside and asked how a fountain of milk could get into an old clay pitcher, Quicksilver pointed to his staff. ★

"There is the answer," said Quicksilver. "And if you can figure it out, please tell me. I can't understand my staff. It is always playing such odd tricks as this—sometimes getting me a supper, and quite as often stealing my supper. If I had any faith in such nonsense, I should say the stick was charmed!"

He said no more, but he looked so slyly at Baucis and Philemon that they almost thought he was laughing at them.

The supper was now over, and Baucis begged the travelers to stay the night. They accepted her offer cheerfully. The good woman showed them to the sleeping room. The magic staff went hopping at Quicksilver's heels as he left the room.

Later that night, the good old couple spent some time talking about the events of the evening, and then they lay down on the floor and fell fast asleep. They had given up their sleeping room to the guests and had no other bed for themselves.

Philemon and Baucis arose with the sun, and the strangers made their preparations to depart. Philemon asked them to remain a little longer so that Baucis could milk the cow and bake some bread. The guests, however, seemed to think it better to set out before the day got hot. Therefore, they set out immediately but asked Philemon and Baucis to walk with them a short distance and show them which road to take.

"Ah, me!" exclaimed Philemon, when they had walked a little way from their door. "If our neighbors only knew what great rewards there are for being kind to strangers, they would tie up all their dogs and never allow their children to fling another stone."

Baucis explained, "It is a sin and a shame for them to behave the way they do! And I'm going to tell some of them what nasty people they are."

With a cunning smile, Quicksilver replied, "I fear you will find none of them at home."

Just then, the older traveler's face took on such a solemn expression that neither Baucis nor Philemon dared to speak another word. They gazed into his face as if it were the sky.

The older traveler spoke. "When men do not treat the humblest stranger as if he were a brother, they are unworthy to exist on Earth." He spoke in tones so deep that they sounded like thunder.

"And anyway, my dear old people," cried Quicksilver, with mischief in his eyes, "where is this village you talk about? On which side of us does it lie? I do not see it."

D MAIN IDEA

For each paragraph, write a complete main-idea sentence.
- Name the main character.
- Tell the main thing that character did.
- Tell when and where the character did that main thing.

1. The Comets were one of the best softball teams in Springfield. In September, they played in the City Championship game. At the end of three innings, they had a five-run lead. But the other team started to come back. In the last inning, the Comets were one run behind, and they failed to score. The Comets were brokenhearted, but they went over to congratulate the other team.

2. It was the Fourth of July. Mr. and Mrs. Dunbar woke up early and began to prepare for the day's big event. Mr. Dunbar made chicken sandwiches and a big potato salad. He put the sandwiches and salad in a large basket, then he woke up the children. Meanwhile, Mrs. Dunbar put gas in the car and checked the oil and tires. Then she picked up the family and the food and drove to Red Rock State Park. When they got to the park, the Dunbars got out of the car and put some blankets on the ground. Then they ate all the food.

E COMPREHENSION

Write the answers.
1. How was the food and drink at supper different from the food and drink the old couple usually had?
2. At first, Philemon didn't believe what Baucis told him about the pitcher. Why did he change his mind?
3. Why do you think Quicksilver said his staff was filling the pitcher?
4. The next morning, why did Baucis want to go to the village?
5. What do you think happened to the village? Why did it happen?

F WRITING

The older traveler said, "When men do not treat the humblest stranger as if he were a brother, they are unworthy to exist on Earth." Do you agree with that statement?
- Write an essay that explains your answer. Tell what you think the statement means. Then explain why you agree or disagree with the statement. Give different examples to explain what you mean.

A WORD LISTS

1
Planet Names
1. Mercury
2. Venus
3. Earth
4. Mars
5. Jupiter
6. Saturn
7. Uranus
8. Neptune
9. Pluto

2
Vocabulary Review
1. inhabitant
2. spacious
3. abundant
4. disagreeable
5. astonishment

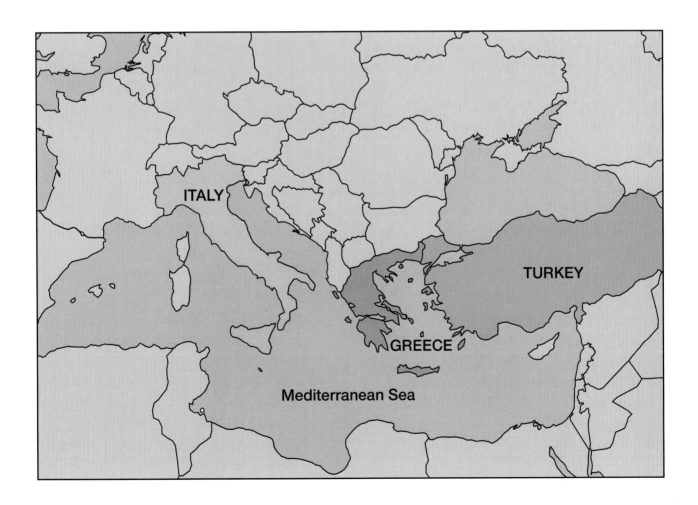

ITALY

TURKEY

GREECE

Mediterranean Sea

Roman Deities

By now, you have probably figured out that the two travelers in "The Miraculous Pitcher" are Zeus (the god of the sky) and Hermes (the god of travelers). You can tell that the older traveler is Zeus because he seems to know everything and has a voice like thunder. You can also tell that the younger traveler is Hermes because he's light-footed and carries a magic staff with wings.

The Greeks began telling myths like "The Miraculous Pitcher" about three thousand years ago. Several hundred years later, the people who lived in Rome also began telling myths. Rome was the biggest city in what is now Italy. The map on page 69 shows where Italy is located. You can see that it's just west of Greece.

Roman myths were similar to Greek myths, but the Roman deities had different names. Some of those names are the same as the names of the planets in our solar system. The list below compares the names of several Greek and Roman deities.

In many ways, the planets are just like their names. Mercury is the fastest planet, just as Mercury was the fastest Roman god. Venus is the most beautiful planet, and Mars, with its blood-red color, is the most warlike. Jupiter is the biggest planet, and Neptune is blue, like the ocean. Finally, Pluto is the darkest and farthest from the sun, just like the underworld.

Two more planets are also named after Roman gods. Saturn was Jupiter's father, and Uranus was his grandfather. The only planet that isn't named after a Roman god is Earth.

Greek and Roman Deities

Greek Deity	Roman Deity	Power
Hermes	Mercury	god of travelers
Aphrodite	Venus	goddess of love
Ares	Mars	god of war
Zeus	Jupiter	god of the sky
Poseidon	Neptune	god of the ocean
Hades	Pluto	god of the underworld

The Miraculous Pitcher
Chapter 4

Philemon and his wife turned toward the valley, where at sunset the day before they had seen the meadows, the houses, the gardens, the clumps of trees, the wide street, and the children. But to their astonishment, there was no longer any village! Even the fertile valley had ceased to exist. In its place they saw the broad, blue surface of a lake, which filled the great valley from brim to brim.

The lake reflected the surrounding hills in its still waters. For an instant, it remained perfectly smooth. Then a little breeze sprang up and caused the water to dance, glitter, and sparkle in the early morning sun.

The lake seemed so strangely familiar that the two old people were greatly puzzled. They felt as if the village had only been a dream. But then they remembered the dwellings and the faces of the inhabitants. It had not been a dream. The village had been there yesterday, and now it was gone.

"Alas!" cried these kindhearted old people. "What has become of our neighbors?"

"The villagers exist no longer as men and women," said the older traveler in his grand and deep voice, while a roll of thunder seemed to echo in the distance.

Quicksilver said with his mischievous smile, "Those foolish people were all changed into fish. It was only a small change, for they were already the coldest-blooded human beings on earth."

The older traveler continued, "As for you, good Philemon, and you, kind Baucis, you have shown us much hospitality and kindness. You have done well, my dear old friends; therefore, request whatever favor you have most at heart, and it is granted." ◆

Philemon and Baucis looked at one another, and then seemed to answer with one voice. They said, "Let us live together while we live, and leave the world at the same instant when we die, for we have always loved one another!"

"It will be so," replied the older stranger, in a deep, kind voice. "Now look toward your cottage."

They did so. But to their surprise, they saw a tall palace of white marble standing where their humble cottage had been.

"There is your home," said the older stranger, smiling at them. "Show your hospitality in that palace as freely as you did in your humble cottage."

The old folks fell on their knees to thank the stranger, but when they looked up, they were amazed to discover that both he and Quicksilver were gone.

• • •

So Philemon and Baucis lived in the marble palace, and they spent much of their time making travelers comfortable.

The milk pitcher was never empty. Whenever friendly guests took a drink from that pitcher, they always found it to be the sweetest milk that ever ran down their throats. But if angry and disagreeable travelers took a sip, they were certain to twist their faces and say that it was a pitcher of sour milk!

Thus, the old couple lived in their palace a long, long time, and they grew older and older. At last, however, there came a summer morning when Baucis and Philemon failed to appear. Their guests searched everywhere, from the top to the bottom of the spacious palace, but they could not find the old couple. ★

Finally, the guests saw two great trees in front of the palace. Nobody remembered ever seeing the two trees before, yet there they stood, with their roots fastened deep into the soil. Their leaves cast a shadow on the palace, and their branches wound together and embraced one another, so that each tree seemed to live in the other.

These trees must have required at least a century to grow, and the guest wondered how they could have become so tall in a single night. Just then, a breeze sprang up and made the branches move. And then there was a deep, broad murmur in the air, as if the two mysterious trees were speaking.

"I am old Philemon," murmured one tree.

"I am old Baucis," murmured the other.

But as the breeze grew stronger, the trees both spoke at once: "Philemon, Baucis, Baucis, Philemon"—as if one were both and both were one, and talking together with a common heart. It was plain enough that the good old couple had been reborn, and were now to spend a quiet and delightful hundred years or so as trees. And oh, what a wonderful shade they gave! Whenever travelers paused beneath the trees, they heard a pleasant whisper of the leaves above their head, and marveled because the sounds seemed to say: "Welcome, welcome, dear traveler, welcome!"

And some kind soul, who knew what would have pleased old Baucis and old Philemon best, built a circular seat around both their trunks, where, for many years the weary and the hungry and the thirsty used to sit and drink milk abundantly out of the miraculous pitcher.

D MAIN IDEA

For each paragraph, write the complete main idea.

1. Last summer, the Chavez family got on a train in Los Angeles. The train pulled out of the Los Angeles station at night and started heading east. The next morning, it passed through Denver. That night, it stopped in Chicago, but the Chavez family did not get off. After one more night, the train finally arrived in New York City. The Chavez family got off the train and walked into the train station.

2. It was springtime, and all the people around Liverpool were talking about the steeplechase that was coming up. People talked about all the different horses, but nobody talked about Chico, a brown horse with white spots. On the day of the steeplechase, Chico lined up with all the other horses and waited for the signal to start. The signal went off, and all the horses started running. Chico was far behind at first, but as the race continued, he came closer and closer to the lead. At the last jump, Chico took the lead, and he was the first horse to cross the finish line.

E COMPREHENSION

Write the answers.
1. What happened to the village during the night?
2. When they were still people, how were the villagers like fish?
3. Why did Baucis and Philemon want to die together?
4. How were the two trees like Baucis and Philemon?
5. What lesson do you think "The Miraculous Pitcher" teaches us?

F WRITING

"The Miraculous Pitcher" teaches us a lesson.
• Write a story that teaches the same lesson as "The Miraculous Pitcher." First write down what you think the lesson is, then make up a story about that lesson. Your story can take place at any time and in any place. If you like, you can include Greek or Roman deities, but you don't have to. Use your imagination!

A WORD LISTS

1
Hard Words
1. soothe
2. persuade
3. pirates
4. poverty
5. conceal
6. dread
7. hasty

2
Compound Words
1. shipwreck
2. horseback
3. anybody
4. halfway
5. courtyard
6. folktale

3
Word Practice
1. ridicule
2. Beauty
3. cautious
4. fatigue
5. excuses
6. ridiculed
7. countries
8. furniture

4
Vocabulary Review
1. vanish
2. original
3. insane
4. glossy
5. dimple
6. greedy
7. victim

5
Vocabulary Preview
1. desolate
2. persuade
3. terrify
4. selfish
5. soothe
6. poverty

B VOCABULARY FROM CONTEXT

1. There was nothing within a hundred miles of this lonely, **desolate** place.
2. She was good at talking people into doing things, but she could not **persuade** anybody to go to the beach with her.
3. The old house was frightening, and the sounds within it **terrified** me.
4. She seemed to be kind, but she was really very **selfish** and thought of nobody but herself.
5. He was so upset that nothing we could do would comfort or **soothe** him.
6. At first he was wealthy, but then he lost all his wealth and found himself in **poverty**.

STORY BACKGROUND

Folktales

The next story you will read is a folktale called "Beauty and the Beast." Like myths, folktales are old stories that people told aloud before someone wrote them down. But folktales are usually much newer than myths. The myths you have just read, for example, take place about three thousand years ago. In comparison, "Beauty and the Beast" takes place just a few hundred years ago.

Another difference is that myths usually include gods and goddesses, but folktales do not. Instead, folktales often have witches, wizards, or other kinds of magic.

"Beauty and the Beast" is one of the most famous folktales of all time. Many movies have been made of the story, and many writers have retold it in their own words. The story comes from France, a large country in Europe.

D **READING**

Beauty and the Beast
Chapter 1

Once upon a time there lived a merchant who was enormously rich. The merchant had six sons and six daughters, and he would let them have anything they wanted.

But one day their house caught fire and burned to the ground, with all the splendid furniture, books, pictures, gold, silver, and precious goods it contained. Yet this was only the beginning of their misfortune. Shortly after the fire, the mer-

chant lost every ship he had upon the sea, either because of pirates, shipwrecks, or fire. Then he heard that the people who worked for him in distant countries had stolen his money. At last, he fell into great poverty.

All the merchant had after those misfortunes was a little cottage in a desolate place a hundred miles from the town in which he used to live. He moved into the cottage with his children. They were in despair at the idea of leading such a different life. The cottage stood in the middle of a dark forest, and it seemed to be the most dismal place on earth.

The children had to cultivate the fields to earn their living. They were poorly clothed, and they missed the comforts and amusements of their earlier life. Only the youngest daughter tried to be brave and cheerful. She had also been sad at first, but she soon recovered her good nature. She set to work to make the best of things. But when she tried to persuade her sisters to join her in dancing and singing, they ridiculed her and said that this miserable life was all she was fit for. But she was far prettier and more clever than they were. She was so lovely that she was called Beauty.

After two years, their father received news that one of his ships, which he had believed to be lost, had come safely into port with a rich cargo. All the sons and daughters at once thought their poverty would be over, and they wanted to set out directly for the town. But their father was more cautious, so he decided to go by himself. Only Beauty had any doubt that they would soon be rich again. The other daughters gave their father requests for so many jewels and dresses that it would have taken a fortune to buy them. But Beauty did not ask for anything. Her father noticed her silence and said, "And what shall I bring for you, Beauty?"

"The only thing I wish for is to see you come home safely," she answered.

This reply angered her sisters, who thought she was accusing them of asking for costly things. But her father was pleased. Still, he told her to choose something.

"Well, dear Father," she said, "since you insist upon it, I want you to bring me a rose. I have not seen one since we came here, and I love them very much." ♦

So the merchant set out on horseback and reached the town as quickly as possible. But when he got there, he found out that his partners had taken the goods the ship had brought. So he found himself poorer than when he had left the cottage. He had only enough money to buy food on his journey home. To make matters worse, he left town during terrible weather. The storm was so bad that he was exhausted with cold and fatigue before he was halfway home. Night came on, and the deep snow and bitter frost made it impossible for the merchant's horse to carry him any further.

The merchant could see no houses or lights. The only shelter he could find was the hollow trunk of a great tree. He crouched there all night long. It was the longest night he had ever known. In spite of his weariness, the howling of the wolves kept him awake. And when the day broke, he was not much better off, for falling snow had covered up every path, and he did not know which way to turn.

At last, he made out some sort of path, and he started to follow it. It was rough and slippery, so he kept falling down. But the path soon became easier, and it led him to a row of trees that ended at a splendid castle. It seemed very strange to the merchant that no snow had fallen in the row of trees. Stranger still, the trees were fruit trees, and they were covered with apples and oranges. ★

The merchant walked down the row of trees and soon reached the castle. He called, but nobody answered. So he opened the door and called again. Then he climbed

up a flight of steps and walked through several splendid rooms. The pleasant warmth of the air refreshed him, and he suddenly felt very hungry; but there seemed to be nobody in this huge palace who could give him anything to eat.

The merchant kept wandering through the deep silence of the splendid rooms. At last, he stopped in a room smaller than the rest, where a bright fire was burning next to a couch. The merchant thought this room must be prepared for someone, so he sat down to wait. But very soon he fell into a heavy sleep.

His extreme hunger wakened him after several hours. He was still alone, but a good dinner had been set on a little table. The merchant had eaten nothing for an entire day, so he lost no time in beginning his meal, which was delicious. He wondered who had brought the food, but no one appeared.

After dinner, the merchant went to sleep again. He woke completely refreshed the next morning. There was still no sign of anybody, although a fresh meal of cakes and fruit was sitting on the little table at his elbow. The silence began to terrify the merchant, and he decided to search once more through the rooms. But it was no use. There was no sign of life in the palace. Not even a mouse could be seen.

E MAIN IDEA

For each paragraph, write a sentence that tells the complete main idea.

1. Saturday finally arrived. Janet took her camera out of her closet. Then she went outside to look for her friends. When she had found everybody, she told them to stand together on her porch. She looked through her camera and told everybody to stand closer together. Finally, she said, "Smile," and pressed the button on the camera. The camera went "click," and some of Janet's friends made faces.

2. William liked rowing boats. Last spring, William visited Swan Lake. He rented a rowboat for the whole day. He hopped into the boat and started to pull the oars. The boat started across the lake. William could see the boat rental place getting farther and farther away. William kept rowing. He looked at people fishing and at birds flying near the water. He had fun seeing how fast he could row. After a long time, he came to the opposite side of the lake.

F COMPREHENSION

Write the answers.
1. Why were most of the merchant's children greedy and spoiled?
2. Name at least three ways that Beauty was different from her sisters.
3. Why do you think Beauty asked her father for a rose?
4. Why did the merchant get lost on the way home?
5. Name at least three strange things about the palace.

G WRITING

What objects do you think are beautiful?
• Pick an object that you think is beautiful, such as a flower, a painting, or a river. Then write a poem about the object. Describe what the object looks like and tell why you think it's beautiful.

77

A WORD LISTS

1 Word Endings	2 Word Practice	3 Vocabulary Review	4 Vocabulary Preview
1. permission	1. fault	1. selfish	1. dread
2. solution	2. curiosity	2. terrify	2. hasty
3. condition	3. sensible	3. soothe	3. conceal
4. possession		4. desolate	
5. mention		5. persuade	
		6. poverty	

B VOCABULARY FROM CONTEXT

1. She hated the thought of leaving town, but she **dreaded** leaving her mother most of all.

2. They were in such a hurry that they ate a **hasty** breakfast.

3. She did not want the Beast to know she was afraid, so she **concealed** her fear.

Beauty and the Beast
Chapter 2

After he wandered around the palace, the merchant wondered what he should do. He imagined what it would be like if he owned all the treasures he saw. He considered how he would divide the riches among his children.

Then he went down into the garden. Although it was winter everywhere else, the sun was shining here. The birds were singing, the flowers were blooming, and the air was soft and sweet. The merchant was so overjoyed with all he saw and heard that he said to himself, "This magic must have been put here for me. I will go and bring my children to share it with me."

He turned down a path that led to the gate. This path had roses on each side of it, and the merchant thought he had never seen or smelled such delightful flowers. They reminded him of his promise to Beauty, so he picked one to take to her.

Suddenly, the merchant heard a strange noise behind him. Turning around, he saw a frightful Beast, who seemed to be very angry. The Beast roared in a terrible voice: "Who told you that you could pick my roses? Wasn't it enough that I allowed you to stay in my palace? Wasn't it enough that I fed you and was kind to you? This is the way you show your thanks—by stealing my

flowers! Your selfishness shall not go un-punished!"

The merchant was terrified by these furious words and dropped the rose. He then fell on his knees and cried, "Pardon me, noble sir. I am truly grateful for your hospitality. I did not imagine you would be angered if I took such a little thing as a rose."

But the Beast's anger was not soothed by the merchant's speech. "You are very ready with excuses," he cried, "but that will not save you from the death you deserve."

"Alas," thought the merchant, "if my daughter Beauty could only know what danger her rose has brought upon me." ♦

The merchant feared for his life. In despair, he began to tell the Beast all his misfortunes and the reason for his journey. The merchant also mentioned Beauty's request for the rose.

The merchant explained, "A king's treasure would hardly have bought all that my other daughters asked. But I thought I might at least take Beauty her rose. I beg you to forgive me, for you see I meant no harm."

The Beast thought for a moment, and then he said, in a less furious tone, "I will forgive you on one condition—that you give me one of your daughters."

"Ah!" cried the merchant. "I am not cruel enough to buy my own life at the expense of a child's life. Besides, what excuse could I invent to bring one of my daughters here?"

"No excuse would be necessary," answered the Beast. "She must come willingly. See if any one of them has enough courage and loves you enough to save you. You seem to be an honest man, so I will trust you to go home. I will give you a

month to see if any of your daughters will come back with you and stay here, so that you may go free. If none of them is willing, you must come alone after bidding them goodbye forever, for then you will belong to me. And do not imagine that you can hide from me, for if you fail to keep your word, I will come and get you."

The merchant accepted this offer, although he did not really think any of his daughters would come. He promised to return a month later. Then he asked permission to set off at once. But the Beast declared he could not go until the next day.

"Tomorrow you will find a horse ready for you," the Beast said. "Now go and eat your supper, and wait for my orders."

The poor merchant was feeling more dead than alive. He went back to his room, where a delicious supper was already served on the little table. But he was too terrified to eat much, so he only tasted a few of the dishes. After a while, he heard a great noise in the next room.

The Beast appeared and asked roughly if the merchant had eaten well. The merchant answered humbly that he had, thanks to the Beast's kindness. Then the Beast warned him to remember their agreement and to prepare his daughter for what to expect. ★

The Beast added, "Do not get up tomorrow until you see the sun and hear a bell ring. Then you will find your breakfast waiting for you here, and the horse you are to ride will be ready in the courtyard. It will also bring you back when you come with your daughter a month from now. Farewell. Take a rose to Beauty, and remember your promise."

The merchant was glad when the Beast went away, and although he could not sleep, he lay down until the sun rose. When he heard the bell ring, he ate a hasty breakfast and went to pick Beauty's rose. Then he mounted the horse, which carried him off so swiftly that he lost sight of the palace in an instant. Soon, the horse stopped before the door of his cottage.

The merchant's sons and daughters rushed to meet him. When they saw the splendid horse, they thought his journey had gone well. The merchant hid the truth from them at first. But he said to Beauty as he gave her the rose, "Here is what you asked me to bring you. You have no idea what it has cost."

This statement only excited his children's curiosity. At last, he told them his adventures from beginning to end. All his children were unhappy and wept loudly over their lost hopes. They declared that their father should not return to this terrible castle and began to make plans for killing the Beast. But the merchant reminded them that he had promised to go back. Then the girls were angry with Beauty. They said it was all her fault and declared that if she had asked for something sensible this would never have happened.

Poor Beauty was distressed. She said, "I have indeed caused this misfortune, but who could have guessed that a rose would cause so much misery? It is only fair that I should suffer. I will go back with Father to keep his promise."

At first, nobody would agree to that solution, and Beauty's father declared that nothing would make him let her go. But Beauty was firm. As the time to depart grew near, she divided all her possessions between her sisters and said goodbye to everything she loved. And on the day of departure, she encouraged and cheered her father as they mounted the horse.

D COMPREHENSION

Write the answers.
1. Why did the merchant believe the Beast's garden was magical?
2. Why did the merchant pick a rose in the garden?
3. What did the merchant mean when he said, "I am not cruel enough to buy my own life at the expense of a child's life"?
4. Why did Beauty decide to go back to the Beast with her father?
5. What do you think the Beast will do with Beauty?

E WRITING

When the merchant explained what had happened, Beauty's sisters were angry with her. Then Beauty decided to go to the Beast's palace with her father.

• Write a conversation between Beauty, her sisters, and her father. Have the father explain what happened with the Beast. Then have Beauty's sisters say what they feel. Finally, have Beauty announce her decision.

A WORD LISTS

1	2	3	4
Hard Words	**Word Practice**	**Vocabulary Review**	**New Vocabulary**
1. statue	1. paw	1. conceal	1. long for
2. chandelier	2. pawing	2. dread	2. chandelier
3. bracelet	3. patience	3. hasty	3. portrait
4. portrait	4. impatience		4. grief
5. grief			5. refuse
6. refuse			

B READING

Beauty and the Beast
Chapter 3

The horse seemed to fly rather than gallop. But it went so smoothly that neither Beauty nor her father felt frightened. The merchant still tried to persuade Beauty to go back, but she would not listen. While they were talking night fell, and then, to their great surprise, wonderfully colored lights began to shine in all directions; and splendid fireworks blazed before them. All the forest was lit up, and the air felt pleasantly warm, although it had been bitterly cold before.

The fireworks lasted until Beauty and her father reached the row of orange trees, where statues were holding flaming torches. When they arrived at the palace, they saw that it was lit up from the roof to the ground, and music sounded softly from the courtyard.

"The Beast must be very hungry," said Beauty, trying to laugh, "if he makes all this rejoicing over the arrival of his prey."

But in spite of her anxiety, Beauty could not help admiring all the wonderful things she saw. When the horse stopped in front of the castle, they got off, and the merchant led Beauty to the little room he had been in before. They found a splendid fire

burning and a delicious supper spread on the table.

The merchant knew this supper was meant for them; and Beauty was quite willing to eat, for the long ride had made her very hungry. But they had hardly finished their meal when they heard the Beast approaching. Beauty clung to her father in terror, which became all the greater when she saw how frightened he was. But when the Beast appeared, Beauty made a great effort to hide her terror. She bowed to him respectfully and thanked him for his hospitality.

Her behavior seemed to please the Beast. After looking at her, he said, in a tone that might have struck terror in the boldest heart, "Good evening, sir. Good evening, Beauty."

The merchant was too terrified to reply, but Beauty answered sweetly, "Good evening, Beast."

"Have you come willingly?" asked the Beast. "Will you be content to stay here when your father goes away?"

Beauty answered bravely that she was quite prepared to stay.

"I am pleased with you," said the Beast. "You seem to have come of your own choice, so you may stay. As for you, sir," he added, turning to the merchant, "at sunrise tomorrow you will leave. When the bell rings, get up and eat your breakfast. You will find the same horse waiting to take you home. But remember that you must never expect to see my palace again." ◆

Then the Beast turned to Beauty and said, "Take your father into the next room and help him choose everything you think your brothers and sisters would like to have. You will find two trunks there; fill them as full as you can. It is only fair that you should send them something precious to remember you by."

Then the Beast went away. Beauty dreaded her father's departure, but she was afraid to disobey the Beast's orders. So they went into the next room, which had shelves and cupboards all around it. They were greatly surprised at the riches the room contained. Beauty and her father went from cupboard to cupboard, selecting precious things, which they heaped into the two trunks. There were splendid dresses fit for a queen, and gorgeous jewels that were heaped on every shelf. After choosing the finest riches and filling the two trunks, Beauty opened the last cupboard. She was amazed to discover that it was completely filled with gold.

She said, "I think, Father, that the gold will be more useful to you. We should remove the other things and fill the trunk with gold."

So they removed the precious things and began heaping gold into the trunks. But the more they put in, the more room there seemed to be. They were able to put back all the jewels and dresses they had taken out, and Beauty even added many more jewels. The trunks were soon so heavy that an elephant could not have carried them.

"The Beast was deceiving us," cried the merchant. "He must have pretended to give us all these things, knowing I could not carry them away."

"Let us wait and see," answered Beauty. "I cannot believe that he meant to deceive us. All we can do is fasten the trunks up and leave them here."

When they arose the next morning, they found breakfast ready. The merchant ate his food with a healthy appetite. He secretly believed that he might come back soon and see Beauty. But she felt sure that her father was leaving her forever, so she was very sad when breakfast was over. The time had come for them to part. ★

They went down into the courtyard, where two horses were waiting. One was loaded down with the trunks, and the other was saddled for the merchant to ride. The horses were pawing the ground impatiently waiting to start, so the merchant was forced to bid Beauty a hasty farewell. As soon as he was mounted, he went off at such a pace

that Beauty lost sight of him in an instant. Then Beauty began to cry, and she wandered sadly back to her room.

Beauty was still sleepy. She had nothing better to do, so she lay down and fell asleep. She dreamed she was walking by a brook bordered with trees. In her dream, she was quite sad. Then she saw a Prince, more handsome than anyone she had ever seen. His voice went straight to her heart.

"Ah, Beauty," he said, "you are not as unfortunate as you think. In this palace you will be rewarded for all you have suffered.

Your every wish shall be granted. I love you dearly, and in making me happy, you will find your own happiness. Be as true-hearted as you are beautiful, and we shall be very happy."

Beauty asked, "What can I do, Prince, to make you happy?"

"Only be grateful," he answered, "and do not trust your eyes too much. Above all, do not desert me until you have saved me from my misery."

Beauty did not know what the Prince meant. Suddenly he turned to leave and said, "Dear Beauty, try not to regret all you have left behind you. Just do not be deceived by the way things appear."

Beauty found this dream so interesting that she was in no hurry to wake up. But at last the clock woke her by calling her name softly twelve times. She got up and found dinner waiting in the next room. But eating dinner does not take very long when you are all by yourself, and soon she sat down in the corner on a cozy sofa and began to think about the charming Prince she had seen in her dream.

"He said I could make him happy," said Beauty to herself. "I think that the Beast keeps him a prisoner. How can I set the Prince free? I wonder why he told me not to be deceived by the way things appear?"

C COMPREHENSION

Write the answers.
1. As Beauty approached the castle, what made her think the Beast was rejoicing?
2. How did Beauty behave when she first met the Beast?
3. How can you tell the trunks were magic?
4. What do you think the Prince meant when he said, "Do not trust your eyes too much"?
5. Beauty thought the Beast was keeping the Prince a prisoner. Do you agree with her? Explain your answer.

D WRITING

Pretend that the Beast also had a dream after Beauty arrived at his palace.
- Write the story of the Beast's dream. Describe which characters appear in the dream, such as the merchant, Beauty, or the Prince. Then write about what those characters do and say. Also describe what the Beast does.

A WORD LISTS

1	2
Compound Words	*Vocabulary Review*
1. candlesticks	1. long for
2. lifetime	2. portrait
3. riverbank	3. chandelier

B READING

Beauty and the Beast
Chapter 4

Beauty began to explore some of the rooms in the palace. The first room she entered was lined with mirrors, and she saw herself reflected on every side. She had never seen such a charming room. Then a bracelet hanging from a chandelier caught her eye. She took it down and was greatly surprised to find that it held a portrait of the Prince she had dreamed about. With great delight, she slipped the bracelet on her arm and went into a large room filled with pictures. She soon found a portrait of the same handsome Prince, as large as life. It was so well painted that he seemed to smile kindly at her.

Beauty tore herself away from the portrait at last. She then went into a room that contained every musical instrument under the sun, and here she amused herself for a long while trying them out and singing until she was tired. The next room was a library. She saw everything she had ever wanted to read, as well as everything she had already read. There were so many books that a whole lifetime would not be long enough even to read the names of them.

By this time it was growing dark, and candles in diamond and ruby candlesticks were beginning to light themselves in every room. Beauty found her supper served at the exact time she preferred to have it, but she did not see anyone or hear a sound.

Although her father had warned her she would be alone, she realized her life would not be dull.

After a while, Beauty heard the Beast coming, and she wondered if he meant to harm her. However, the Beast did not seem at all terrifying. He said gruffly, "Good evening, Beauty."

Beauty answered cheerfully, concealing her terror. The Beast asked her how she had been amusing herself, and she told him about all the rooms she had seen.

Then the Beast asked her if she was happy in his palace, and Beauty answered that everything was so wonderful that she was quite happy. After about an hour's talk, Beauty began to think the Beast was not nearly so terrible as she first thought.

At last, the Beast got up to leave and said in a gruff voice, "Beauty, will you marry me?"

Beauty was astonished by his question. She did not know what to say, for she was afraid to make the Beast angry by refusing.

"Say yes or no without fear," the Beast went on.

"No, Beast," said Beauty hastily.

"Since you will not marry me, Beauty" he replied, "I will say good night."

And Beauty answered, "Good night, Beast." She was glad her refusal had not made him angry. ♦

After the Beast had gone, Beauty was soon asleep in bed, dreaming of her Prince. She dreamed he came to her and said, "Ah, Beauty, why are you so unkind to me?"

And then Beauty's dreams changed, but the charming prince was in all of them. When morning came, her first thought was to look at the portrait and see if it really looked like the Prince, and she found that it did.

That morning, Beauty decided to work in the garden. The sun was shining, and all the fountains were spraying trails of sparkling water. She was astonished to find that every place was familiar to her from her dream. She came to the brook where she had first met the Prince in her dream. It made her think more than ever that he must be the Beast's prisoner.

After supper that evening, the Beast paid her another visit and asked the same question as before. Then with a gruff "Good night," he left, and Beauty went to bed to dream of her mysterious Prince.

The days passed swiftly. Every evening after supper, the Beast came to see her, and always before saying good night, he asked her in his terrible voice, "Beauty, will you marry me?"

Now that Beauty understood him better, it seemed to her that he went away quite sad. But her happy dreams of the handsome young Prince soon made her forget the poor Beast.

So the days and nights passed in the same way for a long time, until at last Beauty began to long for her father and brothers and sisters. One night she seemed so sad that the Beast asked her what was the matter.

Beauty was no longer afraid of the Beast. She knew that he was really gentle in spite of his terrifying looks and dreadful voice. So she explained that she wanted to see her home once more. The Beast seemed greatly distressed when he heard this, and he replied, "Ah, Beauty, do you have the heart to desert an unhappy Beast? Is it because you hate me that you want to escape?"

"No, dear Beast," answered Beauty softly, "I do not hate you, and I should be very sorry never to see you anymore. But I long to see my father again. Only let me go for two months, and I promise to come back to you and stay for the rest of my life." ★

The Beast, who had been sighing while she spoke, now replied. "I cannot refuse anything you ask, even though it might cost me my life. Take the four boxes you find in the room next to yours and fill them with everything you wish to take. But remember your promise to come back when two months are over. If you do not come in good time, you will find your faithful Beast dead."

The Beast stopped for a minute and gave Beauty a ring. "You will not need a horse to bring you back," he said. "Only say goodbye to all your brothers and sisters the night before you leave, and when you have gone to bed, turn this ring around your finger and say, 'I wish to go back to the palace and see the Beast again.' Good night, Beauty. Fear nothing, sleep peacefully, and before long you shall see your father once more."

As soon as Beauty was alone, she hurried to fill the boxes with all the rare and precious things she saw about her, and only when she was tired of heaping things into the boxes did they seem to be full.

Then she went to bed, but she could hardly sleep. And when at last she did begin to dream of her beloved Prince, she was sorry to see him stretched upon a grassy bank, sad and weary, and hardly like himself.

"What is the matter?" she cried.

He looked at her sadly and said, "How can you ask me, cruel one? You are leaving me to my death."

"Don't be so sorrowful," said Beauty. "I am only going to show my father that I am safe and happy. I have promised the Beast faithfully that I will come back. He would die of grief if I did not keep my word."

"What would that matter to you?" said the Prince. "Do you really care about him?"

"I should be ungrateful if I did not care for such a kind Beast," cried Beauty. "I would die to save him from pain. It is not his fault he is so ugly."

But the Prince said nothing, and only turned his face from her.

C MAIN IDEA

Write the main idea for the following paragraph.

The year was 1896. A boat with three men in it floated down the Klondike River. At one point, the boat stopped and the men got out. They had seen something at the bottom of the river. One of the men scooped up a handful of dirt and pebbles from the bottom of the river. He sifted through the material and saw something that glistened yellow in the sun. He looked more closely, then let out a whoop of joy. "We're going to be rich," he said. The other men began to scoop up the pebbles as fast as they could.

D COMPREHENSION

Write the answers.
1. Why do you think there was a portrait of the Prince in the palace?
2. Why do you think Beauty would not agree to marry the Beast?
3. Why did Beauty want to return home?
4. How did the Prince feel about Beauty's return home?
5. How did Beauty feel about the Beast at the end of the chapter?

E WRITING

Do you think Beauty should marry the Beast?
• Write an essay that explains your answer. First give reasons why Beauty should marry the Beast. Then give reasons why she shouldn't. Finally, give your own opinion and explain why you feel that way.

A WORD LISTS

```
           1
    Word Endings
    1. joyfully
    2. constantly
    3. loudly
    4. dearly
    5. apparently
```

```
           2
    New Vocabulary
    1. trust appearances
    2. trace of
    3. spell
    4. despite
```

B READING

Beauty and the Beast
Chapter 5

In Beauty's dream, she was about to speak to the Prince, but a strange sound woke her. Someone was speaking nearby. When Beauty opened her eyes, she found herself in a room she had never seen before. It was nearly as splendid as the rooms in the Beast's palace. Where could she be?

She got up and dressed hastily, and then saw that the boxes she had packed the night before were all in the room. While she was wondering how she got to this strange place, she suddenly heard her father's voice. She rushed out and greeted him joyfully.

Her brothers and sisters were astonished because they never expected to see her again, and there was no end to the questions they asked her. They told her what had happened to them while she was away.

When Beauty's family heard she had only come for a short stay, they sobbed loudly. Then Beauty asked her father what he thought her strange dreams could mean, and why the Prince constantly begged her not to trust appearances.

Her father thought for a while, then answered. "You tell me that the Beast, frightful as he is, loves you dearly. You say that the Beast deserves your love for his kind-

ness. I think the Prince wants you to marry the Beast in spite of his ugliness."

Beauty thought her father's answer was right, but still, when she thought of her dear, handsome Prince, she did not want to marry the Beast. For two months she did not have to decide, so she could enjoy herself with her family. Although they were rich now and lived in a town again with plenty of friends, Beauty found that nothing amused her very much. She often thought of the palace where she was so

happy. Furthermore, she never once dreamed of her dear Prince, and she felt quite sad without him.

Her sisters had grown quite used to being without her, and they even found her in the way. But her father begged her to stay and seemed very sad at the thought of her leaving. So Beauty put off her departure. ♦

On the night Beauty was to return to the palace, she had a dismal dream. She dreamed she was wandering on a lonely path in the palace gardens and heard groans coming from a cave. She ran quickly to see what was the matter and found the Beast stretched out upon his side, apparently dying. He said Beauty was the cause of his illness, and he moaned pitifully.

Beauty was so terrified by this dream that the next morning she announced she was going back at once; and that very night she said goodbye to her father and all her brothers and sisters.

As soon as Beauty was in bed, she turned the ring around her finger and said, "I wish to go back to the palace and see the Beast again."

Then she fell asleep instantly, and only woke up to hear the clock saying, "Beauty, Beauty," twelve times. She knew at once that she was in the palace again. Everything was just as before, but Beauty had never known such a long day. She was so anxious to see the Beast again that she felt supper time would never come.

But when it did come and no Beast appeared, she was frightened. After listening and waiting for a long time, she ran down into the garden to search for him. No one answered her calls, and she could not find a trace of him. At last, she stopped for a minute's rest and saw she was standing near the cave she had seen in her dreams. She entered the cave, and sure enough, there was the Beast, fast asleep. Beauty was glad to have found him. She ran up and stroked his head, but to her horror he did not move or open his eyes.

"Oh, he is dead, and it is all my fault," said Beauty, crying bitterly. But then she looked at him again and saw that he was still breathing. She got some water from the nearest fountain and sprinkled it over his face. To her great delight, he began to wake up. ★

"Oh, Beast, how you frightened me," she cried. "I never knew how much I loved you until just now, when I feared I was too late to save your life."

"Can you really love such an ugly creature as I?" asked the Beast faintly. "Ah, Beauty, you came just in time. I was dying because I thought you had forgotten your promise. But go back now and rest. I shall see you again soon."

Beauty had expected him to be angry with her, but she was reassured by his gentle voice. She went back to the palace, where supper was awaiting her. Afterward, the Beast came in as usual, and they talked about the time she had spent with her father. The Beast asked if she had enjoyed herself, and if her family had been glad to see her.

Beauty answered politely and quite enjoyed telling him all that had happened to her. At last, the time came for him to go, and he asked, as he had so often asked before, "Beauty, will you marry me?"

Beauty answered softly, "Yes, dear Beast."

As she spoke, a blaze of light sprang up before the windows of the palace. Beauty turned to ask the Beast what it could all mean but found that he had disappeared. In his place stood her long-loved Prince!

"Ah, Beauty," he said. "You have rescued me at last from my terrible spell."

Beauty looked at him in amazement and begged him to explain.

The Prince said, "When I was young, a witch put a spell on me and changed me into the Beast. She said that I would keep that form until I met a woman who had enough courage to love me despite my ugliness. You are that woman, and now we will be husband and wife."

The Prince came up to Beauty and kissed her. They were married the next day, and they lived happily ever after. And every day, the Prince would go into his garden and bring Beauty a rose.

C COMPREHENSION

Write the answers.
1. How had the Prince been changed into the Beast?
2. What was the only way the Beast could change back into the Prince?
3. At first, why was it so difficult for Beauty to love the Beast?
4. Why did she change her mind?
5. Why were roses so important in this story?

D WRITING

A famous poem begins, "My love is like a red, red rose."
- Write an essay, a poem or a story that describes how love is like a rose. Think about people who are in love. How do they behave? What kinds of problems do they have? How do they fix those problems? Then think about how their love might be like a rose.

A WORD LISTS

1
Hard Words
1. ne'er
2. 'tis
3. I'm
4. I've
5. I'll
6. you're
7. you've

2
New Vocabulary
1. parlor
2. weary
3. pantry
4. pearly

The Spider and the Fly
by Mary Howitt
Part 1

"Will you walk into my parlor?" said the spider to the fly,
"'Tis the prettiest little parlor that ever you did spy;
The way into my parlor is up a winding stair,
And I've many curious things to show when you are there."
"Oh, no, no," said the little fly, "to ask me is in vain,
For who goes up your winding stair can ne'er come down again."

"I'm sure you must be weary, dear, with soaring up so high;
Will you rest upon my little bed?" said the spider to the fly.
"There are pretty curtains drawn around; the sheets are fine and thin,
And if you like to rest a while, I'll snugly tuck you in!"
"Oh, no, no," said the little fly, "for I've often heard it said,
They never, never wake again, who sleep upon your bed!"

Said the cunning spider to the fly, "Dear friend, what can I do
To prove the warm affection I've always felt for you?
I have within my pantry good store of all that's nice;
I'm sure you're very welcome—will you please to take a slice?"
"Oh no, no," said the little fly, "kind sir, that cannot be;
I've heard what's in your pantry, and I do not wish to see!"

"Sweet creature," said the spider, "you're witty and you're wise,
How handsome are your pearly wings, how brilliant are your eyes!
I have a little looking-glass upon my parlor shelf,
If you'll step in one moment, dear, you shall behold yourself."
"I thank you, gentle sir," she said, "for what you're pleased to say
And bidding you good morning now, I'll call another day."

C COMPREHENSION

Write the answers.

1. Why do you think the spider keeps offering food and other treats to the fly?
2. What do you think the spider actually plans to do with the fly?
3. Do you think the fly knows what the spider is doing? Explain your answer.
4. Why would a looking-glass be tempting to the fly?
5. What do you think will happen in the next part of the poem? Explain your answer.

D WRITING

At the end of the fourth stanza, the spider leaves the fly.

- Write a new fifth stanza for the poem. Your stanza should show what happens after the fly thinks about the spider's offers. Tell what the fly does, then tell what the spider does.
- Write your stanza in the same form as the first four stanzas, with six lines and three rhyming couplets.

A WORD LISTS

1	2
Vocabulary Review	*New Vocabulary*
1. parlor	1. subtle
2. weary	2. hither
3. pantry	3. alas
4. pearly	4. aloft
	5. hue

B READING

The Spider and the Fly
Part 2

The spider then turned round about, and went into his den,
For well he knew the silly fly would soon come back again;
So he wove a subtle web, in a little corner sly,
And set his table ready, to dine upon the fly.
Then he came out to his door again, and merrily did sing,
"Come hither, hither, pretty fly, with the pearl and silver wing;
Your robes are green and purple—there's a crest upon your head;
Your eyes are like the diamond bright, but mine are dull as lead!"

Alas, alas! how very soon this silly little fly,
Hearing the cunning, flattering words, came slowly flitting by;
With buzzing wings she hung aloft, then near and nearer drew,
Thinking only of her brilliant eyes, and green and purple hue—
Thinking only of her crested head—poor foolish thing! At last,
Up jumped the cunning spider, and fiercely held her fast.
He dragged her up his winding stair, into his dismal den,
Within his little parlor—but she ne'er came out again!

And now, to all you people, who may this story read,
To idle, silly, flattering words, I pray you ne'er give heed;
And unto evil creatures close heart and ear and eye,
And take a lesson from this tale of the spider and the fly.

C COMPREHENSION

Write the answers.
1. What were some of the "cunning and flattering" things the spider told the fly?
2. What was the fly "thinking only of" as she hung aloft near the spider?
3. What happened to the fly at the end of the poem?
4. What lesson does this poem teach us about flattering words?
5. What lesson does this poem teach us about evil creatures?

D WRITING

"The Spider and the Fly" teaches us lessons about flattering words and evil creatures.

- Write a story that teaches a lesson. The lesson can be about flattering words, evil creatures, or whatever you want.
- First write down the lesson you want your story to teach. Then think of a story that teaches the lesson. You can use animals or people for your characters, and you can set the story wherever you want. It can take place in a make-believe land or in the real world.

83

A WORD LISTS

1	2	3
Hard Words	*Place Names*	*New Vocabulary*
1. suburbs	1. Halsted Street	1. suburbs
2. Italian	2. Hull House	2. slum
3. Russian	3. Chicago	
4. exist	4. Michigan	
5. memory		

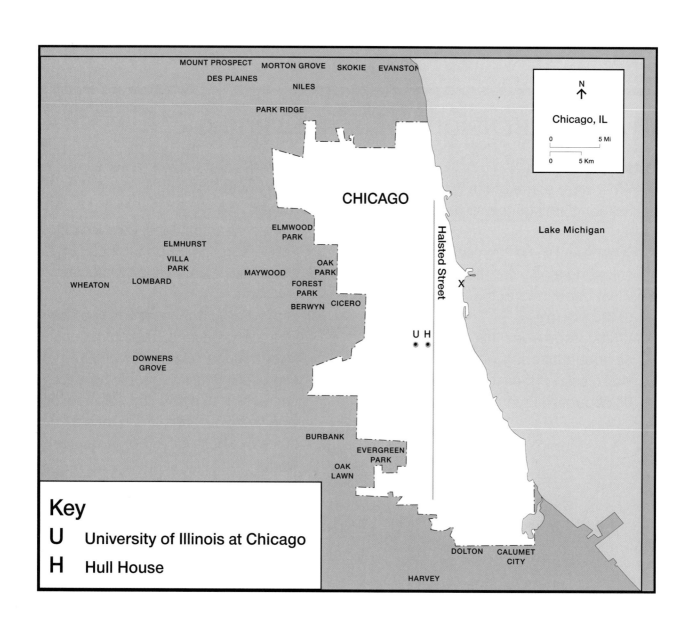

Key

U   University of Illinois at Chicago

H   Hull House

Hull House

Chicago is a huge city—one of the largest cities in the United States. The city itself has about three million inhabitants, and almost five million more people live in the suburbs that surround the city on the north, south, and west. There are no suburbs on the east side of Chicago because that side of the city is on the shore of Lake Michigan.

Chicago is like many other modern cities. The downtown part of the city has towering buildings filled with offices, apartments, and hotels. The rest of the city is made up of houses and factories.

You will be reading a biography that begins in Chicago in 1889. The biography is about a woman named Jane Addams. At that time, she was twenty-nine years old, and she worked in one of the city's poorest neighborhoods.

It's easy to get to the neighborhood where Jane Addams worked. Just go to the middle of downtown Chicago, which is called the Loop. Then go exactly one mile to the west. You'll come to a street called Halsted Street, where Jane Addams lived.

Halsted Street looks greatly different now than it did in 1889. The University of Illinois at Chicago stands right in the middle of the neighborhood where Jane Addams lived. On the edge of the university is a big old house. Today that house is a museum, but in 1889, it was where Jane Addams lived. She made that house into one of the most famous places in the world. It was called Hull House.

Presidents of the United States visited Hull House, and so did kings and queens from all over the world. The house was important because it changed the way that people thought about neighborhoods. Although many people worked at Hull House, it existed because of just one person. That person was Jane Addams.

You're going to read about the things Jane Addams did, but different narrators are going to tell you the story. One narrator will tell the first part, another narrator will tell the second part, and a third narrator will tell the last part. The narrators are fictional. But the things the narrators tell about are facts. The first fictional narrator is Maria Rossi, who was a young girl in 1889, when Jane Addams moved into Hull House.

Jane Addams
Chapter 1

Maria Rossi's Story

I lived a few blocks from Hull House in 1889, and I knew Jane Addams well. You cannot appreciate the story I have to tell unless you come back with me to 1889 and share some of the things I saw and felt and lived with.

The neighborhood around Hull House was different then. People who did not live there called it a horrible slum—and it was horrible in a lot of ways. But I lived there, and for me, it was not all bad. I lived with Mama and Papa on the first floor of a little building. We had three rooms, which was not much room for our family because there were eight children. Grandmother Rossi also lived with us.

My parents did not speak English. On our street and in our house, we spoke Italian. My parents had come from Italy when I was just one year old. They had thought it would be easy to get rich in the United States, but it was not easy. It was hard to get a good-paying job, so we had to live in the poor neighborhood near Hull House. ♦

Mama did not have a job, but Papa did, and so did all the children after they became twelve years old. When I turned twelve years old in 1889, I worked in a candy factory on Halsted Street. I worked there from seven in the morning until seven at night. Papa worked even longer hours than I did. We did not see him until nine at night, when he was very tired. Six days a week he worked these long hours, but he earned so little money that we could hardly purchase enough food.

Our neighborhood was packed with small wooden houses. We had no lawns or playgrounds. We had no indoor toilets, and some of our houses had no inside water. The whole neighborhood had a bad smell in the summertime. ★

The smell came from the garbage. The garbage collectors only came once in a while, so the garbage sometimes stayed around for weeks at a time. We would throw the garbage in wooden boxes next to the street, and there it would stay, attracting swarms of flies and thousands of rats. There were also rats in our house. We were careful about trying to catch them in traps, but there were so many rats in the neighborhood that we could not keep them out of our place.

Our neighborhood was all Italian people, and everybody spoke Italian. But you could go a few blocks away and you would be in a Greek neighborhood, and nobody could understand Italian at all. Instead, they would speak Greek. You could go a few more blocks and you would be in a Russian neighborhood. Each neighborhood was like a small world, and I felt most comfortable in my world—my neighborhood.

D COMPREHENSION

Write the answers.

1. Why are there no suburbs on the east side of Chicago?
2. Why didn't Maria's parents speak English?
3. Why did Maria's family live in the neighborhood near Hull House?
4. Why did Maria's neighborhood smell bad in the summertime?
5. Why was it hard for people from the different neighborhoods to understand each other?

E WRITING

What is your neighborhood like?

Write an essay that describes your neighborhood. Be sure your essay answers the following questions:

- Where is your neighborhood located?
- How big is your neighborhood?
- What does your neighborhood look like?
- What kind of people live in your neighborhood?
- How do you feel about your neighborhood? Why do you feel that way?

A WORD LISTS

1	2	3	4
Hard Words	*Word Endings*	*Vocabulary Review*	*New Vocabulary*
1. buon giorno	1. pitifully	1. slum	1. peddler
2. sausage	2. instantly	2. mayor	2. foreman
3. agile	3. bitterly	3. suburbs	3. agile
4. nowhere	4. politely		
5. sewing			
6. Gino			

B READING

Jane Addams
Chapter 2

Maria Rossi continues:

I have told you about the bad in my neighborhood, but you should know about the good as well. In the morning you would wake up to the sounds of horses clumping along the street. Most of the horses were owned by peddlers pulling carts. Some peddlers sold ice; some sold vegetables; some sold milk; some sold coal to burn in the stove. The ragman would sing, "Rags for sale!" as he sat up on his cart behind an old nag that clumped down the street.

During the summer, the other children and I would follow the iceman. When somebody would buy ice, the iceman would go inside the back of his cart and slide out a huge block of ice. Then he'd take an ice pick and cut the ice into smaller blocks. When he did this, small chunks of ice would splinter off and fall. We would rush to pick them up. Then we would suck on them until they were all gone. The ice was wonderful, and so were the bright sun, the yellow ice wagon with the big letters on the side, and the warmth of the street on our bare feet.

And then there were picnics. Sunday was special—always special. It was family

day because it was the only day we had to-gether. Whenever we could, we would have a picnic. We would get on a streetcar that was pulled by horses. Then we would go all the way past downtown to a beach along Lake Michigan. It was like going to a dif-ferent world.

The beach had clean water and clean air. I did not know how to swim, but I think I could have sat there forever, just watch-ing the small waves move in. When we came home, I would try to remember the sound of the beach when it was too hot to

sleep. I would think about the beach and try to ignore the mosquitoes that buzzed all around my pillow.

On those picnic days, we would eat well. To me, there is no food like Italian food. Mama would have some of the special sausage that came from Italy. That sausage is as hard as a brick before it is cooked. But when it is cooked and you eat it with pep-pers and tomatoes, it is delicious.

We ate and we sang, and we tried to make those days last forever. But too soon they would end, and we would return home on the streetcar, with the sun going down and the lamplighters lighting up the street lights. The day was over. But it wasn't really over because I had it in my memory, and I could think about it any time I wished. I could remember the sand on the beach, and the songs, and Papa dancing, and the food.

The morning after a picnic day was a work day. I would wake up to the sound of Mama calling us. The air would be cool, and a gentle wind would be blowing through the open windows into the room. I could hear the sounds of chickens and roosters from the house next door. Peddlers were already calling from the street, and many people were already walking to work.

Most of the people in our neighborhood walked. They did not own horses. It was silly to own a horse because if you had one, you would have to keep it inside the house with you. And we did not like to live that way. But two people on our block did have horses they kept inside at night.

I knew nearly all the people who walked past our place on their way to work. And everybody who was walking knew everybody else. So you would hear them calling greetings to each other in Italian. They would say, "Buon giorno," and then they would laugh and talk to each other. Just looking at them would make you want to smile and talk. ◆

One time I made a bad mistake at work. My job was to wrap pieces of hard candy with red paper. The girl who worked next to me wrapped candy in yellow paper. I got mixed up and wrapped all the hard candy in yellow paper. Oh, how I got yelled at by the foreman!

Everybody in our neighborhood found out about what happened, because every-body knew about everything. People teased me for months about not knowing the difference between red and yellow paper. Sometimes one of the men would pull a red handkerchief from his pocket and hold it up. Then he would say, "Maria, can you tell if this is red or yellow?" Everybody would laugh.

We would not argue with Mama and Papa. You did not want to do that. But people in our neighborhood would argue a lot. In the morning you could hear Mama arguing with a peddler about the prices of eggs and fresh fruit. She was so good at buying things that the people on their way to work would pause just to admire her.

The peddler would tell Mama that the eggs were fifteen cents a dozen. Of course, that was ridiculous. Mama would laugh and wave her arms. She would pick up one of the eggs, hold it up, and say in a very loud voice with a very large smile, "Fifteen cents!" She wasn't talking to the peddler. She was talking to the people who were on their way to work. She was putting on a show for them.

"Fifteen cents!" she would repeat, waving her arms. "You must be in the wrong neighborhood. There are no trees here. And there are no trees that grow money! What do you think? We pick the money from the trees so we can buy eggs for fifteen cents?" ★

The peddler would try to hush her up. "Please, please," he would say softly. "For you, twelve cents."

Mama would shout, "Twelve cents! A penny an egg. You must think that we have money bushes! Look around. You have eyes. Show me the money bush!"

By now the people passing by would be smiling and talking among themselves about Mama's great performance. "Please, please," the peddler would say. "I have a family. I must earn money, too. These are good eggs, and my price is fair."

"He says his price is fair," Mama would announce. "But I ask, who is it fair to?"

Nobody paid the prices the peddler asked. Everybody would bargain and argue. And maybe Mama didn't get things any cheaper than the other people on the street. But she sure put on a better show.

She would come home with the things she purchased, singing and smiling. We would help her fix breakfast. Mama would talk all the time. Sometimes she would get mad at us, but most of the time she was cheerful. Then we would eat breakfast, and when it was over, I would get a sad feeling because now it was time to go to work.

To get to work, I would walk on the wooden sidewalks past the old house on Halsted Street that would become Hull House. I would walk over a mile until I came to the candy factory. Usually, I would walk with some of the other girls and boys who worked there. We would talk and joke with each other until we came to the factory entrance. Then we would become serious, and we would start to speak in English. They didn't like us to speak Italian at work, but I knew enough English to get by.

C COMPREHENSION

Write the answers.
1. Which peddler would Maria and her friends follow in the summer? Why?
2. Describe how the beach was different from Maria's neighborhood.
3. Why did people stop to watch Maria's mother talking to the peddlers?
4. Why do you think the peddlers set their prices so high?
5. Why do you think Maria had to speak English at the factory?

D WRITING

In the story, Maria described the picnics her family would have. What kind of picnic would you like to have?

Write an essay that describes what kind of picnic you would like to have. Be sure your essay answers the following questions:
- Where would you go for the picnic?
- What would the weather be like?
- Who would go with you on the picnic?
- What food would you take?
- What would you do during and after the picnic?

A WORD LISTS

1	2
Word Practice	*Vocabulary Review*
1. kindergarten	1. agile
2. sewing	2. peddler
3. Gino	3. foreman
4. crayon	
5. wad	
6. nowhere	

B READING

Jane Addams
Chapter 3

Maria Rossi continues:

If you did not get to work by seven o'clock, you would lose one hour of pay. You would lose an hour even if you were one minute late. So, I was always on time.

The inside of the factory was dark, even though it had large windows in the ceiling. I didn't like the smell, even though it was the sweet odor of candy. When I first came to work in the factory, I loved the smell. But, we used to eat the candy when we got hungry, and after a while I grew to hate the taste of that candy and its odor.

For many years after I worked in that factory, I would have a terrible feeling if I even smelled candy.

You could not talk when you were working. A foreman walked around to make sure you were not talking and you were working hard. If you stopped for a moment to look at the clock, the foreman would yell at you. "Hey, what do you think we're paying you for? Get to work!"

I had to stand next to the other girls near a large slide. Hundreds of pieces of candy would keep tumbling down the slide.

We'd wrap each piece and then toss the wrapped candy into big boxes. If the pile of candy at the bottom of the slide got too big, the foreman would yell, "Come on! Work faster!"

I was fast. My fingers were agile, and I practiced with them. I could tie my shoes in less than three seconds, which is faster than anybody I'd ever seen. And I could wrap a piece of candy in less than one second. Most of the other girls were nowhere near that fast, so they got yelled at a lot more than I did.

In the morning, we stood at the line for two hours, then we got five minutes off. We could talk during the break. Then we went back to work until our lunch break at noon. We got twenty minutes for lunch. After that, we kept working until six o'clock.

We spent the last hour cleaning up. They let us talk when we cleaned up, so that was fun. Everybody was tired, and we were glad the day was over. We walked home slowly, feeling happy to be done.

That's how it went every day—summer and winter. But in September 1889, we had something new to talk about. Mama was the first to tell us. One morning, she came in laughing after talking to Gino, who sold milk. She said, "Some rich young ladies are moving into our neighborhood." Then she bowed low, and we all laughed.

I asked, "Why would rich young ladies want to live here?"

Mama gave a sly smile. "To help us live better." She laughed. "Gino says that they are going to turn the old Hull place into a settlement house."

"What's a settlement house?" we asked.

"I don't know," said Mama, with big eyes. "But whatever it is, it will help us live better." She shook her head and added, "Crazy women."

That day on the way to work, I stopped in front of the old Hull place to see if I could get a glimpse of those crazy women. And I did. There they were, standing out in front of the old place, talking to some workmen. The women were well dressed. I had never seen women like these outside of downtown Chicago. One of them took a few steps toward the house as she said something to the workmen. I didn't know this woman was Jane Addams and the other one was her friend, Ellen Starr.

But before the day was over, I had heard all about them. At work, the girls passed messages down the line. One girl would whisper the message when the foreman was not looking. Then the next girl would pass the message on.

From the messages, I learned that Jane Addams and Ellen Starr were going to help the people in the neighborhoods around Hull House. Even more amazing, these women were not going to be paid for anything they did. When I heard these things, I could not understand these women, but I said to myself that if they were really going to do these things, I would admire them. ♦

As I stood there on the line wrapping candy, I thought about what I would do if I were a rich woman. Maybe I would do what Jane Addams was trying to do. Perhaps I would try to make things better so the people in my neighborhood could have a better life. But in the back of my mind, I couldn't really believe Jane Addams would do this nice work.

The only rich people I ever saw in my neighborhood were the ones who came in and out of the factory. I saw the owner, Mr. Flannigan, a few times. He was a bad person. He did not care about anything but making candy. He did not care if you were sick, if you had to work until your fingers were covered with blisters, or if you did not earn enough money each day to buy food. Because he did not care, I thought all rich people did not care. I had a lot to learn about some rich people.

Two weeks went by. Each time I heard some news about the activities that were going on in Hull House, I tried to imagine what it would be like inside. The girls at work told me there was expensive furniture. They told me Jane Addams was going to start cooking and sewing classes. They told me there were activities for young boys.

But the news I found most amazing was that Hull House was going to have a free kindergarten for young children. The children would play games, learn to speak English, and have a good meal. One morning, Mama commented on the kindergarten. She shook her head and said, "This cannot be true. How can they afford to run a free school? There is nothing free in this whole world." ★

But Mama was wrong. The day after she told me about the kindergarten, I paused in front of Hull House on my way to work. As I stood there, part of my mind told me Mama was right. But another part was so curious that I decided to go inside and look around. After all, lots of other people were going in and out of Hull House. They were smiling and talking in three different languages—Greek, Russian, and Italian.

I was anxious as I walked up the front steps, following a mother with a little boy and a little girl. Jane Addams was at the top of the stairs, just inside the doorway, talking to an old man. When she saw the woman with the two children, she said, "I see we have two new children for our kindergarten."

The woman could not speak English, but you could see she was apologizing because her little boy was crying.

"He'll be fine," Jane Addams said, taking the boy by the hand. Then she led him into the parlor. I followed them and peeked inside. What the girls had told me about the house was correct. There was expensive furniture, and the floors were clean and polished. I imagined it was just like being inside a rich person's house.

Suddenly I heard somebody talking to me. It was Jane Addams. She said, "What can I do for you?"

I wanted to apologize for coming inside. I wanted to tell her I had a younger brother who was the right age for kindergarten. I wanted to tell her I was curious. But before I could say anything, she said, "Welcome to Hull House."

I could not talk for a moment. Then I managed to say, "Your house is beautiful."

She laughed and replied, "Well, thank you. But it is not beautiful yet; and it is not my house. It is our house—yours and mine and all the other neighbors."

I don't remember what I said next, but I do remember that before I left I asked if my brother could come to the kindergarten. She said, "Yes, but he's not the only one. Everybody in your family can come here. And you can come any time."

C COMPREHENSION

Write the answers.
1. At the factory, why did the other girls get yelled at more than Maria?
2. Why do you think Maria's mother made fun of Jane Addams?
3. What did Maria admire about Jane Addams?
4. Why did Maria think Mr. Flannigan was a bad person?
5. Jane Addams said Hull House "is not my house." What did she mean?

D WRITING

Maria worked in a candy factory. What kind of job would you like to have when you grow up?

Write an essay that explains your answer. Be sure to answer the following questions:
• What would you do in your job?
• Why would the job interest you?
• Why would the job be better than other jobs?
• How would you prepare yourself for the job?

A WORD LISTS

1
Hard Words
1. community
2. fashion
3. fashioned

2
New Vocabulary
1. shawl
2. draped

B READING

Jane Addams
Chapter 4

Maria Rossi continues:

Every season was so different when I was a child, and each one brought some good and some bad. Hull House opened in the fall, which was always the most beautiful season. Not far from where I lived were streets with large trees. In the fall, they turned gold and red like a magnificent sunset.

Then winter came. The good that came with winter was the way it made everything seem clean. The terrible smells of summer were gone, and just after a snowfall, everything looked like a beautiful painting. The snow covered the dirt and even made the buildings look freshly painted.

The bad that came with winter was the

cold. We had just one small stove in our house. We covered the windows with old blankets so the heat would not escape, but at night the inside of our house would get nearly as cold as the outside. It was dreadful getting up in the morning. Sometimes Mama would pull back our covers and laugh. We would get dressed very quickly.

By winter, Mama no longer doubted Jane Addams and Ellen Starr were trying to be good neighbors. Mama had been to Hull House many times. In fact, she had even helped out in one of the evening cooking classes for young girls.

Mama talked about going to the English classes at Hull House, but she never went. Most of the people who went to these classes were people who had just come from Europe and had moved into the neighborhood around Hull House. Jane Addams and Ellen Starr taught them to speak English, and some of them soon knew a lot more English than Mama.

One December day, the factory where we worked closed down because something went wrong with the heating system. The factory was closed for over a month while the heating system was repaired. When I found out that I would have a vacation, I jumped up and down and screamed for joy. I could not believe my good fortune. Imagine, I would have days with nothing to do.

What made my vacation even more exciting was the snow. A thick blanket of fresh snow had just fallen, and the air was not too cold. So, you could make snowballs or snowmen. You could make piles of snow and dive into them. You could run and chase each other in the snow, and play until you were exhausted.

I would have to go inside around four in the afternoon and help Mama with dinner. But after dinner I would go out again. What a beautiful sight—the green light from the gas street lamps, and the soft snowflakes floating down. I would stand with my mouth open and try to catch some falling snow in my mouth. The large snowflakes would land on my tongue and seem to shrink into a little drop of cold water. ♦

One evening, I noticed some of the girls I worked with were all dressed up and walking toward Halsted Street. "Where are you going?" I asked.

They told me they were on their way to Hull House to practice singing. They were going to sing a concert in the dining room on Sunday evening. I ran inside and asked Mama if I could go with them. At first she said no, but after I pleaded with her, she said, "Stop standing around. You certainly don't plan to go there in the clothes you are wearing." I changed clothes as quickly as I could and joined my friends.

All kinds of things were going on inside Hull House that evening. Artists were hanging up pictures they had painted. The parlor was filled with people learning English, and Jane Addams was teaching them. Ellen Starr was in another room with a group of women who were reading stories aloud. It was as if all the Greek, Russian, and Italian neighbors were not separate neighbors any more. They all had come together inside Hull House to become part of one neighborhood.

Ellen Starr talked to us about the songs we would sing on Sunday. Then we practiced for a little while. The practice went badly because some boys kept looking at us and making faces. Every time we sang, they would put their hands over their ears. Then we would start giggling and feel embarrassed.

Singing in front of all the people that Sunday was terrifying. I wanted to look as beautiful as I could, and I was concerned because my dress looked old. It was not really my dress. It had been my mother's, and it had belonged to three of my sisters before it was mine. The dress was a little small for me, but Mama let me wear her best shawl. When I draped that shawl around my neck and looked at myself in the living room mirror, I thought I looked like a grown-up woman. I just hoped nobody would notice that my shoes had holes in them. ★

The largest downstairs room in Hull House was filled with people. Inside the

room were many ladies and gentlemen dressed in splendid clothes. Ellen Starr led us into the room and introduced us. The people in the audience nodded and smiled, and then we sang. I think we sounded beautiful. People in the audience could not understand the words of our songs, but I could see in their eyes that they understood what the songs said. When we finished, they clapped and asked us to sing more. So we did.

At last, Jane Addams stood up and thanked us. Then she held out a large tray of hard candy and offered some to us. The first girl smiled and shook her head. "No, thank you, Miss Addams," she said.

Jane looked a little puzzled and offered the candy to the next girl, who also refused. Then Jane offered the candy to me. I did not mean to be rude, but I said, "I cannot stand the sight of that candy."

She asked why I felt that way. I explained that we all worked in the candy factory. Her face suddenly became serious.

"You should be in school," she said. "How long do you work each day?"

We told her how many hours we worked. "How many girls work there?" she asked.

"About two hundred," I replied.

She turned to Ellen Starr and said, "We must change this situation." At that moment, I knew that she was strong enough to do anything she set out to do.

It took Jane Addams, Ellen Starr, and their friends a great deal of work to change the situation. But four years later, in 1893, a law was passed that made it illegal for any child under fourteen to work in the factories. That law did not help me, because by then I was already sixteen and was used to hard work. But it helped three of my brothers and one sister. They had a chance to go to school, and by then our neighborhood was much nicer than it was when I was their age.

Despite the poverty and the work, I have many fond memories of my neighborhood, and a lot of these memories are of Jane Addams and the other women who lived at Hull House. They taught me what it means to be a good neighbor.

C COMPREHENSION

Write the answers.
1. Name at least three reasons why Maria liked winter in her neighborhood.
2. Why didn't Maria have to work one December?
3. What were some of the activities Hull House offered people?
4. Why did the girls refuse the candy Jane Addams offered?
5. What did Jane do to change the situation for children who worked in factories?

D WRITING

People at Hull House taught classes in different subjects. What kind of class would you like to teach?

Write an essay that describes what kind of class you would teach and why you would be a good teacher. Be sure your essay answers the following questions:
• What class would you teach?
• Why do you want to teach that class?
• What do you know about that subject?
• What exactly would you teach?
• Why would you be a good teacher?

A WORD LISTS

1	2	3	4
Hard Words	*Word Practice*	*Vocabulary Review*	*New Vocabulary*
1. resident	1. exhibit	1. shawl	1. resident
2. fascinated	2. nurse	2. draped	2. fascinated
3. supervisor	3. nursery		3. ward
4. infant	4. soup		4. profit
5. dedicated	5. community		5. supervisor
6. Irish			6. infant

B READING

Jane Addams

Chapter 5

Rita Hansen's Story

I became a resident of Hull House in 1893. I had read about Hull House in several magazine articles, and I was fascinated by the idea of a house to help the poor and needy. But, when I heard Jane Addams talk, I knew Hull House was more than a place. It was a new idea—the idea of trying to make the world a better place for everybody.

At that time, Jane was making speeches about the need for a new law that prevented young children from working in factories. I heard her talk at a club meeting in downtown Chicago. She told about the difficult lives of the people who lived near Hull House. By now, that part of the city was well known, thanks to the efforts of Jane and the people who worked with her. Hull House was in Ward 19, and hardly a week went by without an article in the newspaper about that ward.

I had read the newspaper articles and understood the hardships of the people in Ward 19; but it wasn't until I heard Jane talk that I actually felt their problems. Jane talked about children who were eleven and twelve years old working in factories.

She said, "Shortly after Christmas in 1889, just a few months after Hull House opened, a young boy was killed in a factory accident. The life of this fine young boy was lost because the laws permit factories to hire children who should be in school."

Jane paused and then continued slowly. "That boy was killed four years ago. Since then, Hull House has been dedicated to changing laws that permit factory owners to make a profit by hiring children and paying them almost nothing. But the factories still hire children. Some children still work twelve to fourteen hours a day."

Jane then told about the school situation in Ward 19. She explained that she and the other residents at Hull House had counted the children of school age in Ward 19. There were about seven thousand children. Then she said, "But there are less than three thousand seats in the schools in Ward 19."

Jane reported that she had talked with parents in Ward 19 and had explained how important it was for their children to go to school. The parents understood the need for school, but there was no space for their children in the schools. Besides, many of the families needed the money their children brought home from the factories.

Jane then explained that Hull House was able to operate because people gave money to the house or worked without pay. Finally, she said, "Hull House is a bridge bringing you and your neighbors together."

When Jane finished her speech, I introduced myself and asked how a person could become a resident at Hull House. Jane smiled and explained that most of the residents had jobs in downtown Chicago, but they lived at Hull House and worked at the house in their spare time. ♦

I thanked Jane and told her I would think about it. Over the next few days, I thought a lot. In one way, I thought the poor people in Ward 19 were a great deal like me and many other young women of that time. In 1893, women did not have the same rights men had. Women were not able to vote, and there were not many jobs for them. I had just finished college, and I was at the top of my class. But like other women, I was not able to get a good job. The good jobs were for men, and I resented that. In a way, the people in Ward 19 had the same kind of problem. They had to suffer, simply because they were poor and had to live in a poor part of the city.

I worked as a clerk in a downtown bank. My supervisor was a young man who had graduated from the same college I had. He had not been a good student, and he was not very intelligent. One day at work, he blamed me for a mistake he had made. I tried to point out to the bank manager that I had not made the mistake, but he didn't believe me.

When I went back to my desk, I was furious. I sat there trying to hold my temper. Suddenly, almost without thinking, I decided I would become a resident at Hull House. I stood up and told my supervisor that I would like to take the rest of the day off.

Outside, I called a taxicab and told the driver to take me to Hull House. Although it was not much more than a mile from the bank, I had never been there before. To get there, you had to travel through an unpleasant part of the city. The odor was terrible. ★

Halsted Street, near Hull House, was lined with little shops. The street was so crowded with colorful peddlers that the taxi could hardly move at times. Each neighborhood the taxi passed through was different—Greek, Italian, Russian. But the people who lived there seemed to be proud. And in the middle of the neighborhood was Hull House.

As soon as I saw the house, I understood what Jane Addams had meant when she called it a bridge that brings neighbors together. Men, women, and children from the neighborhood were walking up the steps. Some of the carriages in front of the house were owned by wealthy people. Hull House had attracted them to Ward 19 and made them neighbors too.

Every square inch of the house was occupied with clubs, activities, and exhibits. Behind the house was a cottage with a nursery school for infants and young children. And next to the house was a large building that was just being completed. The upstairs would become a gym. Downstairs would be a lunchroom that would be open to everybody. Jane planned to send out hot lunches to the factories from this lunchroom. For five cents, factory workers would be able to buy a bowl of soup and two rolls.

Jane was busy talking to the workmen when I arrived, so I strolled inside the house and looked around at the activities and the art exhibits. Some of the best painters in the United States had their

paintings on display there. As I was wandering through the rooms, a young woman came up and asked if she could help me. I told her I wanted to become a resident. I found out the young woman's name was Julia Lathrop. She was one of the first residents.

Julia showed me to the residents' bedrooms on the top floor of the old house. And then she left. I sat on a small bed, and I had the strange feeling I had just begun a new life—one that was completely different from anything I had ever known.

C COMPREHENSION

Write the answers.
1. Why were factory owners able to increase their profits when they hired young children?
2. Why did so many children in Ward 19 not attend school?
3. Name at least two ways women in the United States were treated unfairly in 1893.
4. What incident made Rita decide to work for Hull House?
5. How was Hull House like a bridge that brings neighbors together?

D WRITING

Rita felt that women and poor people were not treated fairly in 1893. Do you think any groups of people are still treated unfairly?

Write an essay that explains what you think. Try to answer the following questions in your essay:
- Which group do you think is treated unfairly, if any?
- Who treats them unfairly?
- In what ways is the group treated unfairly?
- How could the group get fairer treatment?
- Why should the group get fairer treatment?
- If you think everybody is treated fairly, explain why you think so and give examples.

A WORD LISTS

1 *Hard Words*	2 *Word Practice*	3 *Vocabulary Review*	4 *New Vocabulary*
1. donate	1. range	1. ward	1. filth
2. stubborn	2. arrange	2. supervisor	2. stubborn
3. inspector	3. sicken	3. infant	3. fined
4. fiery	4. sickening	4. resident	4. invest
5. wages		5. fascinated	5. wages
		6. profit	6. distressed

B READING

Jane Addams
Chapter 6

Rita Hansen continues:

As a resident of Hull House, I had two jobs—my regular job at the bank and my job at Hull House. I had never worked so hard in my entire life, but I don't believe I've ever been as happy.

Residents at Hull House worked around the house. They also worked on problems in the neighborhood, and they tried to raise money. Hull House depended on gifts from wealthy people, and the gifts had to keep coming in.

Jane was a marvel. She worked all day and late into the night. She made speeches, contacted wealthy people, and still had time to go into the neighborhood and work on problems. The other residents and I tried to imitate her, but it was almost impossible. She seemed to have endless energy. She had no husband, and her whole life was wrapped up in Hull House.

I got up early every morning and helped set up things for the activities that were scheduled at Hull House. Sometimes, I would work in the kitchen. Other times, I would go into the neighborhood in the

evening and talk to families about problems, such as garbage collection.

The city garbage collectors were supposed to pick up garbage regularly, but sometimes weeks would go by before the collectors came. And when they did come, they filled up their wagons so quickly that they didn't get to all parts of the neighborhood. In the meantime, the garbage would overflow the boxes that were next to the street. In some places the streets were almost blocked by mounds of garbage.

When I worked in the bank, I wondered if my work made any difference in anybody's life. I asked myself whether banking was really important. And I would usually answer no. But when I worked at Hull House, I had no doubt that I was working on important things.

Each day after work, I went back to Hull House. I ate with the residents and then planned the things we were going to work on. Julia Lathrop was the leader of the residents. When residents complained that things weren't going well, she'd make a joke or say something like, "Now that we've heard about the bad, let's talk about the good things we're going to do."

Sometimes I talked to groups of women or to clubs. When I talked to these groups, I tried hard to make them understand that the people in Ward 19 were good people who wanted a better life. They were simply victims of poverty. ♦

Usually, the speeches I made were successful, but I gave several speeches that stirred up trouble. Once I told a large group of people that a wealthy man named William Kent owned all the terrible buildings on one entire block in Ward 19. The houses on that block were in the worst condition of any houses in the entire ward. Old people, sick people, and babies were crowded into dwellings with chickens, pigs, and filth. There was so much filth that I would actually get sick when I went into some of the buildings.

I said, "What kind of man is William Kent that he would have to become a tiny bit richer at the expense of people who are dying in poverty? How important is the rent money that these people give him so they can live in such a sickening place?"

During another speech, I even angered my own parents. They were fairly wealthy, and they lived in one of the nicer suburbs north of Chicago. At first, they were upset when I told them that I had become a resident of Hull House. My mother said she was worried about my walking around in such a terrible neighborhood. My father said I was just being a stubborn child. He said, "Is this why we sent you through college, so you could work in a slum?"

But after a while, my parents changed their minds about Hull House. I told them I would like to make a speech to them and some of their friends. I said their friends might be interested in donating money to Hull House. So my parents arranged a large party at their house. They invited more than fifty people.

On the day I was to give the speech, I found out that the city of Chicago was going to pass the law that made it illegal for children under fourteen to work in factories. I also found out that one of the residents at Hull House would become the factory inspector for the city. Her job would be to go around to the factories. If she found children under fourteen working in a factory, she would take the factory owner to court, where the owner would be fined for breaking the law. ★

I was delighted over this good news, and I was in high spirits that day at the bank. I left early so I would arrive at my parents' home on time. When I got there, my father introduced me to all the guests. Then everybody sat down to a wonderful dinner. After dinner my father said, "And now my daughter is going to tell us about Hull House."

I told the story of Hull House and also told about the law that would be passed. Most of the people seemed quite pleased. After it was over, a man who had a distressed expression on his face came up to me. In a loud voice he said, "My name is Flannigan, and I own a candy company near Hull House. Our plant operates in Ward 19 so we do not have to invest a lot of money in paying high wages to adults. Candy making is a tough business; and if we have to pay our workers high wages, we're out of business, and our workers are out of a job."

By now his face was flushed. Everybody in the room was looking at him. He concluded by saying, "Jane Addams ought to be hanged from the nearest lamppost."

The room became silent. I stood there,

shocked, trying to gather myself together. Then I said. "Jane Addams should not be hanged from anything. She is the most noble person I have ever known. It's too bad you are not more like Jane Addams."

At this point, my father stepped between Mr. Flannigan and me. Father said, "Stop this right now." He put his arm around me and led me to a corner of the room. Then, as he looked at me with a sober expression, his face suddenly broke into a great grin. He bent his head so the people who were watching us couldn't see he was smiling.

Out of the corner of my eye, I saw Flannigan near the front door, grabbing his coat and hat.

C COMPREHENSION

Write the answers.
1. Why did Rita prefer her job at Hull House to her job at the bank?
2. What did Rita mean when she said that the people in Ward 19 were "victims of poverty"?
3. Why did Rita criticize William Kent in one speech?
4. At first, why were Rita's parents upset with her job at Hull House?
5. Why was Mr. Flannigan upset by Rita's speech?

D WRITING

Rita Hansen made speeches to raise money for Hull House. Pretend you have to make a speech to raise money for a group that helps people or animals.

Write your speech. Try to answer the following questions in the speech:
- Which group are you raising money for?
- What good things does the group do for people or animals?
- Why does the group need money?
- What exactly will the group do with the money?
- Why should people give their money to the group?

A WORD LISTS

1 *Job Types*	2 *Word Practice*	3 *Vocabulary Review*	4 *New Vocabulary*
1. investor	1. dilapidated	1. stubborn	1. abandon
2. collector	2. wages	2. filth	2. trance
3. inspector	3. sober	3. fined	3. plump
4. manager	4. abandon		
5. supervisor	5. spectacular		

B READING

Jane Addams
Chapter 7

Camila Perez's Story

In 1935, Jane Addams was seventy-four years old. That was the last year of her life. I went to Chicago that year because I was writing an article on Jane Addams, who was one of the most famous women in the world.

The city had changed greatly since Jane Addams first moved into the old Hull place. Although there were still a few horses pulling milk or ice wagons, trucks were replacing them. The icemen didn't have as much business because electric refrigerators could be found in most homes, even in the homes of poor people. The wooden sidewalks were gone, and so were the horse-drawn streetcars.

The old laws had changed. In 1893, children who were fourteen years old could still work in factories; but by 1935, children that young were not allowed to work in factories. Hull House had also changed. It was no longer a single house but a community of thirteen buildings.

In 1935, the United States was in a depression called the Great Depression. There weren't enough jobs for the people who wanted to work. Although the worst part

of the Depression was over, and companies were hiring again, many people were still out of work. ♦

I flew from New York to Chicago on a passenger plane in May 1935. My parents had come to this country from Mexico, and they were quite old-fashioned. They didn't trust airplanes, and they didn't think that I should ride on one. When I look back, I would have to agree with them.

The strange-looking, slow-moving plane that carried me to Chicago in 1935 was a far cry from modern planes. Today, the plane trip from New York to Chicago takes less than two hours. In 1935, the trip took nearly eight hours. The plane left New York at noon and didn't arrive in Chicago until eight in the evening.

I was excited about this trip because I felt Jane Addams was the most magnificent woman alive, and it was an honor for me to talk to her. As I sat there in the darkness of the plane listening to the steady hum of the engines, I fell into a trance as I thought about her.

I first pictured Jane Addams as a young woman starting Hull House with Ellen Starr. I saw her inviting all the Italian, Greek, and Russian neighbors into the house for the first time. I saw her teaching English classes with Julia Lathrop and the other residents. And I saw her helping to pass a law that prevented children under fourteen from working in the factories of Chicago. ★

Then, in my mind, I saw Jane Addams getting older. By now, she was a famous woman; but she did not let fame pull her away from helping neighbors. When Jane was forty years old, Hull House had both female and male residents, twenty-five in all. By the time Jane was fifty, hundreds of other settlement houses were springing up in different parts of the United States. But Hull House remained the best of them.

My mind moved forward in time, and I saw Jane Addams in 1914, which was twenty-five years after Hull House opened. She was now fifty-four years old and still trying to help people in need. But now she was not simply dealing with one neighborhood. She was dealing with the world.

World War One had begun, and soon the people that Jane loved so much were at war—the people in Germany, Italy, France, and Russia, among others. Jane Addams tried to stop the war. She traveled around Europe, trying to prevent the terrible harm the war was creating. But the war continued for several years. During this time, Jane was deeply saddened. She returned to Chicago, but she did not abandon her work for peace.

In 1918, the war ended, and the countries of Europe were in terrible condition. So Jane went to Europe again, this time to help the people who were starving and diseased. Many people in Europe did not care about the starving people in the countries they had been at war with. But Jane said, "All the people in the world are neighbors. Hull House taught me that. I must go on working for peace among my neighbors worldwide." And she did.

C COMPREHENSION

Write the answers.
1. Why was Camila Perez gathering information about Jane Addams?
2. Describe at least three ways Chicago changed between 1889 and 1935.
3. What happened to jobs during the Great Depression of the 1930s?
4. How was plane travel during the 1930s different from plane travel today?
5. Why do you think Jane Addams tried to stop World War One?

D WRITING

When Camila meets Jane Addams, she will ask Jane some questions.

- Write at least five questions you think Camila will ask. Then write Jane's answers in complete sentences.

A WORD LISTS

1 Word Sounds	2 Word Practice	3 Vocabulary Review	4 New Vocabulary
1. surround	1. stubborn	1. trance	1. interview
2. picture	2. month	2. wages	2. spectacular
3. courage	3. plumbing	3. distressed	
4. scurry		4. plump	
5. harbor		5. invest	
		6. abandon	

B READING

Jane Addams
Chapter 8

Camila Perez continues:

I looked out the window of the plane and noticed the night sky was clear, with stars that glittered brightly. Below was a town that looked like a little toy town, with tiny lights marking all the streets. I watched the town as we moved slowly over it, and I listened to the engines. Most of the passengers around me were sleeping. But I was too excited to sleep. So I returned to my thoughts of Jane Addams. Where did I leave her? Oh yes, after the war, working for her neighbors around the world.

My mind moved forward in time again, to the year 1931. During that year Jane received one of the world's greatest honors: the Nobel Peace Prize. That prize is awarded to only one or two people each year. The people selected to receive the Nobel Peace Prize have done more for peace than anybody else. Nobody ever deserved the prize more than Jane Addams. But by the time she received it, she was seventy-one years old, and her health was failing.

Jane had never been a healthy person.

Before she opened Hull House, she had gone to college to become a doctor, but she had to drop out of school because of her poor health. ◆

The plane was now flying over Lake Michigan, and I could see the lights of Chicago. Slowly, the city grew larger and brighter until we were flying right over it. We were so low that I felt I could almost reach out of the window and touch the cars and the buildings below. It was a spectacular sight. The passengers were saying "ooooo" and "aaahh" as they watched the glittering sight of Chicago at night.

After the plane landed, I went to a hotel. I arose early the next morning, phoned Hull House, and arranged to talk with Jane Addams that afternoon. That morning, however, I wanted to visit the house and see how it looked in 1935.

I stood outside Hull House for a long time, looking at the buildings and watching the activities. Then I went inside to interview people who were volunteering their time. Inside the kitchen, I met a charming woman who appeared to be in her fifties. Her name was Maria, and she told me about her experiences with Hull House when she was a young girl.

She told me, "I now live in another part of the city, but I come down every morning to help out in the kitchen for a few hours." She smiled warmly and continued, "Some people say I'm crazy and that I could earn money by getting a job that pays. But I don't agree with them. With the work I do, I am paying back only a small amount of what my family owes to Hull House." ★

Next I talked with a splendid woman who was a retired vice president of a large bank. Her name was Rita, and she told me stories of Hull House in the early days. Then she added, "Now I work here with several of the clubs. I am no longer a resident, but Hull House is still an important part of my life."

Later that afternoon, I talked with Jane Addams. Our talk was short, but I don't think I'll ever forget it. Although her eyes looked tired, I could tell that the spirit behind those eyes was as strong as it had ever been. She told me about a book she was writing about Julia Lathrop. I didn't learn much more than I already knew, but the experience of talking to her was magnificent. She was everything I had imagined—kind, warm, determined, and sincere.

After our brief talk, she said, "You'll have to excuse me now. I have to visit a sick neighbor." She had trouble standing up, and I could see she was weak. Later that evening, she became extremely ill. She died a week later.

I can't describe the grief I experienced when I received news of her death. For several days, I had to fight back the tears as I wrote my article. But then I began to realize she was still with us.

She was still living in my mind and in the minds of people like Maria Rossi, Rita Hansen, and the thousands of other people she helped. I hope that Jane Addams lives forever in this way.

C COMPREHENSION

Write the answers.
1. Why do you think Jane Addams received the Nobel Peace Prize?
2. Why did Maria work in Hull House instead of getting another job?
3. Rita told Camila stories about the early days of Hull House. Tell one of those stories.
4. Why was Camila so impressed by Jane Addams?
5. Why did Camila think Jane Addams was still with us?

D WRITING

Jane Addams received a Nobel Peace Prize. Who do you think should receive the prize?

Write an essay that explains what you think. Try to answer the following questions in your essay:
• Who do you think should win the prize?
• Why does that person deserve the prize?
• What specific things has the person done to improve peace in the world?
• Why is the person better than other candidates for the prize?

Unit 4

Living in History

Everybody was young once. A few dozen years ago, your parents or guardians were the same age you are now. And a few dozen years before that, your grandparents were also your age. If you keep going backward in time, you'll find hundreds of relatives who were once the same age as you.

In this unit, you'll read a famous novel about children who lived more than five hundred years ago. Their world was quite different from yours. But the children themselves were very much like you. They liked to play, learn, and have adventures. As you read their story, you'll discover they were just as alive as you are now.

England in the 1500s

The Prince and the Pauper

Edward the Sixth

A WORD LISTS

1
Word Practice
1. opportunity
2. pauper

2
Vocabulary Review
1. spectacular
2. interview

3
New Vocabulary
1. hardware
2. harbor
3. pauper
4. plumbing
5. prince
6. scurry

B READING

England in the 1500s
Chapter 1

In lesson 96, you will begin reading a novel titled *The Prince and the Pauper*. The novel takes place in England in the 1500s. It describes how a very poor young boy—the pauper—happens to meet the richest boy in all of England—the prince. The two of them have many exciting adventures.

The map shows England in the 1500s. England was just one part of a large island, called Britain, that contained two other countries—Wales and Scotland. Another country, called Ireland, was on an island to the west of England. Before the 1500s, England had conquered the countries of Wales

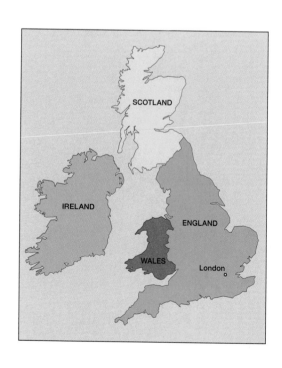

and Ireland. Scotland, however, was still a separate country, and it had many wars with England during the 1500s.

London was already a large city at that time. About a quarter of a million people were crammed into its narrow streets and wooden houses. The houses had no plumbing, no gas, and no electricity. They did, however, have fireplaces. People used the fireplaces to stay warm and to cook their food.

London had a busy harbor. Every day, dozens of sailing ships came into the city on the Thames River. These ships brought goods from many parts of the world and carried other goods away. There was only one bridge across the Thames. It was called London Bridge. The city was so crowded that some people built houses right on the bridge.

The streets of London were filled with beggars and peddlers. There were very few stores, so people had to buy whatever they needed from peddlers. Many sold water, while others sold milk, bread, pots, clothes, coal, or mousetraps. Some streets were paved with stones, but most were made of dirt. Garbage was piled in the streets, and mice scurried from one pile to another. ♦

Dirt roads connected London to other towns in England. Most travelers walked along these roads, but some rode horses, and a few used wagons. The roads were in terrible condition. They were often muddy, and they had deep ruts. If a wagon got stuck in a rut, a traveler might have to spend several hours digging it out. Travelers also had to worry about robbers who hid along the roads and attacked people. To protect themselves, most travelers carried swords or guns.

The biggest wagons on the roads were called stage wagons. These wagons were pulled by six to ten horses and carried goods from one town to another. The wagons moved so slowly that the driver walked along next to the horses and guided them through the ruts and the mud. On a good day, a wagon might go about three miles an hour.

Messengers went much faster. They rode fast horses along the road and shouted at everybody else to get out of the way. It took a messenger about a week to go from London to Scotland. Today, that trip takes about six hours by car and less than an hour by plane.

The countryside around London was quite beautiful. There were gently rolling green hills as far as the eye could see. Small farms dotted the landscape, and sheep were everywhere. During the 1500s, rich English farmers sold a lot of wool, so they kept raising more and more sheep. There were so many sheep, in fact, that the animals began to create problems.

The rich sheep farmers started buying up land for their sheep and even stealing land that didn't belong to them. As a result, many poor farmers lost their farms. These poor farmers tried to fight back, and they came up with a famous saying: "Sheep eat men." Sheep don't really eat men, but because of the sheep, many poor farmers were ruined.

Farther away from London, there were many forests. Loggers were busy in these forests, cutting down trees for houses, ships, and firewood. The demand for wood was so great that some forests were completely destroyed. Fortunately, people discovered how to build fires with coal instead of firewood. During the 1500s, people began digging mines to bring coal out from under the earth. The mines were simple pits or long tunnels dug into hillsides.

People also dug pits to find rocks with iron in them. Workers hauled these rocks to factories that had very hot ovens called blast furnaces. When the rocks were put into the blast furnaces, the iron in them melted and fell to the bottom of the furnace. Workers gathered the hot iron, which was then used to make weapons, tools, and other hardware.

Today, England is very different than it was in the 1500s. But some things are still the same. London is still the biggest city. There are still plenty of sheep and forests. And there are still many coal mines and blast furnaces. But the houses now have gas, water, and electricity; and the roads are much better and safer.

C COMPREHENSION

Write the answers.
1. Why do you think people in London in the 1500s had to buy water from peddlers?
2. Explain why wagons got stuck on English roads in the 1500s.
3. Why did English travelers carry swords and guns in the 1500s?
4. Why were so many poor English farmers forced off their land in the 1500s?
5. Why were some English forests destroyed in the 1500s?

D WRITING

How does life in the 1500s compare to your life today?

Write an essay that compares life in the 1500s to your life today. Try to answer the following questions:
• How was life different back in the 1500s?
• In what ways was life the same in the 1500s?
• What were the good parts of life in the 1500s? The bad parts?
• Which time period would you rather live in? Why?

A WORD LISTS

1
Hard Words
1. opportunity
2. optimistic
3. earl
4. Tudor

2
Vocabulary Review
1. scurry
2. hardware
3. plumbing
4. pauper
5. prince

3
New Vocabulary
1. ruler
2. opportunity

B READING

England in the 1500s
Chapter 2

At the beginning of the 1500s, England was ruled by a king named Henry the Seventh. The king was the richest and most powerful person in the country. He commanded the army and the navy and helped make the laws. He also owned a great deal of land and earned money by collecting taxes from the people. When people talked to the king, they called him "Your Highness" or "Your Majesty."

The king's family was called the Royal Family. His sons were princes, and his daughters were princesses. The firstborn son was called the Prince of Wales. As you have learned, Wales was a country that

England conquered before the 1500s. The English king who conquered Wales decided to call his firstborn son the Prince of Wales. Ever since then, the firstborn son of the English king or queen has been called the Prince of Wales.

When the king sat on the throne, he wore a crown. The crown showed that he was the ruler of England. When the king died, the crown was placed on the head of the Prince of Wales, who then became the new king.

Next in power after the Royal Family were the lords and ladies. Some lords and ladies lived in the king's palace. Others had

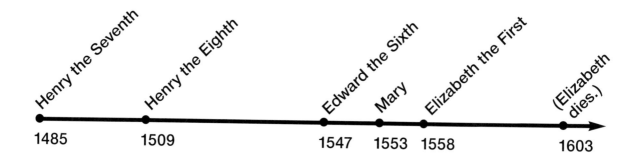

Henry the Seventh   Henry the Eighth   Edward the Sixth   Mary   Elizabeth the First   (Elizabeth dies.)

1485   1509   1547   1553   1558   1603

their own castles and controlled large areas of land. The king gave the lords and ladies different titles to show how powerful they were. The dukes and duchesses were the most powerful, followed by the earls, counts, countesses, barons, baronesses, and knights. Each one had certain powers, but they all obeyed the king.

Henry the Seventh ruled England from 1485 to 1509. He was the first English king to come from the Tudor family. His children and grandchildren ruled England until 1603, when the last Tudor died. The time line shows when each Tudor began to rule England. ◆

Henry the Seventh was a greedy king who collected many taxes and became quite rich. The next Tudor king was his son, Henry the Eighth, who was one of the cruelest kings England has ever known. Henry the Eighth ruled from 1509 to 1547. He was handsome and intelligent, but he was also selfish and mean. His soldiers would kill anyone who dared to criticize him. Some of these people were beheaded, and others were burned to death. It was against the law even to think about harming the king.

More than anything else, Henry wanted a son. England had never been ruled by a queen, and Henry believed that only men were fit to rule the country. Henry was so eager to have a son that he married six times. His first wife gave birth to a girl named Mary, but when the wife failed to give Henry a son, he decided to divorce her. His second wife also gave birth to a girl, named Elizabeth. However, the second wife displeased Henry, so he had her beheaded. His third wife finally gave birth to a boy named Edward, but she died in childbirth. Edward is the prince in *The Prince and the Pauper.*

After Henry's third wife died, he married three more times but had no more children. He divorced his fourth wife and beheaded his fifth wife. His sixth wife, however, outlived him. People became so confused about all of Henry's wives that they made up a saying to remember them by. The saying goes, "Divorced, beheaded, died; divorced, beheaded, survived." The six words in the saying tell what happened to Henry's six wives. ★

The next Tudor king was Edward, who began ruling in 1547. He was called Edward the Sixth. Edward was much kinder than his father and changed some of the harsh laws Henry had made. But Edward soon became seriously ill, and he died in 1553 at the age of fifteen. His older sister, Mary, then became queen. She was almost as cruel as her father and had many people burned alive. People called her "Bloody Mary." In her five years as queen, she had more than three hundred people killed.

After Mary died in 1558, her sister became Queen Elizabeth the First. Elizabeth was the last Tudor to rule England. She was one of the best rulers England has ever had. During her rule, life in England improved greatly. She wrote laws that protected poor people, and she helped to create many new jobs. She also encouraged English sailors to explore the world and trade with foreign countries. People had more freedom during her rule than they had ever had before. Great writers, such as William Shakespeare, were free to say whatever they wanted. During the rule of Henry the Eighth, these writers might have been killed.

Elizabeth ruled England for forty-five years. She refused to marry and have children, so when she died in 1603, there were no Tudors who could become king or queen. Another family took over the throne, and a new king was crowned. Since then, England has had many kings and queens from several different families. Only a few of them, however, have been as great as Elizabeth the First or as cruel as Henry the Eighth.

C COMPREHENSION

Write the answers.
1. Why do you think the king who conquered Wales decided to call his firstborn son the Prince of Wales?
2. Name at least two cruel things Henry the Eighth did.
3. Why was Mary called "Blood Mary"?
4. Why were writers happy during Elizabeth's rule?
5. Why was Elizabeth the last Tudor ruler?

D WRITING

Do you think countries should be ruled by kings and queens?

Write an essay that explains your answer. Try to answer the following questions:
- What good things can happen if a country is ruled by a king or a queen? What bad things can happen?
- How would people feel about having a king or a queen?
- What are other ways of ruling countries?
- Which way do you think is best?

A WORD LISTS

1	**2**	**3**
Job Types	*Vocabulary Review*	*New Vocabulary*
1. collector	1. opportunity	1. carve
2. manager	2. ruler	2. properly
3. investor		
4. supervisor		
5. inspector		

B READING

England in the 1500s
Chapter 3

During the 1500s, England had two main classes of people: rich and poor. The rich people included the Royal Family, the lords and ladies, and some of the merchants. Most of the other people, such as the farmers, the coal miners, and the peddlers, were poor. Rich people led easy and pleasant lives, while poor people led lives that were full of misery and hard work.

Many of the rich lords and ladies had large houses in the country. These houses were made of wood, brick, or stone. They had enough space for about fifty people, including the lord, the lady, their children, their servants, and their guests. Some of the rooms had windows, but glass was so rare and expensive that the windows were often quite small. Almost every room had a fireplace and a stone or tile floor. In the richest houses, there might be wool carpets on the floor or on the walls.

There was not much furniture. In those days, furniture was made of fancy carved wood. It took so long for workers to carve the wood properly that many large houses had only a few chairs, tables, and beds.

The biggest pieces of furniture were the beds for the lords and ladies, their children, and their guests. These beds had tall

posts at all four corners. Curtains were strung between the posts. When people went to bed, they would pull the curtains and sleep in total darkness. It would be a comfortable sleep, because the mattress was made of feathers and the blankets were made of fine English wool.

The lord was the master of the house. His family and his servants had to obey him at all times, or they would be punished. His children had to call him Sir, and they had to kneel down in front of him whenever they wanted to make a request. The lord spent most of his time dealing with the farms and other lands that he owned.

The lady had the job of running the house. Because there were so few stores, many products had to be made right in the house. Some servants made clothes, while others made soap and candles. The lady had to command all these servants. She also had to make medicine and teach her children to read. Her biggest job, however, was to supervise the kitchen servants. About a dozen servants would work in the kitchen all day long preparing food for the lord and his guests. ♦

The food was mainly meat, which was cooked in the kitchen fireplace. Sometimes the meat would be stuck on a long rod called a spit that hung over the fire. Servant boys would spend hours slowly turning the spit so that the meat was evenly cooked. At other times, the meat would be put in a strong iron box and placed directly in the fire.

Rich people spent a lot of money on spices for their meat and on sweets for dessert. They didn't eat many vegetables, however, because they thought vegetables were only for poor people. But in the 1580s, an English explorer went to America and brought back a strange new vegetable called the potato. The rich people loved this new vegetable and started growing it on their land.

Lunch was the biggest meal of the day. It would start at eleven o'clock in the morning and last for up to three hours. The lord, the lady, and their guests would sit in the huge dining room and eat course after course of beef, lamb, chicken, and pork. Their plates were made of silver, and they ate with their fingers, a knife, and a spoon. Forks were not used.

During the 1500s, the lords and ladies wore fine clothes made of velvet, fur, and silk. The ladies' dresses often had silver threads woven into them, and the lords liked to wear belts made of gold. Hats with jewels on them were also quite popular. In the later part of the 1500s, the lords' and ladies' clothes became even more complicated. Ladies wore long dresses with fancy coats and collars. Lords wore tight vests and long stockings. They also wore strange short pants called trunks. These trunks were sometimes so padded with cloth and fur that it was difficult for the lords to sit down. ★

The lords and ladies entertained themselves with different sports and hobbies. They played chess, dice, and cards, and they went hunting for deer and other animals. Behind their houses they had fancy gardens with rare fruit trees, fountains, and even mazes made from hedges. In the evening, they played musical instruments and performed complicated dances. Some of them spent the evening reading by candlelight. The printing press had just been invented, and rich people all over England

had the opportunity to buy books for the first time.

Plays were the one form of entertainment that both rich people and poor people could enjoy. One of the greatest playwrights of all time, William Shakespeare, began writing plays during the 1500s. Groups of actors would travel around the country, putting on plays in every village they visited. The plays would be performed outside, and everyone from around the village, including the lords and ladies, would come to the performances.

Of course, the lords and ladies didn't sit with the poor people. They would sit in balconies or houses overlooking the stage. When the first theaters were built in the 1500s, they always included balconies for the rich and an open area on the ground for the poor. The theaters were just like everything else in England in the 1500s: the best spots were for the rich, while everything else was for the poor.

C COMPREHENSION

Write the answers.
1. In the 1500s, why were windows so small?
2. Why did houses have so little furniture?
3. Why were clothes, soap, candles, and other products made in homes?
4. Why were people able to buy books for the first time?
5. Describe the seating arrangements at theaters in the 1500s.

D WRITING

Pretend you are a lord or a lady in England in the 1500s.

Write an essay that describes what your life is like. Try to answer the following questions:
- What is your house like?
- What do you do during the day?
- What do you eat?
- What hobbies do you have?
- Who works for you?

A WORD LISTS

1	2
Vocabulary Review	**New Vocabulary**
1. spectacular	1. confine
2. opportunity	2. humble
3. properly	3. optimistic

B READING

England in the 1500s
Chapter 4

Most of the people in England in the 1500s were poor. There were poor coal miners and poor ironworkers who earned such low wages that they were almost slaves. There were also thousands of poor farmers.

As you learned in an earlier lesson, many poor farmers lost their land to rich sheep farmers during the 1500s. A few of these poor farmers were able to earn a little money by watching the sheep. Most, however, left their homes and started wandering from town to town looking for work. In the later part of the 1500s, Queen Elizabeth helped the poor farmers by telling the rich farmers to stop raising so many sheep. She asked them to raise cows and grow wheat instead.

A farmhouse in the 1500s was just a one-room wooden house with a dirt floor and a roof made out of dead branches and straw. Most had a simple fireplace that was used for heating and cooking. The fireplaces were often quite smoky, and the air in the farmhouse was usually pretty bad. During the winter, the family would sit around the fireplace to stay warm. They would cook soup and vegetables in pots that hung over the fire. If they were lucky, they might eat meat once a week.

The farmhouse had almost no furniture. There were no beds, tables, or chairs. The family slept on piles of straw and ate while sitting on the ground or on stools. Some families had a simple wooden chest

for their blankets and other valuable items.

Poor people usually had only one set of clothes, which were made of wool or coarse cotton. A man would wear a plain shirt and a pair of pants, while a woman would wear a long dress that touched the ground. Adults wore leather shoes to protect their feet, but children often went barefoot. Poor people were forbidden to wear jewels, fancy shoes, or socks. If a lord didn't like the way a poor person was dressed, the lord could have the poor person whipped. ♦

Some of the farmers who lost their land became beggars, while others became robbers. The robbers would often form into groups and attack rich people on the roads and in the streets. Some robbers carried large hooks. They would stick the hooks through rich people's windows and try to pull out valuable items.

The rich people feared the robbers and carried weapons to protect themselves.

When a robber was caught, he or she was taken to court and tried before a judge. If the robber was found guilty, the judge would say what kind of punishment the robber should receive. These punishments could be quite cruel. Some robbers had their ears cut off, while others lost their hands. If a robber killed a rich person, the robber might be boiled alive or burned to death. ★

The robbers were not the only people to receive punishment from the judges. People without homes were sometimes put into the stocks, which was a device that clamped around their hands and feet. They might be confined in the stocks for several days. Homeless people might also be branded with a hot iron, just like cattle. Whenever the king or queen needed money, the judges would collect large fines from people who wore the wrong clothes or said the wrong things.

Another punishment was the ducking stool. Women who were not seen as humble were strapped to a stool and ducked over and over again into a river.

The punishments were cruelest during the rule of Henry the Eighth. Poor people feared his laws and grew to hate him. When Henry died, some optimistic people hoped his children would be kinder. Although conditions got a little bit better under his son, Edward the Sixth, they soon got worse under Bloody Mary. It was not until the rule of Elizabeth the First that poor people's lives began to improve for good. During her rule, the cruelest punishments were stopped, and laws were passed to protect poor people. Life was still not easy for the poor, but it was not as bad as before.

C COMPREHENSION

Write the answers.
1. Name at least three differences between a poor person's house and a rich person's house in the 1500s.
2. Name at least three differences in the clothing worn by rich people and poor people in the 1500s.
3. Explain how robbers used hooks in the 1500s.
4. Name at least three of the punishments robbers received from judges.
5. Why did poor people think Elizabeth was better than the other Tudor rulers?

D WRITING

Pretend you are a poor person in England in the 1500s.

Write an essay that describes what your life is like. Try to answer the following questions:
- What is your house like?
- Where do you work during the day?
- What do you eat?
- Where do you sleep?
- How do you feel most of the time?

A WORD LISTS

1	2	3	4
Hard Words	**Compound Words**	**Place Names**	**New Vocabulary**
1. captain	1. steamboat	1. Mississippi	1. craft
2. section	2. newspaper	2. Hannibal	2. fathom
3. surface	3. overnight	3. Missouri	3. humorous
4. celebrated	4. railroad	4. Nevada	4. bankrupt
5. experience		5. Calaveras	5. lecture
6. innocent		6. California	
		7. Hartford	
		8. Connecticut	

Pauper Clemens and Prince Twain

In 1857, a young man named Sam Clemens stood next to the steering wheel of a steamboat and watched the captain guide the huge craft up the Mississippi River. At the front of the boat, a sailor held a long rope that was marked off into sections. Each section was exactly one fathom (six feet) long. Tied to the end of the rope was a heavy lead weight.

The sailor dropped the lead weight into the water and let out the rope. When the weight hit the bottom of the river, the sailor noted which mark on the rope was even with the surface of the river. "Mark three!" he called out. The river in that spot was three fathoms deep.

"Three fathoms is good," said the captain to Clemens. "That's deep enough for this boat. But we'll have to be careful."

A few minutes later, the sailor yelled, "Mark TWAIN!" (*Twain* is an old word for two.)

"Mark twain!" exclaimed the captain. "That means we're right on the edge of danger! If we stay on this path, we'll scrape the bottom of the river, and we might even sink." Wasting no time, the captain grabbed the steering wheel and turned hard to the right, out of danger.

The Edge of Danger

Sam Clemens never forgot the phrase "mark twain" and the danger it signaled. Like the phrase, his own life was always on the edge of danger. Born in 1835, he grew up in the small town of Hannibal, Missouri, on the banks of the Mississippi River. There were no highways or railroads along the Mississippi in those days, so people traveled up and down the river on steamboats.

Even though his family was poor, Sam Clemens longed to be a steamboat captain. But when Clemens was eleven years old, his father died. One year later, he quit school and started working to help support his mother and his six brothers and sisters. He had always been interested in writing, so he got a job helping out at a local newspaper. Within a few years, he was writing news and travel articles for several local papers.

Readers loved his sense of humor and adventure. Clemens would travel around the country and write about what he saw. During one of those trips, he ended up on a steamboat and remembered his boyhood dream. He gave up writing for a few years and became a steamboat captain instead.

In 1861, however, the Civil War began. Steamboat traffic nearly stopped, and Clemens lost his job. Always ready for new adventures, he headed west to Nevada, where he began writing for newspapers again. Some of his articles were serious news items about murders and fires. But others were tall tales and complicated jokes.

To help his readers understand which was which, Clemens decided to sign his humorous articles with the name Mark Twain. The new name stuck, and he hardly ever used his real name again. ♦

The Jumping Frog

In 1864, Twain moved to California, where he wrote his best-known short story, "The Celebrated Jumping Frog of Calaveras County." The story tells about a jumping contest between two frogs that are helped along by their human owners. The story was reprinted in newspapers all over the country, and Twain became famous overnight. People came from miles around to hear him lecture and tell jokes.

A few years later, the biggest newspaper in California hired Twain to travel to Europe and write letters about his experiences. These letters made him even more famous. When he returned home, they were gathered into a full-length book, *The Innocents Abroad.*

By now, Twain was rich beyond his wildest dreams. He fell in love with a woman named Olivia Langdon and married her in 1870. The next year they moved into an enormous house in Hartford, Connecticut, where they lived for more than twenty years.

Boom and Bust

In Hartford, Twain wrote the novels and other books that made him one of America's greatest writers. The most famous ones are

- *Roughing It* (1872)
- *Tom Sawyer* (1876)
- *The Prince and the Pauper* (1881)
- *Life on the Mississippi* (1883)
- *Huckleberry Finn* (1884)

Twain made lots of money from all these books, but he spent it foolishly. His worst mistake was investing in a new type of printing press that never worked. By the 1890s, Twain was bankrupt. He decided to earn money by giving lectures around the world. Slowly but surely, he paid off all the money he owed. ★

In the last years of his life, Twain was bitter and gloomy. His wife and two of his three daughters died. His books became quite serious, and they were filled with questions about the meaning of life. Writing up to the end, he died in 1910.

The Prince and the Pauper

You will be reading *The Prince and the Pauper*, which Twain wrote after visiting England in the late 1870s.

The Prince and the Pauper takes place in England in the 1500s. Although the novel includes real people, such as Henry the Eighth and Edward the Sixth, it also includes characters Twain made up, such as Tom Canty and Miles Hendon. Likewise, it describes real events, such as the death of Henry the Eighth, but it also describes

events that never happened, such as Edward's meeting with Tom.

Twain mixes fact and fiction to come up with a good story. You have to remember, however, that it's only a story. The real story was quite a bit different.

On the next two pages are the title page and the table of contents for *The Prince and the Pauper*. You can preview the novel by studying these pages now. You'll begin reading the first chapter in lesson 96.

C COMPREHENSION

Write the answers.
1. Why did Sam Clemens quit school when he was twelve years old?
2. Why did Clemens sign some of his articles with the name Mark Twain?
3. Why was Mark Twain a good second name for Clemens?
4. How did Twain become bankrupt?
5. In what ways is *The Prince and the Pauper* different from a true story?

D WRITING

Mark Twain's most famous story was about a jumping contest between two frogs.

Make up a story about a contest. The contest can be a race, a game, or any other event in which people or animals compete against each other. Think about the following questions as you write the story:
• Who are the main characters?
• Why do they have a contest?
• What happens during the contest?
• Who wins or loses the contest?
• What is the point of the story?

The Prince and the Pauper
by Mark Twain*

*Adapted for young readers

F TABLE OF CONTENTS

Chapter	Page

A WORD LISTS

1 *Hard Words*	**2** *Word Practice*	**3** *Vocabulary Review*	**4** *Vocabulary Preview*
1. presence	1. jewel	1. confine	1. ignorant
2. gifted	2. ancient	2. humble	2. unleash
3. abilities	3. beggar		3. ability
4. wisdom	4. jeweled		4. gifted
5. Westminster	5. ate		5. wisdom
	6. create		
	7. imitation		
	8. dilapidated		

B VOCABULARY DEFINITIONS

1. **ignorant**—If a person is *ignorant,* that person does not understand things. A person who does not understand arithmetic is *ignorant* about arithmetic.
   - A person who does not understand steeplechases is ▮▮▮ .
2. **unleash**—When you *unleash* something, you let it run free. If you let your feelings run free, you *unleash* your feelings.
   - If you let your imagination run free, you ▮▮▮ .
3. **ability**—If you have the *ability* to do something, you are able to do that thing. If you are able to write, you have the *ability* to write.
   - If you can run as fast as a dog, you ▮▮▮ .

4. **gifted**—Somebody who has a lot of ability is *gifted.* She had a lot of running ability, so she was a *gifted* runner.
   - He had a lot of speaking ability, so he ▮▮▮ .
5. **wisdom**—Great knowledge is *wisdom.*
   - If a person has great knowledge, that person has ▮▮▮ .

Chapter 1
The Birth of the Prince and the Pauper

In London, during the year 1537, two boys were born on the same day. One boy was born to a poor family named Canty. This family did not want their boy. The other boy was born to a rich family named Tudor. This family did want their boy. In fact, everybody in England wanted him so much that they were nearly crazy with joy when he was born.

People took holidays to celebrate the birth of the Tudor boy, and they hugged people they scarcely knew. They feasted and danced and sang for days and days. And they talked and talked about the Tudor baby. For, you see, the Tudor baby was a prince—Edward Tudor, Prince of Wales, who lay wrapped in silk, with lords and ladies watching over him.

But there was no talk about the other baby, Tom Canty, who was wrapped in rags. The only people who discussed this baby were in his family. They weren't happy about little Tom, because they were paupers, and the presence of the baby meant more work and less food for them.

• • •

When Tom Canty grew old enough, he became a beggar. He and his family lived in a small, dilapidated house near Pudding Lane. The house was packed full of terribly poor families. Tom's family occupied a room on the third floor. His mother and father slept in a bed in one corner of the room. But Tom, his grandmother and his twin sisters, Bet and Nan, did not have beds. Instead, they slept on the floor in any place they chose. They covered themselves with the old remains of blankets or some bundles of ancient, dirty straw.

Tom was nine years old when the year 1547 began. His sisters were fifteen. They were good but ignorant girls. Tom's father, John Canty, was a thief, and his mother was a beggar.

Tom grew up with a lot of yelling and fighting. He was hungry much of the time, but he was not unhappy. Although he never went to school, he learned to read and write from a priest named Father Andrew. In the summer, Tom spent most of his time listening to people tell charming old stories about enchanted castles and kings and queens. At night when he lay in the dark on his straw, tired and hungry, he unleashed his imagination and dreamed of becoming a prince.

As Tom became more and more fascinated with princes, he developed a strong desire to see a real prince. He mentioned his plan to some of his comrades, but they

only laughed at him. They teased him so much that he decided not to share his plans with them.

Then Tom found some old books about princes. He read them again and again until he began to act like a prince, and he amused his friends with his princely imitations.

As time passed, a strange thing happened. The young people who knew Tom began to show him more and more respect. They treated him as if he were a special person. Most of them couldn't read but Tom could, and he seemed to know a great deal. He could also say marvelous things.

When stories of Tom's abilities reached the parents of his comrades, they began to discuss him and to regard him as a most gifted person. Adults brought their problems to Tom and were often astonished at his wisdom in solving them. He became a hero to all who knew him, except his family. They saw nothing special about him. ♦

After a while, Tom started to play prince with some of his comrades. Tom was the prince, of course. His best friends were earls, guards, horsemen, lords, or ladies. As a prince, Tom would imitate the things a real prince or king would do. He would make laws and send messages to his army.

When the game was finished each day, Tom would go out into the streets, wearing his rags, and beg for a few pennies. At home each night, he would eat some stale bread, stretch out on his dirty straw, and continue his dream of being a prince.

One January day in 1547, Tom tramped up and down a neighborhood that had many food shops. He was barefoot and cold. A slow rain was falling through a thick fog. The smells of the pork pies and other dishes reached Tom, and he imagined how good they would taste. He had to use his imagination because he had never tasted any of the things that he saw in the shop windows.

When Tom came home that night, he had a lot of difficulty escaping into his dream world. The cold, the wet, and the hunger seized him so firmly that he just lay awake for a long time, listening to the arguing, singing, and yelling, and to the sound of horses on the street below. But at last his thoughts drifted to a faraway land, and he fell asleep in the company of jeweled kings and queens who lived in great palaces.

When Tom awoke in the morning and looked around, his life seemed so cruel that he tried to remember his magnificent dream to keep from crying. But the dream seemed very distant. He got up and wandered around London, hardly noticing where he was going or what was happening around him. People pushed him, and some talked sharply to him. Tom ignored them all. ★

As Tom walked aimlessly through the city, he suddenly noticed he was approaching a beautiful road. As he moved down the road, he walked past a small palace and then continued toward a far larger one, called Westminster. Tom stared in wonder at the huge palace and the marvelous gate, with stone lions on each side. "This is the king's palace," he said to himself. "Wouldn't it be something if I saw the king or a prince?"

Guards dressed in armor stood beside the gate, and a small crowd of people had gathered in the road to watch them. From time to time, the guards would admit people in splendid carriages through the gate.

Poor little Tom, in his rags, approached the gate, slowly and timidly. As he drew near, he caught sight of something that almost made him shout for joy. On the other side of the gate was a boy dressed in lovely silk clothing. At his side was a jeweled sword. Several splendidly dressed servants stood near. Tom said to himself, "He is a prince, a prince, a real, living prince."

Tom's eyes grew big with wonder and delight. As he stood there, staring at the prince, he had only one desire—to have a closer look at this marvelous boy. Before Tom realized what he was doing, he had pressed his face against the bars of the gate. In the next instant, one of the guards grabbed him and sent him spinning among the crowd.

"Mind your manners, you young beggar," said the guard.

The crowd laughed, but suddenly the young prince ran to the gate. His eyes were flashing with anger. Then he said something to the guard that changed Tom's life.

D COMPREHENSION

Write the answers.
1. Why were people in England so happy when Edward Tudor was born?
2. Why weren't the Cantys happy when Tom Canty was born?
3. What skills did Tom have that impressed his friends?
4. Why did adults bring their problems to Tom?
5. Why do you think Tom was so fascinated with kings and queens?

E WRITING

Would you want to be a prince or a princess?

Write an essay that explains what you think. Try to answer the following questions:
- What are the advantages of being a prince or a princess?
- What are the disadvantages?
- If you were a prince or a princess, what would you do all day long?
- How would your life be different than it is now?

97

A WORD LISTS

1
Hard Words
1. salute
2. hustle
3. dignity
4. alley

2
Word Endings
1. gifted
2. feasted
3. dilapidated
4. enchanted
5. drifted
6. suspected

3
Word Practice
1. entertain
2. entertainment
3. wrestle
4. bruise
5. shove
6. wrestling

4
Vocabulary Review
1. ability
2. wisdom
3. unleash
4. ignorant
5. gifted

5
Vocabulary Preview
1. rude
2. salute
3. priest
4. trade
5. tattered
6. hustle

B VOCABULARY DEFINITIONS

1. **rude**—The opposite of polite is *rude.* The opposite of a polite party is a *rude* party.
   - What's the opposite of a polite student?
2. **salute**—When you *salute,* you make a gesture that shows respect.
   - Show how soldiers *salute* officers.
3. **priest**—A *priest* is an important man who works in a church. When you talk to a *priest,* you call him Father.
4. **trade**—What do you do when you *trade* with another person?
5. **tattered**—Something that is torn and shredded is *tattered.* A torn and shredded coat is a *tattered* coat.
   - A torn and shredded shirt is ______.
6. **hustle**—When you move quickly, you *hustle.*
   - What are you doing when you move quickly?

C SUPPORTING DETAILS

Here's a paragraph with a main idea:

It was Saturday, and Miguel had a lot of work to do. First of all, he grabbed a broom and swept all the floors. Then he cleaned the bathroom sink. Finally, he mopped the kitchen floor.

- Here's the main idea of the passage: **On Saturday, Miguel cleaned the house.**
- The main idea tells the main thing that Miguel did. To do this main thing, Miguel had to do some other things.
- Those other things are called **supporting details** of the main idea.
- Here's how to write a main idea and three supporting details:

1. On Saturday, Miguel cleaned up the house.
   a. He swept the floors.
   b. He cleaned the bathroom sink.
   c. He mopped the kitchen floor.

D READING

Chapter 2
Tom's Meeting with the Prince

When the prince ran to the gate, the people in the crowd took off their hats. In a single voice, they shouted, "Long live the Prince of Wales!"

Ignoring them, the prince cried out to the guard, "How dare you treat anyone in this kingdom so rudely! Open the gates and let that pauper in!"

The guard quickly saluted as Tom Canty, the Prince of Poverty, passed in, with the rags of his costume fluttering behind him.

The Prince of Wales, Edward Tudor, said to the pauper, "You look tired and hungry. You have been treated poorly. Come with me."

Half a dozen lords who were in the courtyard sprang forward to object to allowing a beggar inside the gates, but the prince waved his hand in a gesture that told them to hold their tongues. The lords stopped in their tracks and stood silently, like half a dozen statues.

Edward led Tom inside the palace, past rows of guards, lords, and ladies. After passing through several halls, the boys entered Edward's beautiful apartment. Edward then commanded servants to bring food for Tom. Within a few minutes, they returned with food that Tom had only read about. Edward waved his hand for the servants to leave so that Tom would not be embarrassed by their presence. As Tom ate, Edward sat near him and asked questions.

"What is your name, lad?"

Tom replied, with his mouth full.

"Where do you live?"

Tom explained that he lived near Pudding Lane with his parents, his grandmother, and his twin sisters, Bet and Nan.

"Is your life hard?" Edward inquired.

Tom replied, "During the winter things are bad, but during the summer my life is pretty good." Tom went on to describe his family's filthy room and his straw mattress.

As Edward listened, a fierce look came into his eyes, and he cried out, "This is terrible! Are your servants good to you and your sisters?"

Tom answered meekly, "We do not have servants."

"What?" demanded Edward. "How do your sisters dress in the morning without the help of servants?"

"They don't need to get dressed," Tom said. "They have only one outfit."

Edward looked shocked.

"That is not a problem," Tom explained. "They each have only one body, so they don't need more than one outfit."

Edward laughed, then said, "Pardon me for laughing. But I shall see to it that your sisters have many changes of clothes."

Tom started to object, but Edward raised his hand. "Do not thank me. It is nothing." Then Edward frowned and continued. "You speak very well. Have you had a great deal of schooling?"

Tom explained how Father Andrew had taught him to read and write and how he had learned about the world from books. ◆

"Tell me, what do you do for entertainment?" Edward asked.

Tom explained the races, games, swimming, and other things he did for fun. "We have the most fun in the river," Tom observed. "We play tag and dunk each other in the water."

Edward leaned back and looked up at the ceiling. "Oh," he said slowly, "I wish I could have such pleasant experiences."

Tom continued. He told Edward about the neighborhood dances, about making mud pies, and about being buried in the sand.

"Don't tell me any more," Edward said at last. "I cannot do any of those things. All my experiences must be here, inside the walls of this palace. I can enjoy no mud pies, neighborhood dances, or games in the river. I just wish I could dress as you dress and delight in the mud with nobody to scold me and tell me that a prince does not behave that way."

"I have a different dream," Tom said. "If I could dress as you are dressed, just once, and . . ."

"Would you like that?" Edward interrupted. "Then you shall have it. We'll trade outfits. Take off your rags and put on the clothes I am wearing. I'll put on your rags, and for a short while, we'll trade places."

A few minutes later, the little Prince of Wales was wearing Tom's fluttering rags, and the Prince of Poverty was wearing the splendid clothes of a real prince. The two boys stood side by side in front of a great mirror. At first they smiled, but then their expression changed to wonder. They could not tell that a change had taken place. Edward looked exactly like Tom, and Tom looked exactly like Edward.

Edward looked at Tom with a puzzled expression and said, "What do you make of this?"

"I'm afraid to say anything," Tom replied.

"Then I will say it," Edward said. "Everything about us is the same—the same voice, the same face, the same hair. If we were both without our clothes on, nobody in the world could tell us apart." ★

Tom stood in amazement as Edward continued. "Now that I look like you, I should be able to experience some of the things that you experience." Suddenly Edward stopped. He pointed to Tom's hand. "That bruise on your hand is the only thing that makes you look different from me. Where did you get it?"

"When the soldier at the gate pushed me back into the crowd . . . "

Edward stamped his bare foot. "That was a shameful and cruel thing," he cried. "You stay here until I return. I shall go to the gate and deal with this matter."

Tom tried to object, but Edward said, "I command you to stay here."

As Edward left the apartment, he picked up a strange, heavy object the size of a small shoe. Tom had no idea what this object was, but it would soon become very important to both boys.

Edward quickly hid the object, and Tom observed where he put it. A moment later, Edward was out the door and running across the palace grounds in his tattered rags. As soon as he reached the great gate, he pointed a finger at the guards on the other side and shouted, "Open this gate!"

The guard who had shoved Tom away opened the gate. As Edward walked through the gate, he began to scold the guard, saying, "How dare you treat poor beggars . . . "

Suddenly, the guard gave Edward a rude shove that sent him whirling into the street. "Take that, you beggar!" he shouted. "I ought to give you more for getting me into trouble with the prince."

The crowd roared with laughter. Edward picked himself up and shouted to the guard, "I am the Prince of Wales! You shall hang for laying your hand on me!"

The guard saluted Edward and said in a mocking voice, "I salute Your Gracious Highness." Then his voice became harsh, "Now get out of here, you filthy beggar," he growled.

Some people in the crowd grabbed Edward and hustled him down the street, laughing and shouting, "Make way for His Royal Highness! Here comes the Prince of Wales!"

E COMPREHENSION

Write the answers.

1. When the lords sprang forward to object to Edward's actions, the story says he "waved his hand in a gesture that told them to hold their tongues." Explain what that sentence means.

2. Why did Tom think his sisters needed only one outfit?

3. When Tom described what he did for entertainment, Edward felt envy. Why?

4. Why did the two boys decide to trade outfits?

5. Why did the guard shove Edward into the street?

F WRITING

Edward and Tom talked about how their lives were different. Which person would you want to be?

Write an essay that explains what you think. Try to answer the following questions:

- What were the good parts of Edward's life? The bad parts?
- What were the good parts of Tom's life? The bad parts?
- Which life do you think would be more interesting? Why?

A WORD LISTS

1	2	3	4
Word Endings	**Word Practice**	**Vocabulary Review**	**Vocabulary Preview**
1. dirty	1. remodel	1. salute	1. torment
2. sorry	2. whisk	2. rude	2. sole
3. poverty	3. remodeling	3. hustle	3. saucer
4. crazy	4. whisked	4. tattered	4. dignity
5. misery	5. merciful		5. alley
6. mercy	6. sauce		6. foul
	7. saucer		
	8. sword		
	9. stricken		

B VOCABULARY DEFINITIONS

1. **torment**—The crowd teased and annoyed him so much that he could hardly stand the *torment.*
   • What does *torment* mean?
2. **sole**—A *sole* is the bottom part of your foot or your shoe.
   • Touch the *sole* of your shoe.
3. **saucer**—A *saucer* is a little plate that is placed under a cup.
   • What is a *saucer?*

4. **dignity**—When somebody acts with confidence and good manners, that person acts with *dignity.*
   • The queen acted with confidence and good manners, so the queen acted with ■■■■.
5. **alley**
   • What is an *alley?*
6. **foul**—Another word for *very bad* is *foul.* A very bad sight is a *foul* sight.
   • A very bad smell is a ■■■■.

C SUPPORTING DETAILS

Mr. Griffin turned on his television set at six o'clock. A television reporter told about the news. Then another reporter told about sports. Then another reporter told about the weather. After the program was over, Mr. Griffin turned off his television set.

- Here's the main idea of the paragraph: **At six o'clock, Mr. Griffin watched the news.**
- Name three supporting details of the main idea.

D READING

Chapter 3
The Prince's Troubles Begin

The crowd teased Edward for more than an hour. They invited others to join in, saying, "This beggar went to see the Prince of Wales, and when he came out, he thought he was the prince."

The crowd continued to make fun of Edward as long as he insisted he really was the Prince of Wales and that all who touched him would be punished. At last Edward realized the crowd would continue to torment him as long as he spoke. So he became silent, and his tormentors quickly left.

Edward now looked around and could not recognize where he was. He was somewhere in the city of London, but that was all he knew. He moved aimlessly down the streets until he came to a place where the houses were far apart. The soles of his bare feet were not used to walking on rough stones, so they were very sore.

As Edward approached a large church, he suddenly knew where he was. His father, the king, had taken over a church and had been remodeling it into a home for poor people. Edward said to himself, "They will serve me here and give me shelter. After all my father has done for them, they will certainly serve me."

Soon he was among a crowd of poor boys, who were running, jumping, playing ball, and making a great deal of noise. All the boys were dressed alike. They all wore black caps about the size of a saucer. Each boy's haircut looked as if someone had placed a bowl over the boy's head and cut off all the hair that stuck out beneath the bowl. Each boy wore a blue gown that hung below the knees, a broad red belt, bright yellow stockings, and low shoes with large metal buckles.

When the boys saw Edward, they stopped playing and flocked around him. With great dignity, Edward said, "Good lads, tell your schoolmaster the Prince of Wales wants to talk to him."

Great shouts of laughter went up from the boys. Then one of them said, "What are you, the messenger for the prince?"

Edward looked at the boy with sharp anger, and without thinking, he reached for the sword at his hip. Nothing was there. Again, a storm of laughter went up from the boys. One of them said, "Did you see him reach for his sword, just like a real prince?"

This comment brought more laughter. Edward stood up tall, with his chest out, and said, "I am the prince, and you would do well to treat me like a prince."

The boys only laughed. "I am serious," Edward shouted, and he waved his arm angrily.

Slowly, the boys stopped laughing. One of them said, "This game has gone far enough. Let's get this loud beggar out of here."

Edward cried out as the boys pushed and shoved him until he was in the middle of the street. "And don't come back," one of the bigger boys said in a threatening tone. ♦

As night approached, Edward found himself wandering through a dark and poor part of the city. His feet were so sore that he could hardly walk. As he slowly limped along, he thought of where he would find shelter for the night. He thought back to the questions he had asked Tom and how Tom had answered. He asked himself, "What was the name of that lane near Tom's house?" In a moment, he remembered.

A plan formed in his mind. "If I can find Tom's place, I will explain the situation to his parents. They will take me back to the palace and prove I am not Tom but the Prince of Wales."

The lights began to twinkle in the houses as people lit their lamps. Now came a heavy rain, blown by a raw wind. Edward moved on slowly through the disgusting alleys where people lived in hives of poverty and misery.

Suddenly, a large man grabbed Edward by the collar and said, "Here you are out at night again, and you haven't brought a thing home for me and your poor mother, not even a crust of bread."

Edward twisted himself loose and began to brush himself off. "So you are Tom's father," he said. "I'm so glad I found you. We must go back to the palace so you can pick him up and I can once again take up my duties as prince." ★

John Canty slowly shook his finger at Edward. "Don't you play those games with me, Tom Canty, or you'll be one sorry boy."

"Oh, please," Edward pleaded. "I'm not joking. I'm tired and sore. I can't take any more. Please, just take me to the king, and he will make you a rich man. Please, believe me. I am not your son. I am the Prince of Wales."

John Canty stared down at Edward with a shocked expression. Then he shook his head and muttered, "This boy has gone mad."

With a rude sweep of his arm, he grabbed Edward by the collar and began to walk quickly down the dirty alley, dragging Edward behind him. "I don't care if you're crazy or not," he growled. "You're coming home with me right now."

As John Canty dragged Edward past the paupers who peeked from the shadows of buildings, he shouted, "Tom's going to get it tonight!" Some boys in rags followed them down Pudding Lane, shouting and laughing at Edward. Finally, John Canty whisked the prince up the stairs and into the disgusting room the Canty family occupied.

"Be glad," John Canty said as he shoved Edward into the room. "Be glad you're not getting the whipping of your life."

E COMPREHENSION

Write the answers.
1. At the beginning of the chapter, why did the crowd make fun of Edward?
2. Describe the haircuts of the boys Edward met outside a church.
3. Why did Edward try to find Tom's family?
4. Why didn't John Canty believe Edward's story?
5. Name at least three ways the Cantys' home is different from Edward's.

F WRITING

Edward will probably try to convince Tom's family that he really is the Prince of Wales.

Write a conversation between Tom's family and Edward. Have Edward try to convince them that he really is the prince. Have the different family members give their replies.

A WORD LISTS

1	2	3	4
Word Endings	*Word Practice*	*Vocabulary Review*	*Vocabulary Preview*
1. poverty	1. pose	1. saucer	1. regain your senses
2. alley	2. magnificent	2. foul	2. pose
3. crazy	3. magnificence	3. torment	3. merciful
4. misery	4. activity	4. sole	4. stricken
5. dignity	5. activities	5. dignity	5. patrician
	6. posing		

B VOCABULARY DEFINITIONS

1. **regain your senses**—If you lose the power to think clearly, you lose your senses.
   - If you regain the power to think clearly, you ▇▇▇▇.

2. **pose**—When you *pose,* you try to look very attractive. A boy who is trying to look very attractive in front of a girl is *posing* in front of the girl.
   - A boy who is trying to look very attractive in front of a mirror is ▇▇▇▇.

3. **merciful**—The opposite of cruel is *merciful.*
   - What's the opposite of a cruel king?

4. **stricken**—When you are struck by a powerful emotion, you are *stricken* by that emotion. If you are struck by horror, you are horror-*stricken.*
   - If you are struck by grief, you are ▇▇▇▇.

5. **patrician**—A *patrician* is a lord, a lady, or a member of the royal family.
   - The Prince of Wales is one type of ▇▇▇▇.

Chapter 4
Tom as a Patrician

As Edward was having his terrible adventure, Tom Canty was having a very different kind of experience. Left alone in Edward's apartment, he spent some time standing in front of the great mirror admiring his fine clothes. He practiced walking like a prince as he observed himself sideways in the mirror. Next, he drew the jeweled sword and bowed in the gesture of a great knight. After he became tired of posing, he admired all the ornaments and decorations in the room. He sat in the grand chairs and felt the fine drapes that hung next to the windows.

After half an hour had passed, Tom realized that Edward had been gone a long time. Suddenly, Tom felt uneasy and strangely alone. He stopped looking around the apartment and began to worry. What if the guards came into the apartment and caught him in Edward's clothes? Edward wasn't around to explain. Tom guessed the guards would hang him first and ask questions later. As his fears rose, he quietly opened the door to the servants' chamber. He had almost resolved to run from the palace and find Edward.

Six finely dressed gentlemen and two young boys sprang to their feet and bowed as soon as they saw Tom. He quickly stepped back into the room, shut the door, and said to himself, "They're making fun of me. Now they'll tell on me, and I'll be in great trouble."

Tom paced up and down the floor, feeling fears he could not name. Every tiny sound made him jump. Just then, the door swung open, and a finely dressed boy said politely, "Lady Jane Grey is here to see you, my prince."

A young girl in rich clothes bounded through the door. She stopped suddenly in front of Tom and said in a distressed voice, "Oh, what's wrong with you, my lord?"

Tom could hardly catch his breath, but he managed to stammer, "Be merciful. I am only poor Tom Canty. Talk to the real prince, and he will explain. I didn't intend to do anything wrong."

The boy was now on his knees. The young girl seemed horror-stricken. She cried out, "I can't believe it! My lord is bowing to me!"

She ran from the apartment in fright, and Tom sank down to the floor, murmuring, "There is no hope for me now. They will come and take me away."

"The prince has gone mad!" Lady Jane Grey announced as she fled down the hall, and that message followed her across the palace. "The prince has gone mad!" was on everyone's lips.

Soon, groups of gentlemen and ladies formed in every marble hall. After a while,

a splendid gentleman came marching by these groups, saying solemnly, "In the name of the king, nobody is to talk about this foolish matter unless he or she wants to leave the palace forever." ♦

The whisperings ceased. Then suddenly, a buzz of voices sounded through the halls: "The prince! The prince is coming!"

Poor Tom walked slowly past the bowing groups, trying to bow in return. Soon, a group of people formed around him and led him to the king's apartment.

When they arrived, Tom gazed upon a large, fat man who had a wide face and a stern expression. His clothing was of rich material, and one of his swollen legs lay on a pillow. Everybody bowed and became silent.

The man was King Henry the Eighth. His face grew gentle as he said to Tom,

"What is this, my prince? Why are you playing jokes on me?"

Tom listened as well as he could, but when he realized he was in front of the king of England, he felt as if he had been shot. "Oh," he cried. "Now I'm really in trouble!"

The king looked stunned. His eyes settled on the confused boy before him, and he spoke in a tone of disappointment, "I think you are sick," he said. "Come here to your father." He held out his arms.

Tom approached the king, who held Tom's face between his hands and gazed earnestly into it, as if looking for evidence that his son was regaining his senses. After a while, the king said, "Don't you know your father, child?"

Meekly, Tom replied, "Yes, you are the king of England."

"That's right. But why are you trembling? Nobody here would hurt you. We love you."

Tom said, "I am the lowest of the people in your kingdom, a pauper. But I am too young to die. Please tell them not to kill me."

"Die?" exclaimed the king. "Rest your troubled mind. You shall not die."

Tom sprang up and turned a joyful face toward the lords and ladies in the room. "You heard it," he announced. "I am not to die. The king said so." ★

The lords and ladies bowed deeply to Tom. Then he turned toward the king, saying, "May I please go now?"

"Of course," the king said. "Where do you want to go?"

Tom looked down and answered timidly, "I must go back to the place where my mother and sisters wait for me. I am not used to all the magnificence of this palace. I belong in the filth of Pudding Lane. Please let me go."

The king was thoughtful for a while, and his face showed his uneasiness. Then he said, "Perhaps his mind is all right in other ways. We will find out."

The king asked Tom a question about history, and Tom answered it correctly. The king was delighted, and so were the lords and ladies.

"Let's have another test," the king said. He turned to Tom and asked a question in French.

"I don't know that language," Tom replied.

The king fell back upon his couch. Then he raised himself back up and said to Tom, "Don't worry. You will soon be well."

As he turned to the lords and ladies, the king's gentle manner changed, and he seemed to have lightning in his eyes. "Listen carefully," he said sternly. "My son is mad, but he will get over it. You have done this by keeping him penned up too much. He is reading too many books and listening to too many teachers. This boy needs sports and activities that will build up his health."

The king continued in a sharper tone, "If any of you speak of this madness, you will be severely punished."

After more discussion, Tom was led from the king's apartment and down the hallways, which once more buzzed with the words, "The prince! Here comes the prince!"

As Tom went sadly back to Edward's apartment, he realized that he was a prisoner, and he longed for the freedom of the streets.

D COMPREHENSION

Write the answers.
1. Why was Lady Jane Grey so shocked when Tom bowed to her?
2. Describe what the king looked like.
3. Why did the king ask Tom a series of questions?
4. Why do you think Tom answered the question about history correctly?
5. How did the king plan to cure Tom's "madness"?

E WRITING

If Tom meets Lady Jane Grey again, he might try to prove to her that he's not the prince.

Write a conversation between Tom and Jane. Have Tom try to explain who he really is. Show Jane's answers and questions. Think of ways that Tom could prove who he really is.

A WORD LISTS

1 Hard Words	2 Word Practice	3 Vocabulary Preview
1. identical	1. Elizabeth	1. page
2. Hertford	2. hesitate	2. dismiss
3. banquet	3. cause	3. mad
4. advantage	4. hesitating	4. identical
	5. causing	
	6. hesitant	

B VOCABULARY DEFINITIONS

1. **page**—A *page* is a young boy who serves a royal person.
   - What do we call a young boy who serves a royal person?
2. **dismiss**—When you *dismiss* somebody, you tell that person to leave. If you tell a servant to leave, you *dismiss* a servant.
   - What do you do if you tell a class to leave?

3. **mad**—*Mad* is another word for *insane.*
   - What's another way of saying *She was insane*?
4. **identical**—Things that are *identical* are the same in every way. Shoes that are the same in every way are *identical* shoes.
   - What are houses that are the same in every way?

C VOCABULARY REVIEW

foul
stricken
pose
ability
regain your senses
abandon
merciful

1. The opposite of cruel is ▬▬.
2. What's the opposite of a cruel act?
3. When you are struck by a powerful emotion, you are ▬▬ by that emotion.
4. If you are struck by horror, you are ▬▬.
5. If you regain the power to think clearly, you ▬▬.
6. When you try to look attractive, you ▬▬.
7. A boy who is trying to look attractive in front of a girl is ▬▬.

D READING

Chapter 5
Tom Receives Instructions

When Tom returned to the prince's apartment, he learned he would have just one teacher, an earl named Hertford. All the other teachers who usually instructed the prince were ordered to leave.

Hertford explained to Tom, "You have lost your memory. We will take things slowly, and soon you will remember everything. We will not spend time reading books. Instead, we will entertain ourselves in other ways. After all, we don't want you to be all worn out when you go to the banquet."

Tom gave Hertford a puzzled look. Gracefully, Hertford said, "I guess you have forgotten about the banquet this evening. But don't worry about it. I was referring to the Lord Mayor's Banquet. The king said you would attend. Do you remember it now?"

"No," Tom said in a hesitating voice.

At that moment, a page announced, "Princess Elizabeth and Lady Jane Grey are here to see the prince."

Hertford stepped quickly toward the door. As the girls passed him, he told them in a low voice, "Do not pay attention to the odd way he behaves, and do not act surprised if he forgets things."

Then Hertford walked over to Tom and whispered in his ear, "Act as if you remember everything. Don't let your sister or Lady Jane Grey know your memory is as poor as it is."

Lady Jane Grey approached Tom and

asked pleasantly, "Have you seen the queen today, my prince?"

Tom didn't know what to say. Hertford said, "Indeed, he has. Is it not so, Your Highness?"

Tom nodded his head yes.

Then Lady Jane Grey said, "It's a shame you are not continuing with your studies, my lord. I'm sure you will someday be as well learned as your father."

"My father!" cried Tom. "That thief doesn't know anything. He's . . . "

Hertford was slowly shaking his head, so Tom continued calmly, "I beg your pardon. It is hard for me to remember, and my mind sometimes wanders. I certainly didn't mean to call the king a thief."

"We know that," Elizabeth said, holding Tom's hand tightly.

As the conversation continued, Tom grew more and more at ease, seeing that the girls were kind and helpful. When they mentioned they would be accompanying him to the Lord Mayor's Banquet that evening, his heart jumped with delight. ◆

Hertford and the girls then left, and two lords and three servants entered the room. Feeling thirsty, Tom reached for a pitcher of water. The instant his fingers touched the pitcher, a servant respectfully picked it up, dropped to one knee, and poured out a glass of water for Tom.

Because Tom didn't know how to dismiss his attendants with a wave of his arm, they stayed with him in the room, standing stiffly and waiting for their prince to command them. But Tom didn't command them. He didn't know what to do.

Tom also didn't know he was causing serious problems in the kingdom. After Hertford left Tom, he met with an official named Lord Saint John to discuss the prince's condition. Hertford said, "I fear King Henry is so sick that he will soon die. The prince is obviously mad. If the king dies, a madman will become king of England. What a horrible thought!"

Lord Saint John replied, "Do you have any doubts that the prince is . . . ?" His voice trailed off.

"Speak up," Hertford said. "We are alone. Tell me what you are thinking."

"All right," Lord Saint John said. "I find it strange that the prince seems to be perfectly healthy in many ways, yet he seems to have forgotten French. He also doesn't seem to know his own father, and he does not behave like a prince. Although his voice is the same, his manners are different. I was wondering if he really is the . . . " ★

"Don't say it," Hertford interrupted. "Do you want us both to be hanged? If word got out that you were even thinking such thoughts, you might lose your life."

"I beg your pardon," Lord Saint John said. "Perhaps I was hasty in thinking such thoughts. I shall not mention the subject again."

After this meeting, Hertford went to his chambers and paced the floor. "He must be the prince," he said to himself. "The only other explanation is that there are twin boys who are so identical in every way that it is impossible to tell them apart. But . . . "

Hertford shook his head. "But if that were true, how could it be possible for the other boy to take the place of the prince? And if so, where is the real prince?" Again he shook his head. "No, it's not possible," he concluded. "No person could look so much like the prince that he could fool his father and all the others who have known him since birth."

Hertford tried to dismiss the thought that there could be a boy who looked so much like the real prince. But the thought would not leave his head. At last, he pounded his fist into his hand and said aloud, "No. He must be the real prince. But if he is, he has gone completely mad."

E COMPREHENSION

Write the answers.
1. How was Tom's father like Henry the Eighth?
2. Why was Tom happy that Jane and Elizabeth were going to the Lord Mayor's Banquet?
3. Why did the attendants stay in Tom's room?
4. Why were Hertford and Lord Saint John worried about the king and the prince?
5. Which two explanations did Hertford have for the prince's behavior? Which one was correct?

F WRITING

Pretend you are Henry the Eighth.

Write a letter to the prince explaining your plan for helping him get better. Try to answer the following questions:
- Why are you worried about the prince?
- How do you expect the prince to behave?
- What do you think has caused the prince's problems?
- How do you want to solve those problems?
- How do you feel about the prince?

A WORD LISTS

1
Hard Words
1. diaper
2. crisis
3. improper

2
Vocabulary Preview
1. butler
2. inspect
3. grave
4. pester
5. rose water
6. diaper

B VOCABULARY DEFINITIONS

1. **butler**—A *butler* is a male servant who's in charge of other servants.
   - The chief male servant in the castle was the ▇▇▇.
2. **inspect**—When you *inspect* something, you look at it closely.
   - What's another way of saying *She looked at the spoon closely*?
3. **grave**—One meaning of *grave* is serious. If you speak *gravely,* you speak in a serious tone of voice.
   - If you look at someone in a serious way, you look at them ▇▇▇.
4. **pester**—*Pester* is another word for annoy.
   - What's another way of saying *The flies are annoying me*?

5. **rose water**—*Rose water* is a kind of perfume made with water and roses. People rub *rose water* on their hands and face.
   - What kind of perfume is made with water and roses?
6. **diaper**—*Diaper* is a soft fabric that is used for napkins and towels. Baby wrappings made from this fabric are called *diapers.*
   - Napkins and towels are sometimes made of ▇▇▇.

Chapter 6
Tom's First Royal Dinner

Sometime after one in the afternoon, servants dressed Tom for "dinner," even though it was only lunch. He was clothed as finely as before, but everything was changed, from his collar to his socks. The servants then accompanied him to a fancy, spacious dining room where a table was already set—for one.

The room was half-filled with servants. Tom was quite hungry and was about to begin eating, but he was interrupted by the Lord Chief Diaperer, who fastened a napkin around his neck. Another servant stood to the side, ready to pour water into Tom's glass. The Taster to his Highness was there also, prepared to taste any dish when asked—and run the risk of being poisoned.

The Lord Chief Butler stood behind Tom's chair, overseeing the meal under the command of the Lord Head Cook, who stood nearby. The prince had three hundred and eighty-four servants beside these, but they were not all in that room, not even a quarter of them.

All the servants present had been well-drilled to remember that the prince was acting strangely and to show no surprise at his behavior. Tom soon displayed some of these odd manners, but the servants were only moved to pity, not laughter. It pained them greatly to see their beloved prince so stricken with madness.

Poor Tom ate with his fingers, mainly, but no one smiled or even seemed to notice. He inspected his napkin with deep interest, for it was made from a dainty and beautiful fabric. Then he said, "Please take it away. It might get dirty."

The Lord Chief Diaperer quickly took away the napkin without a word of complaint.

Tom examined the turnips and the lettuce, and asked what they were, and if they were to be eaten. Farmers had only recently begun to raise these vegetables in England, and the poor boy had never seen them before. His question was answered with grave respect.

When Tom finished his dessert, he filled his pockets with nuts, but nobody tried to help him. This lack of assistance worried Tom. Pocketing the nuts was the only act he had been permitted to do with his own hands during the meal, and he wondered if he had done something improper. ♦

At that moment, the muscles of Tom's nose began to twitch. The twitching continued, and tears came into his eyes. He gave a distressed look to the servants who stood around him. They sprang forward and begged to know his trouble.

"Please," said Tom, "my nose itches! What is the custom for this emergency? Hurry!"

All the servants were flustered, and they looked to each other for help. But no one was able to solve this serious problem. Alas, there was no Lord Chief Scratcher!

Meanwhile, tears had begun to trickle down Tom's cheeks. His twitching nose pleaded for relief. At last, Tom begged everyone's pardon and scratched his nose himself, bringing joy to his servants' heavy hearts.

When the meal was over, a lord came and held a shallow golden dish in front of Tom. The dish was filled with rose water for the prince to clean his face and fingers with, and the Lord Chief Diaperer stood by with a napkin for his use. Tom gazed at the dish a puzzled moment or two, then raised it to his lips and gravely took a sip. He returned the dish to the waiting lord and said, "It likes me not, my lord. It has a pretty flavor, but it's too weak."

This new evidence of the prince's ruined mind made all the hearts about him ache.

By his own request, Tom was now conducted to his apartment and left there alone. Hanging upon hooks on the wall were several pieces of a suit of shining steel armor, covered with beautiful designs and bits of gold. Tom put on the boots, the gloves, and the helmet. He thought about calling the servants to help him put on the rest of the suit, but then he remembered the nuts he had brought away from lunch.

What a joy it would be to eat the nuts with no crowd to eye him and no Lord Chiefs to pester him! Tom hung the armor back on the wall and was soon cracking nuts. For the first time since becoming a prince, he felt almost happy.

When the nuts were gone, Tom stumbled upon some inviting books in a closet. One was a book about how to behave in the English court. This was a prize. He lay down on a well-stuffed couch and proceeded to teach himself with honest pleasure.

Tom read for the rest of the afternoon. As night approached, he put the book aside and yawned. He wondered when the Lord Mayor's Banquet would begin, but he was too tired to think about it now. A moment later, he was fast asleep.

Let us leave him there for the moment.

D COMPREHENSION

Write the answers.
1. Why were there so many servants in the dining room?
2. Why didn't the servants laugh at Tom's strange behavior?
3. Why did Tom think he had done something wrong when he pocketed the nuts?
4. Why was Tom so happy when he ate the nuts in his apartment?
5. Do you think the writer is making fun of all the royal servants? Explain your answer.

E WRITING

Tom had hundreds of servants, and each one had a particular job. What kind of servants would you like to have?

Make up a list of servants you would like to have. Give each servant a title, such as Lord Chief Dishwasher. Then explain what the servant has to do and how he or she helps you.

A WORD LISTS

1
Word Endings
1. sternly
2. gently
3. gracefully
4. pleasantly
5. hesitantly

2
Vocabulary Preview
1. take advantage
2. lumbering
3. stout
4. retreat
5. seaman
6. toils

B VOCABULARY DEFINITIONS

1. **take advantage**—When a person is helpless and you make that person do what you want, you *take advantage* of that person.
   - How could a bully *take advantage* of a weak boy?
2. **lumbering**—When you walk with heavy steps, you are *lumbering.*
   - What are you doing when you walk with heavy steps?
3. **stout**—Something that is thick and sturdy is *stout.* A thick and sturdy stick is a *stout* stick.
   - What's a thick and sturdy person?

4. **retreat**—When you *retreat,* you move backward.
   - What's another way of saying *He moved backward toward the door*?
5. **seaman**—Another word for *sailor* is *seaman.*
   - What's another way of saying *The sailor was stout*?
6. **toils**—A *toils* is a trap.
   - What's another way of saying *The fox was in the trap*?

C VOCABULARY REVIEW

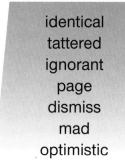

identical
tattered
ignorant
page
dismiss
mad
optimistic

1. A young boy who serves a member of the Royal Family is called a ▦.
2. When you tell people to leave, you ▦ them.
3. If you tell a servant to leave, you ▦.
4. Things that are the same in every way are ▦ things.
5. Shoes that are the same in every way are ▦.
6. Another word for insane is ▦.
7. What's another way of saying *The king was insane*?

D OUTLINING

The outline in the next column shows three main ideas for *The Wonderful Wizard of Oz.* Later, you will write three supporting details for each main idea.

- The first main idea is *Dorothy visited the Land of the East.* Tell which people lived there. Tell what color the land was. Tell what Dorothy did there.
- The second main idea is *Dorothy visited the Emerald City.* Tell which person lived there. Tell what color the city was. Tell what Dorothy did there.
- The third main idea is *Dorothy visited the Land of the West.* Tell which people lived there. Tell what color the land was. Tell what Dorothy did there.

1. Dorothy visited the Land of the East.
   a. ▦
   b. ▦
   c. ▦
2. Dorothy visited the Emerald City.
   a. ▦
   b. ▦
   c. ▦
3. Dorothy visited the Land of the West.
   a. ▦
   b. ▦
   c. ▦

Chapter 7
The Prince in the Toils

While Tom was sleeping in Westminster Palace, the true Prince of Wales was trapped in the Cantys' dismal room. In the corner stood Tom's mother. Bet and Nan were sprawled on the floor, and Tom's grandmother was propped up in another corner, staring at Edward with fierce eyes. Long gray hair streamed over her shoulders.

John Canty shoved Edward to the floor and said, "I will not stand for any more of your games. This is the last time you'll go wandering around by yourself without bringing home even a penny. If you do anything like that again . . . " He raised his hand in a threatening gesture.

Edward lifted his eyes and looked at Canty with a steady gaze. Then he said, "You are very ill-mannered. I will tell you again what I told you before. I am Edward, Prince of Wales, and nobody else."

Canty looked stunned for a moment, then burst into laughter. But Tom's mother and his sisters responded differently. They huddled around Edward, saying, "Oh, poor Tom, poor Tom."

Tom's mother put her hands on Edward's shoulders and looked into his face. "Oh, my poor boy," she said. "Your foolish reading has ruined your mind."

Edward replied gently, "Your son is well and has not lost his mind. If you will take me to Westminster Palace, my father, the king, will quickly return him to you."

"Your father, the king!" Tom's mother cried. "Oh, my child. Stop these horrible games. Try to remember who you really are. Don't you know? I am your mother, and he is your father." She pointed to Canty.

Edward said slowly, "I don't wish to sadden you, but I have never seen you or him before."

Tom's mother sank down, covered her face with her hands, and began to cry.

"Enough of this nonsense!" shouted Canty. "Get away from him!"

Nan said, "Oh, please, Father. Let him rest and sleep so his memory will come back."

"Yes, Father," said Bet. "He's worn down. He'll be himself again tomorrow. If he rests today, I'm sure he'll bring some money home tomorrow."

Canty turned sternly to the girls. "Let me remind you," he said, "that our rent is due tomorrow. If we do not pay two pennies for this hole, out we go." ♦

Canty grabbed Edward and pulled him to his feet. The frightened girls retreated to their corner, but Tom's mother stepped forward to help her son. Edward waved her away, saying, "You shall not suffer for me. I am not afraid of this man."

"Back to the street!" yelled Canty. "We must get money for the rent!" As Tom's

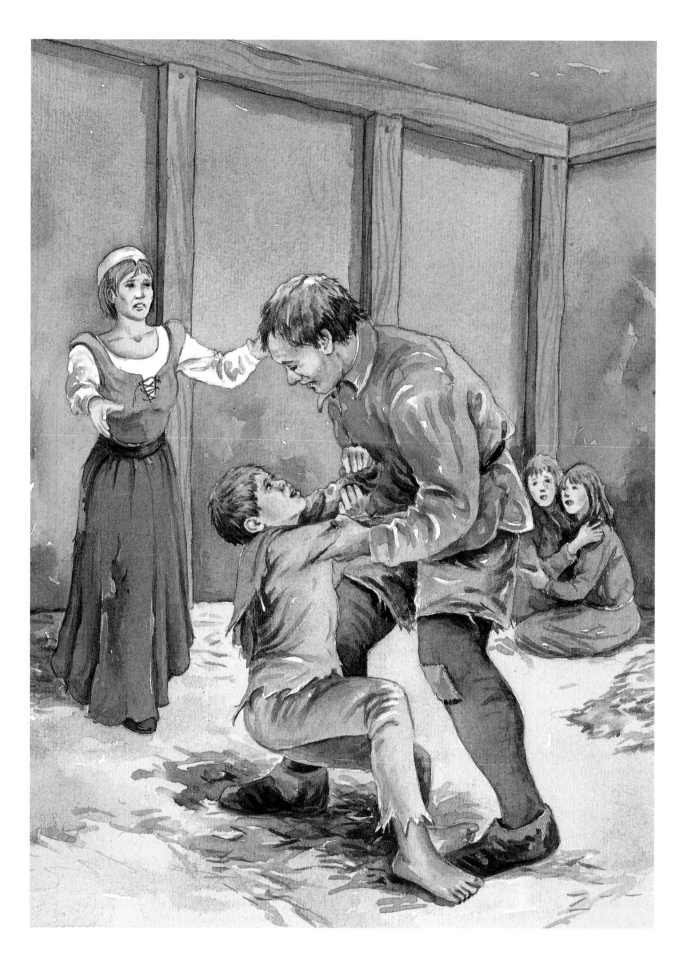

father pulled Edward out the door, Tom's mother slipped the poor boy a crust of bread.

After the two had left the room, Tom's mother began to think strange thoughts. "I have known that boy since the day he was born," she said to herself, "but he doesn't seem to be himself. He does not stand or move in his usual manner, and he's never spoken quite like that before. Could it be that he is not . . . "

She couldn't force herself to finish the question. How could she believe that the boy she had just seen was not her son?

• • •

Canty held Edward firmly by the wrist as they walked down the alley. "Tonight," he said, "I'm going to keep a good eye on you."

No sooner were the words out of Canty's mouth than another voice said, "So there you are, John Canty. I've been looking for you."

Edward turned and saw a large man lumbering toward them with a determined expression on his face. The man yelled out, "When you owe me money, you pay—or I'll pound it out of you." ★

"Run," Canty said, and he began to dodge through the swarms of people in the alley, still hanging onto Edward's arm. They slowed down after a few blocks, but then a towering form could be seen behind them, over the heads of the other people.

"He won't give up," Canty said. "If we get separated, go to the far end of London Bridge and wait for me there. Remember that!"

Canty shook a warning fist at Edward. Then he began to plow rudely through the crowd, still holding onto Edward. They soon ran into a stout sailor, who grabbed Canty and said, "What's the hurry? Slow down and stop shoving people around."

When Canty turned to answer the seaman, he let go of Edward. The boy wasted no time in scampering off through the crowd. He ran until he was a safe distance away; then he slowed to a walk and began to form a plan.

All around Edward, people were talking about the Lord Mayor's Banquet that would take place that evening at Guildhall. It was going to be a fine affair, and the Prince of Wales would attend.

The Prince of Wales! Edward's head spun. It seemed that Tom Canty had taken advantage of him and was pretending to be the real prince!

Edward stopped for a moment and thought up a simple plan. He would go to Guildhall. There he would make himself known and declare that Tom Canty was a pretender, a humbug. After the people realized Edward was the real prince, he would deal harshly with Tom. He would see to it that Tom was severely punished for taking advantage of him.

D COMPREHENSION

Write the answers.
1. Why was John Canty so mad at Edward at the beginning of the chapter?
2. Why was it so hard for the Cantys to believe Edward when he claimed to be the Prince of Wales?
3. What made Tom's mother think Edward might not be her son?
4. What did Edward plan to do at Guildhall that evening?
5. Do you think Edward's plan will work? Why or why not?

E WRITING

Tom's mother suspects that Edward is not her son.

Write a conversation between Tom's mother, his sisters, and his grandmother. Have Tom's mother explain why she thinks Edward is not really her son. Then show the answers given by Tom's sisters and grandmother. Have everyone discuss a plan to find out who Edward really is.

A WORD LISTS

1

Hard Words
1. Thames River
2. wand
3. cushion
4. ragged
5. suspicious
6. ruffian

2

Word Practice
1. merry
2. merriment
3. hurl
4. shield
5. hurled

3

Vocabulary Preview
1. vast
2. barge
3. file
4 wand

B VOCABULARY DEFINITIONS

1. **vast**—Something that is very large is *vast.*
   • What's a very large room?

2. **barge**—A *barge* is a large, flat boat that travels on rivers. State *barges* are *barges* that are owned by the state.
   • What do we call large, flat boats that are owned by the state?

3. **file**—A *file* is a line. A line of people is a *file* of people.
   • What is a line of barges?

4. **wand**—A *wand* is a small staff that is decorated.
   • What do we call a small staff that is decorated?

C VOCABULARY REVIEW

rude
lumbering
seaman
dignity
take advantage
retreat
ignorant
stout

1. When someone is helpless, and you make that person do what you want, you ______ of that person.
2. Another word for *sailor* is ______.
3. Something that is thick and sturdy is ______.
4. A thick and sturdy person is a ______.
5. When you move backward, you ______.
6. What's another way of saying *He moved backwards toward the door*?
7. When you walk with heavy steps, you are ______.

D OUTLINING

The outline in the next column shows three main ideas for "The Cat That Walked by Himself." Later, you will write three supporting details for each main idea.

- The first main idea is *Three animals visited the cave.* Name those three animals.
- The second main idea is *The cat and the woman made a bargain.* Tell what would happen if the woman praised the cat once, if she praised him twice, and if she praised him three times.
- The third main idea is *The cat did three things to win the bargain.* Tell what the cat did with the baby outside the cave. Tell what the cat did with the baby inside the cave. Tell what the cat caught for the woman.

1. Three animals visited the cave.
   a. ______
   b. ______
   c. ______
2. The cat and the woman made a bargain.
   a. ______
   b. ______
   c. ______
3. The cat did three things to win the bargain.
   a. ______
   b. ______
   c. ______

Chapter 8
At Guildhall

At nine in the evening, the whole vast riverfront of Westminster Palace was blazing with lights. The Thames River was crowded with boats and barges as far as the eye could see. These boats were fitted with colored lanterns that cast glorious reflections on the water.

A file of fifty state barges drew up in front of the palace. Some barges were decorated with banners and streamers, some with gold cloth and silk flags, and some with hundreds of tiny silver bells that sent out showers of joyous sounds. The barge Tom would occupy was decorated with large shields and silk streamers.

Attendants rolled out a thick carpet from the palace to the river. As a large band began to play, two pages holding white wands walked slowly from the palace along the carpet. They were followed by a group of lords and ladies.

A loud blast from the horns announced the members of the royal family. Lord Saint John appeared, wearing a scarlet robe. Princess Elizabeth was next, wearing a magnificent yellow gown. Then a roar went up that could be heard for miles down the river as Tom Canty, the Prince of Poverty, stepped from the palace and started down the carpet. He was dressed in purple and white, and he wore a long, white, diamond-studded cape.

Tom stepped into the royal barge. Slowly, the file of barges moved down the Thames through the crowds of decorated riverboats. The banks of the river were lighted with torches and bonfires that sent many slim towers of flame into the sky. The barges were met with a roar of cheers as they floated by.

Tom was half-buried in his silk cushions. This incredible sight left him in silent wonder. Soon the barges reached the center of London. Tom and the others stepped from the barges and walked slowly past huge crowds to the enormous dining room in Guildhall.

Inside, the Mayor of London bowed and greeted the royal party. After Tom and the others were seated at a huge table near the front, hundreds of finely dressed men and women filed into the hall and took their seats.

When everybody was seated, Princess Elizabeth reminded Tom that he should stand up. He did, and everybody else in the hall stood up at the same time. Tom drank from a large golden cup. Then Princess Elizabeth drank from it. This drinking signaled that the banquet had begun. ♦

By midnight, the banquet was at its height of merriment. A group of dancers with torches performed, and Tom was dazzled by their skill. But outside the great

hall, the scene was quite different. The real Prince of Wales was at the gates, shouting, "I am the real Prince of Wales. Let me pass and I will prove that the other prince is a humbug."

The crowd outside enjoyed this show nearly as much as the people inside enjoyed the dancers. One man yelled at Edward, "I can see from the way you dress that you are the real prince." This comment brought howls of laughter from the mob.

Another person shouted, "Where is your diamond-studded cape, Prince?" and another howl went up.

Edward stood tall and announced, "I'm not moving from this spot until I am recognized as the real prince."

As the crowd laughed and hurled insults at Edward, a tall, strong gentleman wearing a long sword pushed forward and stood in front of the boy. He said, "My name is Miles Hendon. I don't know if you really are the prince, but I do know you are a brave lad. I will stand by your side and be your comrade, but don't waste your voice on these alley rats."

Another roar of laughter went up from the crowd. "Look here," somebody shouted, "we have another prince. The city is full of them tonight."

Somebody else shouted, "Let's take the little prince and throw him in the river!" ★

A ragged sailor grabbed Edward. In an instant, Miles Hendon drew his sword and held it high. "Remove your hand or else!" Miles threatened. The sailor let go and backed away.

People began to shout, "Get them! Get them!" and slowly the crowd advanced. Edward and Miles backed against the wall. Just as the crowd seemed ready to pounce on them, everyone was stunned by the blast of a loud horn and the thundering of horses' hooves.

"Make way for the king's messenger!" one of the horsemen shouted.

Instantly, Miles grabbed Edward and ran.

Moments later, a solemn scene took place inside the hall. The king's messenger entered, bowed, and exclaimed, "The king is dead!"

A moment of silence followed. Then the lords and ladies sank to their knees and held out their hands toward Tom. In one mighty voice that seemed to shake the building, they shouted, "Long live the king!"

Poor Tom's eyes wandered over this kneeling crowd, then rested on Hertford and Princess Elizabeth, who were kneeling next to him. Slowly he began to realize that everybody thought he was the king of England. Tom bent over and quietly asked Hertford, "Am I really the king?"

"Yes, Your Royal Highness. You are the king of England. Your word is law."

The news was soon carried to the mob of people outside the great hall. A shout burst from the crowd, "Long live Edward, king of England!"

F COMPREHENSION

Write the answers.
1. Why do you think the royal family traveled to Guildhall on the river instead of the road?
2. Edward had a plan for explaining who he was. Why didn't that plan work?
3. Why did Miles Hendon want to be Edward's comrade?
4. Explain what this saying means: "The king is dead! Long live the king!"
5. Now that Tom is king, what do you think he will do first? Explain your answer.

G WRITING

Pretend you are Tom.

Write the thoughts you have about Edward as you sit at the Lord Mayor's Banquet. Try to answer the following questions:
- What do you think you should do about Edward?
- What might happen if you ask people to follow your plan?
- What might happen if you do nothing?
- What do you think is the right thing to do?
- Which action will be best for you?

A WORD LISTS

1 *Word Sounds*	2 *Word Practice*	3 *Vocabulary Preview*
1. blurred 2. curse 3. injury 4. return	1. swallow 2. basin 3. faults 4. swallowed	1. shudder 2. blurred 3. inn 4. regret 5. convince

B VOCABULARY DEFINITIONS

1. **shudder**—Another word for *shiver* is *shudder.*
   - Show how you *shudder.*
2. **blurred**—Things that do not look clear are *blurred.* A picture that does not look clear is a *blurred* picture.
   - What is an image that does not look clear?
3. **inn**—An *inn* is a small hotel that serves meals and has rooms where people stay.
   - What do we call a small hotel?

4. **regret**—When you are sorry about something that happened, you *regret* that thing.
   - What's another way of saying *She was sorry about what she had done*?
5. **convince**—When you make somebody believe something, you *convince* the person that what you're saying is true.
   - What's another way of saying *She made her mother believe that she worked hard*?

C VOCABULARY REVIEW

barge
wisdom
wand
merciful
foul
vast
file

1. Something that is very large is ▓▓▓.
2. A very large room is a ▓▓▓.
3. A large, flat boat that travels on rivers is called a ▓▓▓.
4. A line is a ▓▓▓.
5. A line of people is a ▓▓▓.
6. A small, decorated staff is called a ▓▓▓.

D READING

Chapter 9
The Prince and His Deliverer

As soon as Miles Hendon and Edward ran from the mob, they made their way through the alleys toward the river. When they approached London Bridge, they met another huge crowd of people. Edward learned from a thousand voices that the king was dead.

This news sent a shudder through Edward's body, and he began to cry. He no longer paid attention to the things around him. Everything seemed blurred through the tears in his eyes. Then suddenly, he heard a shout that thrilled him in his sadness. "Long live King Edward!"

He thought, "How grand and strange it seems! I am the king of England!"

• • •

London Bridge was like a little town.

It had stood over the river for six hundred years. Along the bridge were inns and shops of all kinds, with family dwellings above them. Children were born in these dwellings. They grew up there, and they died of old age there.

Miles was staying in a little inn on the bridge. As he and Edward neared the door of the inn, a harsh voice said, "So there you are. You kept me waiting here for hours, and now you're going to pay for it."

John Canty reached out to seize Edward.

Miles stepped between them and said, "Not so fast. What is this boy to you?"

"It's none of your business," Canty replied. "Give me back my son!"

"I'm not your son!" cried Edward.

Miles turned toward Edward and said, "I believe you."

"I don't know this man!" Edward exclaimed. "I would rather die than go with him."

"Then it is settled," Miles replied. "You will stay with me."

Canty pushed forward. "We'll see about that!" he shouted.

"If you touch him, you'll regret it," Miles said in a low voice as he reached for his sword.

Canty backed away, and Miles continued, "I didn't save this lad from a mob so I could turn him over to somebody like you. So be on your way, and do it quickly."

Tom's father moved off, muttering threats. Soon the crowd swallowed up the sight of Canty. Meanwhile, Miles and Edward entered the inn, where Miles ordered a meal to be delivered to his room.

The room was small and a little shabby. Edward went to the bed and dropped down onto it. His mind was blurred with sadness, hunger, and exhaustion. It was now three o'clock in the morning. "Call me when the food arrives," he said, and immediately went to sleep. ♦

Miles began to wonder about the sleeping boy. How could such a friendless little pauper think he was the Prince of Wales and now the king of England? Yet, the way he behaved was like a noble soldier. He had faced the crowd with the bravery of a king. "I like him," Miles said aloud. "I will become like a big brother to him."

A servant entered the room with a hot, steaming meal, which he placed on the table. As he left, he slammed the door. Edward awoke and sprang to a sitting position. For an instant, his eyes flashed around as he tried to remember where he was. Then he saw the meal on the table. He said to Miles, "You are kind to me. Thank you."

Edward got up and walked to the empty wash basin in the corner of the room. Then he stood there, waiting. Miles asked, "What's wrong?"

Edward replied, "Pour the water for me and bring me a towel." Miles laughed, took a towel that was right in front of Edward, and handed it to him without comment. Then he poured water from a large pitcher into the basin.

After Edward had washed, he sat down at the table. Miles was about to sit down as well, but Edward said, "What are you doing? You cannot sit in the presence of the king."

Smiling once again, Miles stood beside Edward and watched him eat. "The lad really does believe he's the king," he thought to himself.

In the middle of his meal, Edward looked suddenly at Miles and said, "You behave like a nobleman. Are you?"

"In a way," Miles replied. "My father is one of the least important lords of England, Sir Richard Hendon." ★

"Tell me more," Edward said as he continued to eat.

"There's not much more to tell," Miles said. "I was full of mischief when I was a lad. My younger brother, Hugh, turned all my faults into great crimes. He convinced my father I was worthless. So my father threw me out of our small castle and told me never to return. For the last seven years, I have been a soldier in France. As soon as I could, I came back to England. I've only just returned. As you can see, I'm quite poor. That's my story."

"You have had terrible experiences," Edward said with flashing eyes. "But I will set things right."

Then Edward told Miles his own story.

Miles was astonished. To himself, he said, "What an imagination this boy has! I think it has ruined his mind." Miles resolved to take care of Edward until the boy's mind was cured.

Edward said, "You have saved me from injury and maybe from death. Name anything you want, and if it is within my royal power to give it to you, you shall have it."

For a moment, Miles stared at Edward, not knowing what to say. At last he said, "Would it be possible for me to sit in the presence of the king?"

"Kneel," Edward commanded. And before Miles realized what he was doing, he kneeled before the young king.

"I declare that from this day on, you are Sir Miles Hendon." said Edward. "You are a knight. You and your children will live in Westminster Palace with me. Unlike any other lords, you may sit in my presence."

Then the little king bowed his head and said to the astonished knight, "You may rise, Sir Miles."

Miles said to himself, "I will not laugh, but here I am—a knight in the kingdom of dreams."

E COMPREHENSION

Write the answers.
1. Why was Edward sad when he heard the king was dead?
2. Why was John Canty waiting for Edward on the bridge?
3. Why did Miles admire Edward?
4. In what ways are Miles and Edward alike?
5. Why do you think Miles asked to sit in the king's presence?

F WRITING

Pretend you are Miles.

Write a letter to one of your friends in France explaining what has happened to you during the past few hours. Try to answer the following questions:
- Whom did you meet outside Westminster Palace?
- What happened there?
- Where did you go next?
- What happened there?
- What are you doing now?

A WORD LISTS

1
Compound Words
1. innkeeper
2. madman
3. grandmother

2
Word Practice
1. plunge
2. worm
3. busy
4. busied
5. wormed
6. yawn
7. plunged

3
Vocabulary Preview
1. ruffian
2. suspicious
3. drowsy

B VOCABULARY DEFINITIONS

1. **ruffian**—A *ruffian* is a rude and rough person.
   - What do we call a rude and rough person?
2. **suspicious**—When you are *suspicious* about something, you don't really believe it is true. If you don't really believe a statement, you are *suspicious* about that statement.
   - If you don't really believe a person, ▆▆▆▆.
3. **drowsy**—It was late at night and she was so *drowsy* she could hardly keep her eyes open.
   - What could *drowsy* mean?

C VOCABULARY REVIEW

lantern
inn
shudder
donate
convince
regret
hustle
blurred

1. Things that do not look clear are ■■■■.
2. A picture that does not look clear is a ■■■■.
3. A small hotel is an ■■■■.
4. When you are sorry about something that happened, you ■■■■ that thing.
5. What's another way of saying *She was sorry about what she had done*?
6. Another word for *shiver* is ■■■■.
7. When you make somebody believe something, you ■■■■ the person that what you are saying is true.
8. What's another way of saying *She made her father believe she should go to the movies*?

D READING

Chapter 10

The Disappearance of the Prince

After the little king had eaten, he stood up and yawned. He took off his rags and plunged into Miles's bed, saying to the man he had just knighted, "I will sleep here. You sleep in front of the door and guard it against anybody who tries to enter."

Sir Miles was going to object, but then he thought to himself, "I have slept in worse places for the last seven years. The lad needs a good sleep, so it will be no great hardship for me to sleep in front of the door." And he did.

Miles awoke late the next morning. He sat up and glanced at the bed, where Edward was still sound asleep. "I will let him sleep a while more," Miles said to himself. "The way the lad acts, he should have been born a real king, not a pauper."

As he stood up, Miles noticed Edward's old rags. "The poor boy needs new clothes," he thought. Taking a piece of string, he measured Edward from head to toe. When he finished, he covered Edward's head with a towel to keep him warm and to block the morning light.

Miles thought he could find some clothes before the boy woke up. Closing the door softly, he went down the stairs and onto the bridge, which was already crowded with people. A half hour later, he returned to the room with a bundle under his arm. He glanced at the bed. The bulging form under the covers and the towel seemed to be resting silently, as if the boy were still in a deep sleep.

Miles sat in the corner and sang softly to himself as he inspected the clothes he had purchased for Edward. They were used, and they needed some mending. Luckily, Miles had a needle and thread. He was not good at sewing, however, and he soon drove the needle into the end of his finger. "Ouch!" he cried.

Afraid that this noise would awaken the sleeping king, Miles glanced over at the bed. The form under the covers did not stir, so the new knight continued sewing.

After mending all the clothes, Miles decided it was time to awaken Edward. "My lord," he said, "it is time to get up. Arise, and we will have a hearty breakfast."

The form in the bed did not stir. Miles stared for a moment, then rushed to the bed and threw back the covers. The bed was empty except for some blankets and pillows under the cover, rolled up to look like the form of a sleeping person.

"What!" Miles yelled. He flew to the door and shouted for the innkeeper. "Get up here!" he demanded. ◆

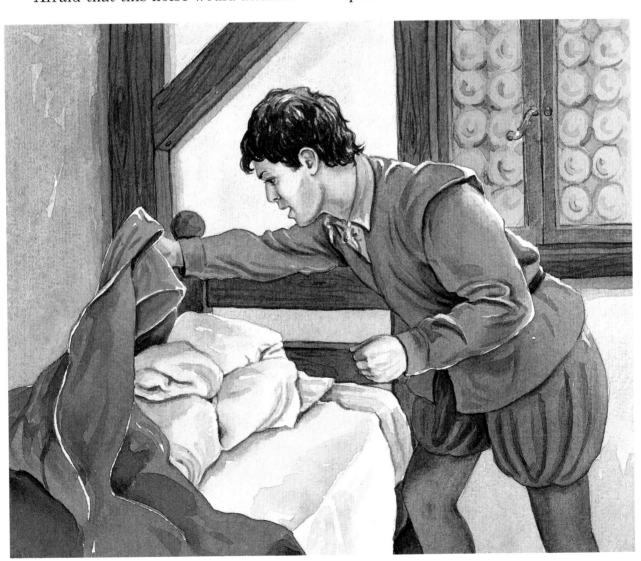

The innkeeper waddled up the stairs as fast as he could, huffing and puffing for breath. "What is wrong?" he asked timidly.

"The boy!" Miles exclaimed. "Where is the boy?"

"A minute after you left the inn, a young boy came here and said he had a message from you. I let him into the room."

"Go on," Miles said impatiently. "Go on."

"Well, the boy who came in woke up the lad who was sleeping in your bed and told him he was to go along with him. So the lad in your bed put on his rags. He said it was very rude of you to send a messenger when you should have come yourself. Then he said . . ."

"What happened, my man? Just tell me what happened."

"They went down the stairs together, and then they set off. That's all."

"That's all?" Miles exclaimed. "That can't be all. Tell me, was the boy who came with the message alone?"

"Yes, quite alone," the innkeeper replied. Suddenly, the innkeeper's expression became thoughtful. "Now that I think about it . . ."

"Out with it!" said Miles.

"Now that I think about it, I remember the two lads walked onto the bridge. And then it seemed that a large ruffian dressed in rags stepped from the crowd and followed the boys."

Miles knew instantly who that ruffian was. "So, that man who claimed to be the lad's father tricked me," Miles said and paced across the room. Then he whirled around and demanded, "Tell me what happened then." ★

"That's all, sir. That's all. There was a large crowd on the bridge, as you know, and soon the crowd swallowed up all sight of them."

"This is horrible!" Miles shouted. Then he pointed to the bed and said, "Who fixed the bed so it would look as if somebody were still sleeping there?"

"The boy who said he was your messenger," the innkeeper replied. "I have no idea why he did that. I thought you had ordered him to do it. I . . ."

Miles didn't wait for the innkeeper to finish. He grabbed his coat, threw it over his shoulders, and dashed down the stairs two at a time.

As Miles plunged into the crowd on the bridge, his eyes flashed this way and that way for signs of John Canty and Edward. He said to himself, "I have lost that poor little mad boy. But I swear he will not stay lost. If I have to turn over every stone in England, I will find him again."

Miles kept thinking about the cruel trick the ruffian had played. If anybody else had sent a messenger, Edward would have been suspicious and would not have gone. But he went because he thought the message had come from Miles. "I will make this up to the brave lad," Miles resolved. "I will make it up."

E COMPREHENSION

Write the answers.
1. Why did Edward ask Miles to sleep in front of the door?
2. How did Miles know which size clothes to buy Edward?
3. Why did Edward agree to go with the messenger boy?
4. How did the messenger boy fool Miles?
5. How do you think Miles can find Edward again?

F WRITING

When the messenger boy came for Edward, he probably had a hard time convincing Edward to come with him.

Write a conversation between Edward and the messenger boy. Have the messenger boy explain what he wants. Then have Edward ask the boy questions. Make sure Edward acts like a king.

A WORD LISTS

1	2	3
Hard Words	*Compound Words*	*Vocabulary Preview*
1. mourn	1. background	1. article of clothing
2. secretary	2. daylight	2. garment
3. Humphry	3. hairdresser	3. ordeal
4. parlor	4. fingernails	4. mourn
		5. shattered
		6. withdraw
		7. assist

B VOCABULARY DEFINITIONS

1. **article of clothing**—An *article of clothing* is a piece of clothing.
   - What do we call a *piece of clothing?*
2. **garment**—Another word for article of clothing is *garment.*
   - What's another word for *article of clothing?*
3. **ordeal**—An extremely difficult experience is an *ordeal.*
   - What's another way of saying *She suffered through an extremely difficult experience?*
4. **mourn**—When you *mourn* the death of a person, you show that you are sad about the person's death.
   - How do people *mourn* a person's death?

5. **shattered**—When something is broken into many pieces, it is *shattered.* A window that is broken into many pieces is a *shattered* window.
   - What is a hope that is broken into many pieces?
6. **withdraw**—When you take something back, you *withdraw* that thing. When you take back your hand, you *withdraw* your hand.
   - When you take back a suggestion, you ▬▬▬.
7. **assist**—When you help somebody, you *assist* that person.
   - What's another way of saying *She helped the students?*

C VOCABULARY REVIEW

merciful
regret
ruffian
drowsy
shudder
suspicious

1. It was late at night, and she was so ▉▉▉ she could hardly keep her eyes open.
2. A person who is rude and rough is called a ▉▉▉.
3. When you don't believe that something is true, you are ▉▉▉ about that thing.
4. If you don't believe a statement, you are ▉▉▉.

D READING

Chapter 11
The Whipping Boy

A few hours before Edward disappeared on London Bridge, Tom Canty woke up suddenly and didn't know where he was. For a moment, he was tempted to call out to Bet and Nan to tell them about his incredible dream. He reached out to feel the straw around him, but his hand touched only the silk sheets of his enormous bed. Then he saw a dark form moving toward him, and a voice said, "What is your command?"

"Tell me," Tom said earnestly. "Who am I?"

There was a pause. Then the voice repeated, "Who are you? Why, until last night you were the Prince of Wales. But now, gracious ruler, you are Edward, king of England."

Tom buried his head among his pillows, murmuring, "Alas, it was not a dream."

The young king ordered the servant away and went back to sleep. After a time, he had a pleasant dream. In his dream, it was summer, and he was digging a hole in a meadow. As he dug, he found twelve bright new pennies.

Tom felt wonderfully rich. Twelve pennies! In his dream, he ran home and gave the pennies to his mother. She was so pleased that she hugged him.

Then a voice said, "It is getting late, Your Majesty. Do you wish to get up?"

Tom's dream was shattered. He opened his eyes and looked around the apartment, which was not quite light. The voice had come from a lord kneeling next to Tom's bed. Other lords were standing in

the room. All were wearing purple cloaks. From the books Tom had read, he knew these outfits were worn to mourn the death of an important person.

It took some time to dress Tom. Of course, Tom didn't do any of the dressing himself. A row of lords assisted him. At the end of the row, one lord selected each article of clothing the young king was to wear. Then he passed the garment to the next lord, and so on down the row, as if they were passing buckets of water at a fire.

Finally the clothes arrived at Tom's bed, where two lords helped him put on each garment, starting with his shirt.

When the lords were about to put on one of Tom's long socks, one of the lords suddenly stopped. He handed the sock back to the next lord in the row, whispering, "It has a snag!"

One tiny piece of thread was out of place in the sock, causing a tiny ripple in the silk! ♦

With much whispering, the lords withdrew the sock to the beginning of the row. The lord who selected the clothes said, "The Head Keeper of the King's Socks shall go to prison for this!" Then he carefully selected a sock that was free of snags and passed it back down the row.

By the time Tom was fully dressed, he wondered how anybody could waste so much time on dressing. But his ordeal was only beginning. He now went to the palace hairdresser. As he walked down the halls, soldiers stood like statues, while lords and ladies fell to their knees. The royal hairdresser curled Tom's hair, trimmed his fingernails, and oiled his hands.

Next, Tom went to the breakfast hall, where lords and ladies again fell to their knees. After breakfast, he was led to the throne room and seated on the throne. Standing next to him was Hertford, who explained that Tom now had to make some important decisions.

The first decision Tom made was about the burial of King Henry the Eighth. Several lords suggested he should be buried two weeks from that day. Tom had seen people die, and he had seen them buried on the same day. He started to say Henry should be buried at once. But Hertford whispered in his ear, and Tom agreed to the plan.

Tom was then asked to approve the amount of money the palace was spending. These numbers shocked Tom so severely that he could hardly talk. His family's rent was only two pennies per month, so he was stunned to hear the palace had spent twenty-five thousand pounds during the last six months. He said, "We can't spend that kind of money. We'll have to let some of the servants go and move into a smaller palace." Then he added, "I know of a nice house just off Pudding Lane that we could . . ." ★

Hertford was shaking his head no, so Tom stopped talking.

The business of the court went on and on. Tom, who didn't understand most of what the lords were talking about, finally became drowsy and fell asleep—right in the middle of a long speech by one of the most important lords in the kingdom. The speaker stopped, and everyone stood in silence as Tom snored.

Hertford dismissed all the lords from the throne room. "The king needs his rest," he said.

• • •

After completing his nap on the throne, Tom ate lunch and returned to his apartment. A young lad about twelve years old was waiting for him. When Tom asked what he wanted, the boy replied, "I fear your memory fails you, Your Highness. I am Humphry, your whipping boy."

"My whipping boy?" Tom asked.

"When you do poorly in your studies," Humphry replied, "I get whipped."

"I had forgotten," Tom said. "Why am I not whipped myself?"

"You cannot be whipped," answered Humphry. "It is not allowed."

"Then you shall not be whipped either," said Tom.

"But," the boy said hesitantly, "if I am not whipped, I will not earn any money, and I will be returned to the streets of London."

Suddenly Tom had a brilliant idea. He told Humphry, "From now on, come here every day, but not for any whippings. We shall just pretend you get whipped so nobody else will know. When you come here, tell me everything you hear from the people in the palace. Tell me everything that's going on. In that way, you will help my memory return, and you will still have a job."

"Oh, thank you!" exclaimed Humphry. "I will keep this secret and tell you everything I learn."

E COMPREHENSION

Write the answers.
1. Why do you think Tom dreamed about his mother?
2. Why did it take so long for Tom to get dressed?
3. Do you think the Head Keeper of the King's Socks deserves to go to prison? Explain your answer.
4. Why was Tom shocked by the amount of money the palace was spending?
5. Explain Tom's plan for Humphry.

F WRITING

Now that Tom is king, he could make commands to improve life in England.

Write several commands that Tom could make. For each command, explain how the command would improve life in England.

A WORD LISTS

1
Hard Words
1. conduct
2. official
3. lawyer
4. Hugo
5. charred

2
Vocabulary Preview
1. conduct
2. official
3. seal
4. evidence
5. misplaced

B VOCABULARY DEFINITIONS

1. **conduct**—When you *conduct,* you lead. When a king *conducts* business, he leads a meeting about business.
   - If you are leading a tour, you are .

2. **official**—When something is *official,* it is the real thing. An *official* license is a real license.
   - What's an *official* law?

3. **seal**—A *seal* is a tool that puts a special mark on a piece of paper. The official papers the king wrote were marked with a royal *seal.* Unless a paper had that mark, it was not official.
   - Which tool puts a special mark on a piece of paper?

4. **evidence**—Facts that make you conclude something are *evidence.*
   - What *evidence* would make you conclude that somebody had walked through fresh snow?

5. **misplaced**—If you don't remember where you put something, you have *misplaced* that thing.
   - If you don't remember where you put your homework, you have .

C VOCABULARY REVIEW

ordeal
garment
assist
convince
mourn
identical
shattered
withdraw
article of clothing

1. When you show that you are sad about a person's death, you ▮▮▮▮ his or her death.
2. When you help somebody, you ▮▮▮▮ that person.
3. An extremely difficult experience is an ▮▮▮▮.
4. Another word for *article of clothing* is ▮▮▮▮.
5. A piece of clothing is an ▮▮▮▮.
6. When you take something back, you ▮▮▮▮ that thing.
7. When you take back a suggestion, you ▮▮▮▮.
8. When something is broken into many pieces, it is ▮▮▮▮.
9. A window that is broken into many pieces is a ▮▮▮▮.

D READING

Chapter 12
Tom as King

Shortly before King Henry the Eighth died, he had misplaced the royal seal, a device that was used to put a special mark on all his letters and other papers. Without the special mark, those papers were not official.

On the day he died, the king told Hertford that the prince might have the seal. So, on Tom's third day in the palace, Hertford and two other lords asked him about the object.

"The royal seal," Tom said thoughtfully. He tried to remember if Humphry, the whipping boy, had mentioned anything about the seal, but he doubted the lad would know about such matters. At last, Tom replied, "What does the seal look like?"

One of the lords groaned and said, "Oh, his memory is still damaged."

Hertford decided to wait a while longer for the king's memory to return. "Don't worry about the seal," he told Tom. "It will turn up."

• • •

By now, Tom was getting used to seeing people drop to their knees in his presence, but he was bored by the business of being king. One day, however, loud noises outside the palace attracted his attention. Tom looked out the window and saw a sheriff leading a large, noisy mob past the palace gates. Three people were being pushed along in front of the mob: a man, a woman, and a young girl.

"Go and see what's happening out there," Tom said to his page, who bowed and quickly disappeared from the throne room. He returned in a few moments. "Your Majesty," he said, as he kneeled before Tom, "the mob is demanding death for the man, the woman, and the girl. They are accused of committing great crimes."

"Bring the three of them to me," Tom commanded. A great deal of activity followed, and within a few moments, a long line of guards marched across the palace grounds to the gate. Judges and lords entered the throne room to be present while the king conducted official business. After entering, each one kneeled. Tom waved his hand to let them rise again.

At last, the guards brought the man, the woman, and the girl into the throne room. The sheriff followed. Tom observed something familiar about the accused man, but he could not place him at first. Then suddenly, he remembered. On New Year's Day, a boy had fallen into the Thames near Pudding Lane. Tom remembered that this man had jumped into the icy river and saved the boy from drowning.

"What crime is this man charged with?" Tom asked.

"He poisoned another man," the sheriff said.

"That is a serious crime," Tom said. "And if it is true, he deserves to die. But what evidence is there that he committed this crime?"

The sheriff replied, "He went to the house of a sick old man. Shortly after he left, the old man died of poisoning."

Tom asked, "Did anyone see this man poison the old man?"

"No, Your Highness," the sheriff said.

"Then you don't have very good evidence against him," Tom observed.

"There is more evidence," the sheriff said. "A witch said the old man would die of poison and that he would be poisoned by a stranger who wore a brown coat."

Tom said, "I suppose this is the only man in England who has a brown coat."

The judges and lords smiled at Tom's comments. Hertford turned to the lord standing next to him and whispered, "This lad has not lost his wits. His questions are brilliant." ♦

Tom continued, "Do you have evidence that this is the kind of man who would take the life of another?"

The sheriff stammered, "Well, not exactly, Your Highness, but we don't have evidence that he *wouldn't* take the life of another."

Tom turned to the man, who was trembling and kneeling, with his head bowed. Tom asked, "Is that true? Can you give us any evidence that you would not take a life?"

"My king," he said without looking up. "On New Year's Day, I saved the life of a youth who had fallen into the river. And I . . ."

"You are free," Tom announced to loud applause from the lords and judges in the room.

One of the judges said, "The king is brilliant."

Next, the woman was brought before Tom. The sheriff explained that she was charged with being a witch. She was accused of causing a great storm that destroyed many houses in a poor neighborhood of the city. Tom looked at the sobbing woman and asked, "And how did she become a witch?"

"She and her daughter made a contract

with a sorceress. The contract gave her the power to make storms," the sheriff replied.

Tom asked if the woman's house had been destroyed by the storm. When the sheriff said that it had, Tom concluded, "I cannot believe she would make a storm that destroyed her own house." Again, the lords and judges applauded.

Tom continued, "And what does this woman do to make such terrible storms?"

"She takes off her stockings, Your Highness," answered the sheriff. ★

Tom looked at the kneeling woman and said, "First, you are freed of all charges. And now that you are free, I want you to make a great storm for the sheriff. Take off your stockings."

The woman took off her stockings and tried as hard as she could to create a thunderstorm or an earthquake. But she didn't even produce a cloud in the sky. The judges again applauded.

Finally, the woman's nine-year-old daughter was brought before Tom. The girl was accused of making a contract with the sorceress. Tom asked one of the judges if English law permitted nine-year-old children to enter into contracts.

"No, Your Highness," the judge replied. "Children cannot make legal contracts. Only contracts made by adults are legal."

Tom stood up and said, "This child is English, and English children cannot make contracts. Therefore, I cannot see how she could enter into a legal contract. She is free."

Again the lords and judges applauded, and one said, "The new king is as wise as he is merciful. There is nothing wrong with his mind."

• • •

That evening, Tom ate in public for the first time since the Lord Mayor's Banquet. Hertford had planned several of these public meals to show everyone that Tom's memory was improving. At first, Tom had dreaded the idea of eating in public, but after his experience earlier that day, he had great confidence.

At the beginning of the meal, Tom made a short speech welcoming the lords and ladies to the palace. The speech went well, and Tom was quite comfortable and relaxed throughout dinner. After the meal was over, he overheard people saying, "There is nothing wrong with our new king. He is gracious and intelligent."

E COMPREHENSION

Write the answers.
1. Why do you think Hertford was so concerned about the royal seal?
2. The man who was accused of poisoning the old man had visited the old man's house. What was wrong with that piece of evidence?
3. How did Tom prove that the woman could not have caused the storm?
4. How did Tom prove that the girl's contract was not legal?
5. Do you think Tom is starting to enjoy being a king? Explain your answer.

F WRITING

Pretend you are a lawyer who is defending one of the people in this chapter: the man, the woman, or the girl.

Write a letter to a judge to prove that your client is innocent. Discuss each piece of evidence against your client, then explain why the evidence is faulty. Also explain why your client should go free.

108

A WORD LISTS

1
Compound Words
1. daylight
2. fingernails
3. innkeeper
4. background

2
Vocabulary Preview
1. charred
2. sling

B VOCABULARY DEFINITIONS

1. **charred**—Wood that is burned is *charred* wood.
   • Houses that are burned are ▇▇▇▇.

2. **sling**—A *sling* is a loop of cloth you put your arm in when it's injured.
   • What is a loop of cloth you put an injured arm in?

C VOCABULARY REVIEW

official
evidence
suspicious
conduct
business
drowsy
mourn
seal
misplaced

1. A tool that puts a special mark on a piece of paper is a ▇▇▇▇.
2. When you lead, you ▇▇▇▇.
3. Facts that make you conclude something are ▇▇▇▇.
4. If you don't remember where you put something, you have ▇▇▇▇ that thing.
5. If you don't remember where you put your shoes, you have ▇▇▇▇ them.
6. When something is the real thing, it is ▇▇▇▇.
7. A rule made by a king is an ▇▇▇▇ rule.

Chapter 13
The Prince in the Barn

Let us return to Miles Hendon. When last we saw him, he was worming his way along London Bridge, asking if anyone had seen Edward, the messenger boy, and the ruffian who claimed to be Edward's father. Miles was able to track the three past the bridge and into a crowded part of London, but then he lost the trail.

By now it was night, and Miles was tired, hungry, and discouraged. He had supper at an inn and thought about how to find Edward. He figured the boy might be able to escape from the ruffian, but he probably wouldn't return to London Bridge.

Miles recalled telling Edward about his family's castle, Hendon Hall. Perhaps the boy would try to reach him there. It was Miles's only hope. He resolved to start the long trip to Hendon Hall that very evening.

• • •

Earlier in the day, Edward had followed the messenger boy through the streets of London and into the country. John Canty had not actually joined them, but stayed a few steps behind, wearing a disguise. His left arm was in a sling, and he wore a large green patch over his left eye. He walked with a limp, using a long stick for support.

At last Edward became impatient. "I'm not going any farther," he said to the youth. "Where is Miles?"

The messenger boy replied, "Your friend is lying wounded in the woods not far from here. You can stay here if you want, but . . . "

"Wounded?" Edward cried out. "Why didn't you say so before? Move on, quickly!"

After a while, the boys reached an open space with a charred farmhouse and a barn that had nearly collapsed from ruin. There was no sign of life anywhere, and the air was strangely silent. The messenger boy led the way into the barn, with Edward following eagerly. No one was inside. Edward shot a suspicious glance at the youth and asked, "Where is he?"

The only answer was a mocking laugh. Edward picked up a large stick and was ready to attack the youth when more mocking laughter came from the barn door. Edward turned just in time to see Canty enter the barn.

"Who are you?" Edward asked.

"Stop this nonsense," Canty said. "My disguise is not so good that you can't recognize your own father." ♦

"You are not my father," Edward insisted. "You have hidden my servant, Miles Hendon. Tell me where he is at once."

Canty replied in a stern voice, "It is plain that you are mad, so I won't punish you. But don't continue with your pretending, or I'll lose my temper. There's nobody around here to pay attention to your silly games."

Canty moved forward and stared into Edward's face for a moment. Then he continued, "I'm in serious trouble. I owe a lot of money to some other thieves. They're after me, so I've changed my name. I am now Hobbs—John Hobbs. And your new name is Jack. You're always pretending, so now's your chance to do some real pretending, Jack."

Edward did not reply. He simply stared back at Canty.

Canty asked, "Now tell me, where are your mother and your sisters? They didn't come to the place where they were supposed to meet me. What do you know about them?"

Edward answered solemnly, "My mother is dead, and my sisters are in the royal palace."

The youth burst into laughter and started to imitate Edward. "My mother and my sisters . . . "

"Stop it, Hugo!" Canty interrupted. "There's no point in angering him. His mind is confused." Then Canty said to Edward, "Sit down, Jack, and be quiet. We'll have a bite to eat in a while."

Canty and Hugo began talking together in low voices, and Edward went to the far side of the barn, where he found a pile of straw. He lay down in the straw and began to think. ★

Edward was full of sorrow, but the greatest sorrow was the loss of his father.

To the rest of the world, the name of Henry the Eighth brought a shiver and suggested a monster who breathed destruction and death. But to this boy, the name brought fond memories of gentleness. Edward remembered some of his experiences with his father, and tears formed in his eyes.

The true king squeezed his eyes shut to escape from his sadness, and he sank gradually into a deep sleep. The sound of rain pattering on the barn roof finally woke him. For a moment he felt snug in his bed of straw, but a moment later his mood was broken by a loud shriek of laughter and cackling. He looked up to see who was laughing.

A bright fire was burning in the middle of the floor. Around it sat the most incredible company of ruffians Edward could ever have imagined. The fire cast a red glare that made them look even more frightening than they already were. There were huge men in tattered rags, with long hair hanging down their backs. There were middle-sized youths with sour expressions, blind beggars with bandaged eyes, and crippled beggars with wooden legs and crutches. There were wrinkled old women and young mothers with red-faced babies. There were even three dogs with strings around their necks so they could lead the blind.

Edward stared blankly at this astonishing group and said to himself, "I can't believe it. I've fallen into a den of thieves!"

E COMPREHENSION

Write the answers.
1. Where do you think Edward will go if he escapes from John Canty? Explain your answer.
2. Why did Edward go with the messenger boy?
3. Why did John Canty change his name?
4. How did Edward feel about the death of Henry the Eighth? Why?
5. What do you think John Canty and the other thieves are planning to do?

F WRITING

Pretend you are Edward.

Write a letter to Miles explaining what has happened and where to find you.
Try to answer the following questions:
- What happened to you at the inn after Miles left?
- Where are you now?
- How could Miles help you escape?
- What would the two of you do after the escape?
- What problems might you have?

A WORD LISTS

1 Hard Words	2 Compound Words	3 Word Practice	4 Vocabulary Preview
1. vagrant	1. eyesight	1. cross	1. capable
2. capable	2. whirlwind	2. crisscross	2. brawl
3. hurriedly	3. outskirts	3. string	3. brand
4. barrel	4. farmhouse	4. stringy	4. prosper
	5. clothesline	5. accident	5. lash
	6. overcast	6. accidental	6. vagrant
		7. accidentally	7. burly
			8. chant
			9. limb

B VOCABULARY DEFINITIONS

1. **capable**—If you are able to do something, you are *capable* of doing that thing. If you are able to swim, you are *capable* of swimming.
   • If you are able to ride a horse, you are ████.

2. **brawl**—Another word for a rough fight is a *brawl.*
   • What's another word for a *rough fight*?

3. **brand**—When you *brand* an animal, you make a mark on the animal with a hot piece of iron.
   • What are you doing when you make a mark on an animal with a hot piece of iron?

4. **prosper**—When you *prosper,* you earn money and do well.
   • What's another way of saying *She earned money and did well*?

5. **lash**—Another word for *whip* is *lash.*
   • What's another way of saying *The man whipped the fence post*?

6. **vagrant**—A *vagrant* is a person who does not have a place to live and has no job.
   • What do we call a person who does not have a place to live and has no job?

7. **burly**—Another word for *stout* and *strong* is *burly.*
   • What's another way of saying *He was a stout and strong man*?

8. **chant**—When you say the same thing over and over, you *chant* that thing.
   • The children said the same thing over and over, so they were ████.

9. **limb**—A *limb* is an arm or a leg.
   • What's another word for an arm or a leg?

C VOCABULARY REVIEW

official
sling
evidence
garment
charred

1. Houses that are burned are ▬▬ houses.
2. A loop of cloth you put your arm in is called a
   ▬▬ .

D READING

Chapter 14
Foo-Foo the First

As the rain continued, the gang started to make merry. They shouted and cackled and sang loud songs. One of the blind men got up and took off the patches that covered his excellent eyes. He tossed aside the sign that told how he had lost his eyesight. Another member of the gang removed a wooden leg. Underneath was a perfectly healthy limb. The blind man and the man with the wooden leg joined the others in roaring out the words of a song.

Conversations followed the singing. These conversations made it clear that John Canty had worked with the gang at an earlier time. Somebody asked what he had been doing lately, and he explained that he owed money to some other thieves. When he didn't pay, they started looking for him. Canty feared they might throw him into the river with a weight tied to his feet or send him to the other side of the world in the belly of a sailing ship.

"London used to be safer for me than the country, but now they've found me out," he explained. "I decided to take my chances with you."

Canty then asked how many people were now in the gang. The chief of the gang answered. He was a large and powerful man called the Ruffler. "Twenty-five," he said. "Most of them are here, but some are already moving eastward. We will follow the same route in the morning."

Canty said, "I do not see the Wen here. Where is he?"

The Ruffler replied, "Dead. He was killed in a brawl, sometime last summer."

"I'm sorry to hear that," Canty replied. "The Wen was a capable man and very brave."

"That's true," the Ruffler said. "His wife is gone, too. She was put to death by the law. But she was brave to the end."

Canty nodded thoughtfully, and the Ruffler sighed.

A moment later Canty asked, "Have any more of our friends had a hard time?"

"Some," the Ruffler replied. "You know what the law does to beggars in the country. Beggars are whipped the first time they are caught begging, but many just beg again. What else can they do to keep from starving? And if they're caught a second time, they are branded on the cheek with a red-hot iron and sold as slaves. If they try to run away, they are hunted down and hanged." ♦

The Ruffler called out, "Yokel Burns, show your decorations."

A man stood up and stripped away some of his rags. He showed his back, which was crisscrossed with thick old scars left by a whip. There was also a large V that had been branded on his shoulder.

The man said, "I am Yokel. Once I was a farmer who prospered. I had a loving wife and children. You can see that I'm different now. My wife and children are gone. They're lucky because they don't have to live in England any more. My mother tried to earn a little bread by nursing the sick. One of the people she nursed died, and the doctors did not know why. So they put her in prison."

Yokel shook his head and yelled loudly, "English law! Let's cheer for that fine English law!" His voice was bitter as he continued. "After I could not farm, I started to beg. But you know it's against English law to beg. My wife and I went from house to house with our hungry children until they caught us. They lashed us through three towns. Another cheer for English law!"

Yokel continued. "My wife died after the last lashing, and my children starved. Those children never harmed any creature, but now they are gone. Then I begged again, just for a crust of bread. When they caught me, I was sold for a slave. A slave! Do you understand that word? I am an English slave, and when I'm found, I shall hang. Another cheer for English law!"

Suddenly, a ringing voice came piercing through the gloomy air. "You shall not hang!" the voice exclaimed. "I shall order an end to that law!"

Everybody turned and saw the fantastic figure of the little king approaching the fire. "Who are you?" asked the Ruffler in surprise.

The boy stood determined in the middle of the gang and answered simply, "I am Edward, king of England."

A wild burst of laughter followed. Some laughed to mock, but others were laughing over the excellent joke. Edward was stung by the laughter and said sharply, "You vagrants! Is this the way you respond to your king?" His words were lost in a whirlwind of laughter and mocking exclamations. ★

Canty tried to make himself heard above the noise, and at last he succeeded. He said, "Mates, this is my son, a dreamer and a fool. He's mad, so don't pay any attention to him. He thinks he really is the king."

"I am the king!" said Edward, turning toward Canty. "And you will be punished for your crimes."

"You would turn against your father?" Canty said as he sprang forward. "Wait 'til I get my hands on you!"

"Tut, tut," the burly Ruffler replied,

stepping in just in time to save the king. Then he turned to Edward and said, "You must not threaten any of the mates here, lad, but you can be king if you want to. Long live Edward, king of England!"

The chant was taken up and came like thunder from the ragged crew. It was so loud that the barn vibrated to the sound. Edward's face lighted with pleasure. "I thank you, my good people," he said.

This comment brought forth another explosion of laughter. The whole company wriggled with delight. After they quieted down, the Ruffler said firmly to Edward, "Drop it, boy. It's not wise to be Edward. Choose some other title for your act."

Someone from the company shrieked out a suggestion, "Foo-Foo the First, King of the Moon!" The title caught on instantly, and a moment later every throat responded with a roaring shout: "Long live Foo-Foo the First, King of the Moon!"

Almost before Edward could draw a breath, he was robed in a tattered blanket and throned on a barrel. In his hand, he held an old iron rod, the wand of Foo-Foo the First. "Oh, noble king," the mob cried, "have mercy on us poor worms."

One old beggar pretended to kiss Edward's foot, but the boy kicked him away. The beggar quickly got up and asked for a rag to cover the part of his face that had been touched by the foot of the great king. He said, "The air must not touch this precious spot on my face." The mob roared with delight.

Tears of shame and anger burned in Edward's eyes. He said to himself, "I tried to help them, but see how they respond to my kindness."

E COMPREHENSION

Write the answers.
1. Why do you think the "blind" man was pretending to be blind?
2. Describe Yokel Burns's "decorations" and explain how he got them.
3. Why do you think Edward wanted to order an end to the laws about begging?
4. How do you think the Ruffler felt about Edward? Explain your answer.
5. How do you think the Ruffler felt about Henry the Eighth? Explain your answer.

F WRITING

Pretend you are one of the members of the gang.

Tell your story to the gang, just as Yokel did. Try to answer the following questions:
• What is your name?
• How did you use to earn your living?
• What happened that changed your life?
• What type of punishments have you received?
• Why did you join the gang?

A WORD LISTS

1	**2**	**3**
Hard Words	*Word Practice*	*Vocabulary Preview*
1. irritable	1. foolish	1. run a risk
2. hospitable	2. foolishness	2. clothesline
3. motley	3. assist	3. motley
	4. assistant	4. eye
		5. irritable

B VOCABULARY DEFINITIONS

1. **run a risk**—When you take a chance that may be dangerous, you *run a risk.*
   • What are you doing when you take a chance that may be dangerous?
2. **clothesline**—A *clothesline* is a thin rope you hang wet clothes on to dry.
   • What is a *clothesline?*
3. **motley**—Something that is made up of many different types of things is called *motley.*
   • What kind of group is made up of many different kinds of people?
4. **eye**—When you *eye* something, you study it with your *eyes.* Here's another way of saying *She studied the painting with her eyes: She eyed the painting.*
   • What's another way of saying *He studied the jewels with his eyes*?
5. **irritable**—When you are *irritable,* you are grouchy.
   • What's another way of saying *John Canty was grouchy*?

C VOCABULARY REVIEW

prosper
chant
brand
limb
regret
brawl

1. When you earn money and do well, you ▮▮▮▮.
2. Another word for a *rough fight* is a ▮▮▮▮.
3. Another word for *arm* or *leg* is ▮▮▮▮.
4. When you make a mark on an animal with a piece of hot iron, you ▮▮▮▮ the animal.
5. When you say the same thing over and over, you ▮▮▮▮ that thing.

D READING

Chapter 15
The Prince with the Tramps

At dawn, the motley troop of vagrants started forward on their march. The sky was dark with low clouds. The ground was sloppy, and the air stung with a winter chill. All merriment was gone from the company. Some were silent, some were irritable, and no one was in good humor.

The Ruffler put Hugo in charge of Edward and commanded Canty to stay away from the boy. He also warned Hugo not to be too rough with the lad.

After a while, the weather grew milder, and the clouds lifted somewhat. The troop ceased to shiver, and their spirits began to improve. They grew more and more cheerful and finally began to joke with each other and insult people who passed by on the road. They were once more appreciating the joy of their lives.

Everybody the troop passed took the insults without answering, even when the troop's members went into farmyards and snatched garments from clotheslines. The farmers said nothing, for they did not want to run the risk of the troop taking the clotheslines as well.

After a while, the gang came to a small farmhouse and made themselves at home while the trembling farmer and his family brought all the food they had to feed them breakfast. The vagrants insulted the farmer, made fun of the farmer's wife, and teased the farmer's daughters. They threw bones and vegetables at the farmer and his sons, kept them dodging all the time, and applauded loudly when they hit someone.

As they left, they warned the family they would come back and burn the house if the farmer reported them.

About noon, the group came to the outskirts of a village. There they scattered themselves so they could enter the village at different places and go about their business of stealing and begging.

Edward and Hugo went together. They wandered around for a while as Hugo looked for something to steal. ♦

At last, Hugo said, "I see nothing to steal in this poor place, so we are going to beg."

"Not I," Edward replied. "You may beg, but I will not."

"You won't beg?" Hugo said, scratching his head and eyeing Edward with surprise. "What's wrong with you? You've begged in the streets of London all your life."

"I have never begged, you fool."

"You'll be a lot better off if you don't talk to me that way," Hugo warned. "Your father told me you've begged. Maybe he lied."

"He's not even my father," Edward replied. "Of course he lied."

"I like your spirit," Hugo said, "but I don't think much of your wisdom. Stop all this foolishness and get to work. Here's what we'll do. You will be my assistant while I beg. If you refuse . . . "

Just then, Hugo noticed a friendly man walking toward them. "Perfect!" he said to Edward. "Here comes somebody with a kindly face. Now I will fall down in a fit. When the stranger turns to me, start crying and wailing. Then fall down on your knees. Tell the stranger I am your brother and that we have no friends and no home. Beg for a penny. Tell the stranger that with-out it we will both die. Remember, don't stop wailing until we get the penny."

The stranger was now near. Hugo stepped forward and suddenly began to moan and groan and roll his eyes. He staggered about, and when the stranger was nearly in front of him, Hugo fell down and sprawled before the stranger with a shriek. Then he began to squirm around as if he were experiencing great pain. ★

"Oh dear, oh dear!" cried the kind stranger. "Oh, this poor boy, how he suffers! Here, let me help you up."

With wide eyes, Hugo looked up. "Oh, noble sir," he said, "please don't touch me because it hurts too much. My brother there will tell you about my terrible condition and about these awful fits I have. Just give me a penny to buy a little food. Then leave me to my sorrow."

"Penny!" the stranger exclaimed. "You shall have three pennies, you helpless creature." He fumbled in his pocket with nervous haste and brought out three pennies. "There, poor lad," he said, "take them. You are most welcome to them."

The stranger, who was carrying a staff, then turned to Edward and said, "Now come here, my boy, and help me carry your poor brother to my house where . . . "

"I am not his brother," said Edward.

"Oh, listen to him," groaned Hugo. "He doesn't even know his own brother."

"Boy," said the man to Edward, "you are indeed a hard one if this is your brother. For shame!"

Edward said, "He is pretending to be in pain. He is a beggar and a thief. He has your money, and he has picked your pocket. If you want to see a miracle, hit him with your staff."

Hugo did not wait for the miracle. In a

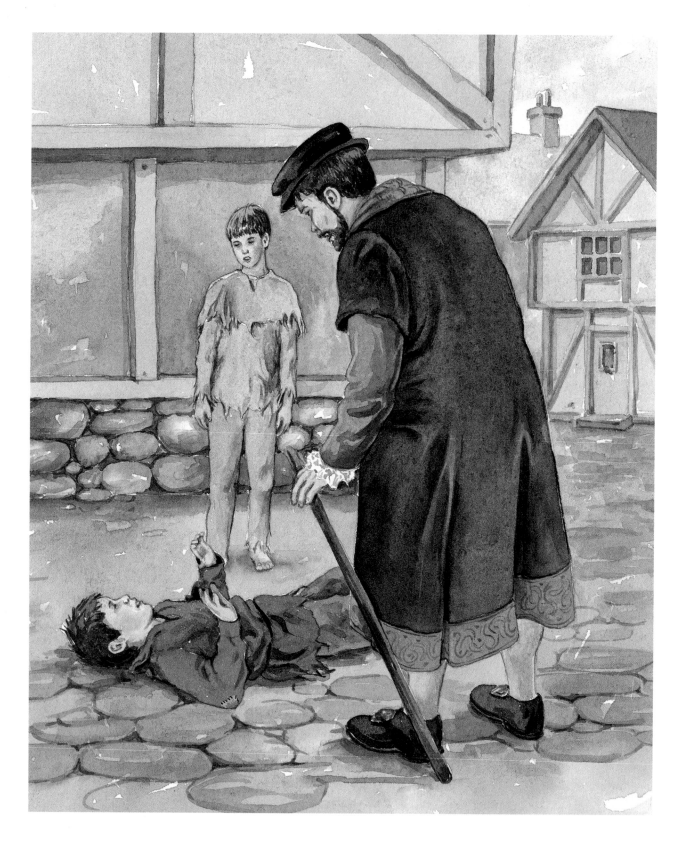

moment, he was up and off like the wind, the gentleman following after him with loud shouts.

Edward breathed a sigh of relief and darted off in the other direction. He did not slow his pace until the village was far behind him.

E COMPREHENSION

Write the answers.

1. Why do you think the vagrants were in such a bad mood in the morning?
2. Why was the gang able to boss the farmer around?
3. Why do you think the gang split up when they came to the village?
4. Explain Hugo's plan for getting money from the stranger.
5. Explain how Edward ruined Hugo's plan.

F WRITING

Hugo and other members of the gang earned money by making up excuses for why they couldn't work.

Write a conversation between a child and an adult. Pretend that the adult wants the child to do a chore, such as cleaning up his or her room, washing the dishes, or doing the laundry. Then have the child make up excuses for why he or she can't do the chore. Try to answer the following questions:

- What chore does the adult want the child to do?
- What excuse does the child give?
- What does the adult say will happen if the child doesn't do the chore?
- What kind of agreement do the child and the adult come to?

A WORD LISTS

1

Vocabulary Preview
1. overcast
2. hospitable
3. grope
4. gasp
5. calf

B VOCABULARY DEFINITIONS

1. **overcast**—When the sky is gray and cloudy, the sky is *overcast.*
   • What's another way of saying *The day was gray and cloudy*?
2. **hospitable**—When you treat guests kindly, you are *hospitable* to them.
   • A person who treats guest kindly is being ▮▮▮▮.
3. **grope**—When you feel your way in the dark, you *grope.*
   • What are you doing when you feel your way in the dark?

4. **gasp**—When you catch your breath loudly, you *gasp.*
   • Show me how you *gasp.*
5. **calf**—A *calf* is a cow or a bull that is not full-grown.
   • What is a *calf*?

C VOCABULARY REVIEW

burly
charred
capable
vagrant
convince
lash

1. Another word for whip is ▨▨▨.
2. What's another way of saying *The man whipped the fence post?*
3. Another word for *stout and strong* is ▨▨▨.
4. What's another way of saying *He was a stout and strong man?*
5. If you are able to do something, you are ▨▨▨ of doing that thing.
6. If you are able to swim, you are ▨▨▨.
7. A person who does not have any place to live and has no job is a ▨▨▨.

D READING

Chapter 16
The Prince in the Straw

Edward hurried along for several hours, keeping a nervous watch over his shoulder to make sure nobody was following him. At last, his fears left him, and he began to feel safe. He recognized that he was hungry and tired, so he stopped at a farmhouse. But when he was about to speak, the farmer drove him away with rude shouts. Edward's clothes were against him.

He wandered on, determined that he would not beg. But hunger is the master of pride, so as evening drew near, he approached another farmhouse. Here he was treated far more rudely than before. The residents called him names and promised to have him arrested as a vagrant unless he moved on promptly.

The night came on, chilly and overcast, and the footsore king kept walking. He was forced to keep moving, for every time he sat down to rest, he was soon tormented by the cold. All his experiences as he moved through the somber gloom were strange to him. Occasionally, he heard voices approach, pass by him, and then fade into silence. Sometimes he would see a twinkling light, always far away and seemingly from another world. Now and then came the howl of a dog. He stumbled along through the night, startled from time to time by the soft rustling of dry leaves. The sounds reminded him of whispers.

Suddenly, Edward noticed the light of a lantern, which was hanging on an open barn door. He waited to see if anyone came for the lantern, but there was no sound and nobody stirring. He got so cold from standing still, and the barn looked so hospitable, that at last he resolved to risk everything and enter. Just as he was walking through the door, he heard voices behind him. He darted behind a barrel inside the barn and stooped down.

Two farm hands came into the barn, bringing the lantern with them. They began to work and talk. As they moved around with the lantern, Edward peeked out from his hiding place and noticed a stall at the far end of the barn. He thought he would sneak over to the stall when it was safe. He also noticed a pile of horse blankets near the stall.

After a while, the men finished their work and left the barn, fastening the door and taking the lantern. The shivering king quickly moved toward the blankets, gathered up four of them, and groped his way safely to the stall. He made a bed using two of the blankets and covered himself with the other two. He was now a very happy king, even though the blankets that covered him were old and thin and smelled strongly of horses. ♦

Edward was at the point of dropping off to sleep when he felt something touching him. The cold horror of that mysterious touch in the dark almost made his heart stand still. He lay motionless and listened, scarcely breathing. But nothing stirred, and there was no sound. After a few moments, he was drowsy once more. Suddenly, he felt the mysterious touch again.

Edward thought quickly. Should he try to escape from the barn? No, the door was fastened from the outside, so there was no escape. The only thing left was to find out what had touched him.

Although he resolved to do this, it was much easier to make the decision than to actually do it. Three times he stretched out his hand a little way into the darkness. Each time he quickly withdrew his hand with a silent gasp, even though he never touched anything. The fourth time, he groped a little farther, and his hand brushed lightly against something soft and warm. He imagined it was part of a dead person, but he had to be sure. Once again, his hand groped into the darkness until it found a bunch of long hair that seemed to be attached to a thick rope.

The king's hand slowly moved up the rope until he could identify the mysterious object. It was a calf, lying down in the stall next to him. Edward was ashamed of himself for being so frightened of a sleeping calf. But a moment later, he felt delighted to have the calf's company. He petted its warm back and arranged his bed so it was right next to the animal. Then he curled up and pulled the covers over himself and the calf.

In a minute or two, Edward was as warm and comfortable as he had ever been upon the splendid couches in the royal palace. Pleasant thoughts came at once. He was free from the gang of vagrants, and he was warm and sheltered. In a word, he was happy.

The night wind rose, and it blew with terrible gusts that made the old barn tremble and rattle. Then it would die down before whining and howling again. But Edward simply snuggled close to his companion and slept. The calf did the same.

E COMPREHENSION

Write the answers.
1. Why were the farmers so rude to Edward when he stopped at their houses?
2. The story says, "Hunger is the master of pride." Explain what that statement means.
3. Why did Edward have to keep moving before he reached the barn?
4. At first, why was the calf so terrifying to Edward?
5. How did Edward put the calf to good use?

F WRITING

Edward was afraid of the calf until he realized what it was.

Write a story about somebody who's afraid of an object until he or she realizes what it is. Maybe the object makes strange noises, looks weird, or has an odd smell.

Tell how the person first becomes aware of the object and why the person is afraid of it. Then show what the person does to figure out what the object is. Finally, show how the person overcomes his or her fear. Use your imagination!

A WORD LISTS

1
Word Endings
1. rattle
2. snuggle
3. trouble
4. cattle
5. terrible
6. hospitable

2
Vocabulary Preview
1. widow
2. cattle
3. tragic

B VOCABULARY DEFINITIONS

1. **widow**—A *widow* is a woman whose husband is dead.
   - What do we call a woman whose husband is dead?

2. **cattle**—Cows and bulls are *cattle.*
   - What do we call cows and bulls?

3. **tragic**—Something that is very sad is *tragic.*
   - A very sad accident is a .

C VOCABULARY REVIEW

eye
overcast
limb
hospitable
grope
irritable
burly
motley
run a risk
brawl

1. When you are grouchy, you are ███████.
2. What's another way of saying *John Canty was grouchy*?
3. When the sky is cloudy and gray, the sky is ███████.
4. Something that is made up of many different types of things is called ███████.
5. When you feel your way in the dark, you ███████.
6. When you study something with your eyes, you ███████ that thing.
7. What's another way of saying *He studied the jewels with his eyes*?
8. When you treat guests kindly, you are ███████ to them.
9. When you take a chance that may be dangerous, you ███████.

D READING

Chapter 17
The Prince with the Peasants

When Edward awoke early in the morning, he found that a wet mouse had crept under his blanket. Now that the mouse was disturbed, it scampered away. Edward smiled and said aloud, "I know now things will get better because they can't get any worse for a king who sleeps with a mouse."

Just as Edward stepped out of the stall, he heard children's voices. The barn door burst open, and two little girls came in. As soon as they saw him, they stopped talking and laughing and stood still, eyeing him with curiosity. At last, they gathered their courage and began to discuss him. One girl said, "He has a nice face."

The other said, "And pretty hair."

"But look at those terrible clothes."

"And look how starved he seems to be."

They timidly approached Edward, circling around him and examining him as if

he were some kind of strange new animal. But they were careful not to get too close. Finally, they stopped in front of him, holding each other's hands for protection. One of them asked, "Who are you?"

"I am the king," Edward answered.

The children blinked, looked at each other, and then stared at Edward for a long moment before one of them asked, "The king of what?"

"The king of England."

This statement seemed to satisfy the girls, and they accepted Edward as the true king. ♦

The girls immediately began to question how he got into such a dreadful situation. They asked him where he planned to go and how he planned to return to the royal palace. He poured his troubles out to them, and as he talked, he forgot his hunger. But when the girls learned how long he had been without food, they stopped his story and hurried him to the farmhouse to feed him breakfast.

Edward was cheerful now and said to himself, "When I return to the palace, I will always remember how these girls believed in me. I'm afraid if they were older and wiser, they would have mocked me."

The girls' mother was kind to Edward and pitied his condition. She was a widow with little money, so she was used to suffering. To her, Edward was a mad boy who had wandered away from his friends. She tried to find out where he had come from, but he seemed to know nothing about the neighboring towns, and he stuck to his story about being the king.

As the good widow prepared breakfast, she kept trying to figure out what kind of work Edward had done before he became mad. She talked about cattle, but he showed no interest. She talked about sheep, but the result was the same. She mentioned weavers, tinsmiths, and merchants, but no matter what subject she raised, the boy showed no knowledge or interest in it.

At last, the widow wondered if Edward had been a servant. She tried to ask questions about servants, but the subject only seemed to weary the boy. Then, quite by accident, she mentioned cooking. Edward's face lit up, and the widow concluded that she had finally discovered what he had done in the past. She was proud of herself for being so clever. ★

Her tongue now got a rest. Edward, because of his terrible hunger, immediately started complimenting the widow on the breakfast she had prepared. From his talk and manner, the widow concluded that he must have worked in a royal kitchen.

Pleased at her discovery, the woman decided to test Edward. She gave him his breakfast, but she left some hot cakes on the stove. Then she crept out of the kitchen and secretly signaled the girls to follow her. She felt confident that the boy would prove he had worked in a kitchen by taking care of the hot cakes.

A short while later, the hot cakes began to burn, but Edward just kept on eating. When the woman returned and saw that he had not lifted a finger to save the cakes, she scolded him loudly. Edward was shocked by her behavior, but before he could respond, her voice softened. She was ashamed of herself for scolding someone as tragic as the ragged little boy who sat at the table.

After breakfast, the woman asked Edward to wash the dishes. This command stunned him for a moment, but then he said to himself, "Kings have had to do worse things than wash dishes." With this, he went to work, but he made a poor job of it. Seeing how badly Edward had done, the woman gave him another task—peeling apples. He was so awkward, however, that the girls giggled at his attempt. Unwilling to give up, the widow asked him to do some yard work.

Edward went into the yard, but his work was rudely interrupted when he saw two figures approaching the front gate—John Canty and Hugo! Before they could see him, he fled from the yard and hurried down a narrow lane.

E COMPREHENSION

Write the answers.

1. Why do you think the girls believed Edward's story?
2. Why did the widow ask Edward questions about different subjects?
3. Why was Edward so interested in the subject of cooking?
4. Why did Edward do such a poor job of washing dishes and peeling apples?
5. How do you think John Canty and Hugo were able to find Edward?

F WRITING

Write an essay about your household chores. Try to answer the following questions:

- What are the different chores that people in your house do, such as cooking, cleaning, and picking up?
- Which chores do you like the most? Why?
- Which ones do you like the least? Why?
- What happens when people in your house don't do their chores?
- How could you make chores easier?

A WORD LISTS

1	2	3
Compound Words	*Word Endings*	*Vocabulary Preview*
1. tiptoes	1. hospitable	1. bound
2. fireplace	2. comfortable	2. gagged
3. sheepskin	3. irritable	3. inform
4. eyesight	4. disagreeable	4. intend
5. clothesline		5. confess

B VOCABULARY DEFINITIONS

1. **bound**—When a person is *bound,* that person is tied up.
   - When a person is tied up, he or she is ▬▬.

2. **gagged**—When a person is *gagged,* that person's mouth is covered and he or she cannot talk.
   - When a person's mouth is covered, that person is ▬▬.

3. **inform**—When you give people information about something, you *inform* them about that thing.
   - What are you doing when you give a girl information about school?

4. **intend**—If you plan to do something, you *intend* to do that thing.
   - A person who plans to go to a party ▬▬.

5. **confess**—When people *confess,* they tell the truth about a secret.
   - What are people doing when they tell the truth about a secret?

C VOCABULARY REVIEW

irritable
widow
calf
tragic
motley
gasp
prosper
cattle

1. A cow or a bull that is not full-grown is a ▬▬.
2. Something that is very sad is ▬▬.
3. A very sad story is a ▬▬.
4. Cows and bulls are ▬▬.
5. A woman whose husband is dead is a ▬▬.
6. Show me how you *gasp*.

D READING

Chapter 18
The Prince and the Hermit

Edward ran quickly down the path. Just before he reached a forest, he glanced back and noticed two figures behind him in the distance. He did not wait to determine who those distant figures were, but hurried on and did not slow his pace until he was far inside the twilight of the woods. Then he stopped and listened intently. His ears heard nothing but stillness.

At first, Edward intended to stay where he was and rest until the following day. A chill soon cut into his sweating body, however, and he began moving again to stay warm. He went straight through the forest, hoping to cross a road, but he continued farther and farther into the forest without finding one.

The gloom began to thicken, and Edward realized that night was coming. The woods were now so thick that he had to move slowly. Even so, he tripped over roots and tangled himself in vines and bushes.

How glad Edward was when he caught a glimpse of light! He approached it carefully, stopping frequently to look around. The light came from the open window of a shabby little hut. He heard a voice inside, and each time it spoke, Edward had to fight the impulse to run away. Finally, he stood just below the window. He raised himself on tiptoes and stared inside.

The room was small, and the floor was nothing but hard-packed earth. In the corner was a bed made of sticks and a ragged

blanket. In front of the fireplace stood an old man. He was holding a large candle. His hair and beard were white, and he wore a robe of sheepskin that went from his neck to his heels.

Edward realized that the man was a hermit, a person who lives by himself far from other people. The young king knocked on the door, and the hermit flung it open, staring at Edward with gleaming eyes.

"Who are you?" the hermit inquired.

"I am the king," came the answer.

"Welcome, king," cried the hermit eagerly. He moved a small bench to the middle of the room, seated Edward on it, threw

some wood on the fire, and paced back and forth as he continued to say, "Welcome, welcome."

After a few minutes, the hermit began muttering. Edward took this opportunity to tell his story, but the hermit paid no attention to him.

Suddenly, he approached Edward and said, "I will tell you a secret."

Then he bent down, looked around the room suspiciously several times, and whispered, "I am a wizard."

Edward groaned and thought, "I have left the company of thieves to be in the company of a madman." ◆

The hermit smiled and told a confusing story about how he became a wizard. The tale lasted for more than an hour, while Edward listened and suffered. Then the hermit's voice softened. He started preparing supper, chatting pleasantly all the time. After supper, he tucked Edward into bed, and then he tapped his forehead as if trying to remember something. "Are you the king of England?" he asked Edward.

"Yes," came the drowsy reply.

"Then Henry is gone."

"That's true," Edward replied.

A dark frown settled over the hermit's face, and he made a hard fist. He said, "Did you know that Henry was responsible for making me become a hermit?"

Edward did not reply because he was sound asleep. As the hermit gazed at the boy, a wild smile replaced the frown on his face. He went back to the fireplace and began muttering again. At last, he said aloud, "His father was responsible for great evil. But his father can no longer be punished, so the boy shall pay for Henry's evil ways."

The hermit went back to the sleeping boy. He quietly tied Edward's ankles to the bed, and then he tied his wrists. As the boy continued to sleep calmly, the hermit tied a rag around his mouth. Then he glided away like a cat and returned with a small bench, which he sat upon, still muttering to himself. He was like a spider viewing a fly that is caught in its web.

Suddenly, Edward woke up and stared with frozen horror at the hermit. He struggled for a moment before realizing that he was tightly bound and gagged. The old man said, "The night is nearly over and daylight approaches. I must take care of you now."

At that moment, thundering knocks came from the door, and a loud voice said, "Open up in there." The voice was like beautiful music to Edward's ears, for it was Miles Hendon's. ★

The hermit moved swiftly to the door and opened it just a crack, blocking Miles's view of the room.

Still standing outside, Miles said, "Where is the boy?"

"What boy?"

"Don't lie to me," said Miles. "I'm not in the mood for it. I caught the two ruffians who were following the boy close to this cabin, and I made them confess. They informed me that they had followed him to the path that leads to your door. Where is he?"

"Oh," the hermit said. "You must mean the ragged vagrant who came here last night. I sent him on an errand before dawn broke. He should return shortly."

"That's a lie," Miles declared. "He would not obey you. He wouldn't obey any man."

"But sir," the hermit said. "I am not a man. I am a wizard."

On hearing this, Edward tried to make as much noise as he could, but he only managed a groan. "What was that noise?" Miles demanded.

"I heard no noise except the wind," the hermit replied.

"I'm going to search this place," Miles said.

"Not so fast," answered the hermit. "The truth is that the boy ran away from me. Come. I will show you where he went." And with that, he slipped out the door and began walking deeper into the forest, with Miles Hendon at his heels.

The little king heard their voices and footsteps fade away. All hope left him. "My only friend has been deceived," he said to himself. "I must escape before the hermit returns."

At that moment, Edward heard the door open once again. An instant later, he stared in amazement. Before him stood John Canty and Hugo!

Edward almost thanked them, but he decided to remain silent. In a moment or two, his limbs were free, and he was being hurried through the forest. Hugo firmly held one of his arms, and John Canty held the other.

E COMPREHENSION

Write the answers.
1. When Edward was in the forest, why do you think he hoped to cross a road?
2. How could Edward tell that the old man was a hermit?
3. Why do you think the hermit believed Edward was the king?
4. Why did the hermit decide to punish Edward?
5. Why did Miles know that Edward did not run an errand for the hermit?

F WRITING

Pretend you meet a person who says, "I am the king of England."

Write several questions you would ask that person to find out if he was telling the truth. After each question, explain why the person's answer will help you.

A WORD LISTS

1	2	3	4
Hard Words	*Compound Words*	*Word Practice*	*Vocabulary Preview*
1. innocent	1. troublesome	1. situation	1. band
2. penalty	2. meantime	2. chuckle	2. mistreat
3. Edith	3. therefore	3. suspicion	3. betray
4. Arthur	4. blacksmith	4. chuckling	4. innocent
	5. courtroom	5. gossip	5. flogged
		6. daily	

B VOCABULARY DEFINITIONS

1. **band**—Another word for *group* is *band.*
   - A group of vagrants is a ▆▆▆▆.
2. **mistreat**—When something is treated poorly, that thing is *mistreated.*
   - If a dog is treated poorly, that dog is ▆▆▆▆.
3. **betray**—You *betray* somebody by pretending to be that person's friend and then tricking that person.
   - What are you doing to a man when you pretend to be his friend and then trick him?
4. **innocent**—Someone who is not guilty of doing something wrong is *innocent.*
   - A person who is not guilty of cheating is ▆▆▆▆.
5. **flogged**—When somebody is beaten with a whip, that person is *flogged.*
   - What's another way of saying *The prisoner was beaten with a whip*?

C VOCABULARY REVIEW

bound
official
intend
tragic
inform
confesses
gagged

1. When a person tells the truth about a secret, the person ▮▮▮▮ that secret.
2. When you give people information about something, you ▮▮▮▮ them about that thing.
3. What are you doing when you give a man information about the weather?
4. If you plan to do something, you ▮▮▮▮ to do that thing.
5. A person who plans to stop at the inn ▮▮▮▮ to stop at the inn.
6. When a person is tied up, that person is ▮▮▮▮.
7. When a person's mouth is covered, that person is ▮▮▮▮.

D READING

Chapter 19
A Victim of Treachery

Once more, King Foo-Foo the First lived with the wandering band of vagrants and thieves. They ridiculed and teased him, but only two people in the entire troop truly disliked him—John Canty and Hugo. They were as cruel to Edward as they could be without getting caught by the Ruffler, who would send them flying to the ground if he discovered that they were trying to mistreat the boy.

Hugo would "accidentally" step on Edward's foot from time to time. One time, following one of these "accidents," Edward hit Hugo with a stout stick and sent him sprawl-ing, much to the delight of the other members of the troop. Hugo sprang to his feet and grabbed a large stick. Immediately a ring of people formed around the two boys.

The onlookers wanted a good fight, but Hugo was no match for Edward, who had been trained for many years in the use of swords and other battle weapons. With graceful ease, the young king blocked the rain of blows that Hugo tried to deliver. Every time Hugo left an opening, Edward delivered a lightning-fast strike, producing a storm of cheers and laughter from the crowd.

At last, the bruised Hugo tossed his stick aside and pushed his way from the ring with his head down. The vagrants lifted Edward to their shoulders and carried him to a place of honor beside the Ruffler.

• • •

After a few days, the Ruffler decided it was no use requiring Edward to beg. Instead, he announced that the boy would be given better work—he would learn to steal, with Hugo as his teacher. Hugo was pleased because now he had a chance to betray Edward and turn him over to the law.

The next morning, the two boys strolled off to a neighboring village and drifted slowly up and down the streets. One boy watched sharply for a chance to steal something, while the other watched just as sharply for a chance to escape. ♦

At last, a woman approached, carrying a large package in a basket. This was just the chance Hugo had been waiting for, and his eyes sparkled with pleasure. He waited and watched until the woman had passed by and the time was right. Then he said to Edward, "Wait here until I return," and he darted after the woman.

Edward's heart filled with joy. Now he could make his escape! Just then, however, Hugo snatched the package from the woman and came running back toward Edward. Before the surprised woman could turn around to see who had stolen her bun-

dle, Hugo tossed the object to Edward and said, "Catch!"

Instantly, Hugo had turned the corner and darted down a crooked alley. Edward threw the bundle to the ground, just as the woman and a crowd of people approached. The woman seized Edward's wrist with one hand and her bundle with the other, all the while yelling loudly at the boy.

Meanwhile, Hugo crept back up the alley and peeked out. His enemy was captured, and the law would take care of him now. Hugo slipped away, chuckling to himself as he started back toward the camp, ready to lie to the Ruffler about what had happened.

For his part, Edward continued to struggle in the woman's strong grasp. The crowd closed in, threatening the boy and calling him names. A burly blacksmith approached Edward and prepared to seize him. But the blacksmith stopped short as another man flashed a long sword in the air and laid its flat side on the blacksmith's arm. Edward's eyes grew wide as the man holding the sword spoke in a pleasant tone. "Good people," the man said, "let us not be hasty. This is a matter for the law. Let go of the boy's arm, good woman."

The blacksmith backed away, and the woman released Edward's wrist. The boy quickly sprang to the side of the person who had saved him. "It took you long enough to get here, Sir Miles," he said.

Miles Hendon smiled as he looked down at the pitiful little boy. "That's right," he said. "I had almost forgotten that I am now Sir Miles, a knight in the kingdom of dreams."

At that moment, the crowd opened, and a police officer approached. He was about to lay his hand on Edward's shoulder when Miles said, "Go easy, good friend. I am responsible for the boy. Lead the way, and we will follow." ★

The officer led, with the woman, Miles and Edward following. Behind them was the crowd. Edward wanted to flee, but Miles said to him in a low voice, "Be patient, my king. They think you have broken the law, and you will only make matters worse if you try to escape."

Soon, the group came to a courtroom, where a judge sat behind a large table. He ordered everybody but Miles, Edward, the officer, and the woman to leave. Then he asked the woman, who was still holding the bundle, whether it was worth more than thirteen pennies.

"Indeed it is," she replied firmly. "Inside the bundle is a large piece of ham worth sixteen pence. That's how much I paid the farmer for it this morning."

The judge turned pale and said, "Good woman, do you know that when a person steals an object worth more than thirteen pennies, the law says that person shall hang?"

The little king's eyes popped wide open with amazement. The woman cried out, "That's horrible! I would not hang the poor boy! He seems so innocent, and I'm sure he stole the ham just because he was hungry. Besides, I have it back. What shall I do?"

The judge said, "Well, maybe you were mistaken about how much the ham is worth."

"Yes," the woman said, "I was mistaken. The ham is worth only eight pennies. Only eight pennies." Miles threw his arms around Edward in delight. The judge thanked the woman, who then left the courtroom. The officer followed her into a narrow hall.

Miles wondered why the officer had followed the woman, so he softly slipped into the hall and listened, just as the officer was saying to the woman, "That ham will make me some fine meals, so I will buy it from you. Here are eight pennies."

"Eight pennies!" the woman cried. "You will not buy it for that amount. You know very well that it cost a lot more."

"Oh," the officer said slowly. "So you lied when you swore that it cost only eight pennies. You have committed a terrible crime. Come back with me and answer for the crime—and then the lad will hang."

The woman frowned and shook her head. "Say no more," she said. "Just give me the eight pennies and take the ham."

Miles slipped back into the courtroom, and the officer followed after he had hidden his prize. Inside the courtroom, the judge sentenced Edward to stay in jail for a few days, after which he would be flogged for his crime. Edward was ready to cry out, but Miles told him to be quiet.

Soon, Miles and Edward were following the officer toward the jail. Miles whispered to the boy, "Be patient. We'll soon have a chance to escape."

E COMPREHENSION

Write the answers.
1. Why did Hugo want to turn Edward over to the law?
2. Why did the woman think Edward had stolen her package?
3. Why did the woman say the ham was worth only eight pennies?
4. How did the police officer take advantage of the woman?
5. How do you think Miles could help Edward escape from the police officer?

F WRITING

The judge in Edward's trial didn't ask many questions. If he had, he might have discovered the truth.

Write a short play that shows what happens when the judge questions the woman and Edward closely. Have the judge try to figure out exactly what happened by asking the woman and Edward what they saw and did. Show their answers, then show what the judge finally decides.

A WORD LISTS

1	2
Word Endings	*Vocabulary Preview*
1. irritable	1. duties
2. comfortable	2. reel
3. hospitable	3. armed
4. disagreeable	4. penalty
	5. slumber

B VOCABULARY DEFINITIONS

1. **duties**—Your *duties* are the things you must do. If a girl must be at school on time, she has a *duty* to be at school on time.
   - If a boy must fix dinner, he ▬▬▬.

2. **reel**—Another word for *stagger* is *reel.* If a man staggers from a blow, he *reels* from the blow.
   - If a woman staggers around the room, she ▬▬▬.

3. **armed**—Somebody who has a weapon is *armed.*
   - A soldier who has a weapon is an ▬▬▬.

4. **penalty**—A *penalty* is the punishment somebody receives for breaking the rules.
   - What do we call the punishment somebody receives for breaking the rules?

5. **slumber**—Another word for *sleep* is *slumber.*
   - What's another way of saying *He slept in the afternoon*?

C VOCABULARY REVIEW

innocent
mistreated
flogged
band
bound
inform
betray

1. When a person is beaten with a whip, that person is ▇▇▇▇.
2. Someone who is not guilty of doing something wrong is ▇▇▇▇.
3. A person who is not guilty of stealing is ▇▇▇▇.
4. Another word for *group* is ▇▇▇▇.
5. A group of vagrants is a ▇▇▇▇.
6. When a person is treated poorly, that person is ▇▇▇▇.
7. If a dog is treated poorly, that dog is ▇▇▇▇.
8. When you pretend to be somebody's friend and then trick that person, you ▇▇▇▇ that person.

D READING

Chapter 20
The Escape

The short winter day had nearly ended by the time Edward, Miles, and the police officer approached the jail. Only a few people were on the street, and nobody paid attention to the party. Edward wondered if the sight of the king of England going to jail had received so little interest before.

Near the jail steps, Miles put his hand on the officer's shoulder and said, "Slow down a minute. I would like to have a word with you."

"I cannot do that," the officer said. "I must do my duty. Now take your hand off me."

"This matter concerns you," Miles said. "I want you to turn your back and let the boy escape."

"How dare you suggest such a thing!" the officer replied. "I should arrest you in the . . ."

"Don't be so hasty," Miles said. Then he lowered his voice to a whisper. "You may have to pay a great deal for the ham that you purchased for eight pennies."

The poor officer was speechless at first. When he found his tongue, he began to threaten Miles, but the knight remained calm until the officer had finished. Then

Miles said, "I like you, friend, and would not harm you if I didn't have to. But I heard it all—every word. I will prove it to you."

Miles then repeated the conversation the officer had with the woman in the hall. He ended by asking, "Have I reported it correctly? I can tell the story the same way to the judge, if that's what you want."

The officer said nothing for a moment. Then he laughed nervously and said, "You're making a great deal over a little joke that I played on the woman."

"It was a pretty good joke because you kept the ham."

The officer insisted that it was an innocent joke. Miles replied, "Well, why don't you just wait here a moment while I run back to the courtroom and ask the judge what he thinks of that kind of joke?" ♦

"Wait a minute," the officer said as Miles started to move away. "That judge doesn't understand jokes very well. What do you want of me?"

"Just close your eyes and count to a thousand—very slowly."

The officer muttered, "This will ruin me. I . . ."

In a sharp voice, Miles said, "Just remember that the penalty for your little joke is death, according to the law."

"Oh, good sir," the officer said. "Go with the boy. I will see nothing. I will say that you snatched the boy from me and ran off."

Hearing that, Miles and Edward fled. As soon as they were out of sight of the officer, they sat down to figure out what to do. Edward wanted to go back to London, but Miles longed to see his father at Hendon Hall. He convinced Edward to go there before returning to London.

A few hours later, the two friends were

riding toward Hendon Hall on two donkeys that Miles bought from a farmer. Edward was warm. He was no longer wearing rags but rather the suit of used clothes that Miles had brought from the inn on London Bridge.

When Miles and Edward had journeyed about ten miles, they reached a large village and stopped there for the night. They stayed in a comfortable inn, where Miles had the same duties as before. He waited on Edward, helped him get ready for bed, and then slept on the floor in front of the door.

The next day, as the two rode along, Miles told the story of how he had searched for Edward with the hermit. When they didn't find him in the forest or the hut, the hermit had seemed brokenhearted.

"I'm sure he was disappointed," Edward said. He then explained how the hermit had bound him to the bed and gagged him with the rag.

As the two companions approached Hendon Hall, Miles's spirits rose. He talked and talked about his father, his brother Arthur, his brother Hugh, and Edith, the woman Miles planned to marry. Finally, when the donkeys made their way over the top of a high hill, Miles pointed excitedly and said, "There, my king, is the village. You can see Hendon Hall nearby. It's a splendid mansion with seventy rooms and twenty-seven servants."

The travelers reached the village around three o'clock in the afternoon. Miles's tongue ran constantly, describing every building to Edward. Soon, they stopped before a noble mansion.

"Welcome to Hendon Hall, my king!" Miles exclaimed, springing to the ground. He helped Edward down, then took him by the hand and rushed inside the entry hall, where they were greeted by an elegantly dressed young man.

"Hugh, it's me!" Miles cried. "I'm home again. Give me a hug."

But Hugh drew backward and stared firmly at Miles. Presently, he said in a mild voice, "I'm sorry, stranger. You must think I am someone else."

"No," said Miles sharply. "I think you are Hugh Hendon." ★

Hugh said, "And who do you think you are?"

"Don't you even know your own brother?" Miles replied.

Hugh smiled with mock surprise. "How could you be my brother when he is dead?" He slowly circled Miles and examined him closely. At last he sighed and said, "This is very disappointing."

"Why?" Miles demanded.

"Because you are not my brother. We received a letter from France six years ago that brought the sad news of my brother's death in battle."

Miles replied excitedly, "Call our father. He will know me."

"It's not possible to call someone who is dead," Hugh said.

Softly, Miles said, "Dead . . . my father dead. This is terrible news." Looking down, Miles continued, "Call our brother Arthur, He will know me."

"He is also dead."

"Oh, no!" Miles exclaimed as he slumped into a chair, holding his hands over his face. "And what about Lady Edith? Is she . . . ?"

"No, she lives," Hugh answered flatly.

"Bring her to me," Miles said. "And bring the servants. They will know me."

A few moments later, a richly dressed,

beautiful young lady followed Hugh into the room. After her came several servants. "Oh, Edith, my darling," Miles said, as he stood up and began walking toward her.

But Hugh raised his hand and said to Edith, "Look at him. Do you know him?"

The woman's face was flushed, and she was trembling. Slowly, she lifted her head and looked into Miles's eyes with a frightened gaze. Her face turned deathly pale. With a voice as dead as her face, she said, "I don't know him." Then she turned away and ran from the room.

After a pause, Hugh said to the servants, "You have observed him. Do you know him?" They shook their heads no, and Hugh said to Miles, "You have made a mistake. Neither the servants nor my wife know you."

"Your wife?" Miles exclaimed, and in an instant he had pinned Hugh to the wall with an iron grip on his throat. "Now I understand. You wrote the letter about my death so you could marry Edith. Get away from me before I give you the punishment you deserve!"

Hugh reeled to a chair and commanded the servants to seize and bind the stranger. They hesitated, and one of them said, "But he is armed."

"Don't tell me that!" shouted Hugh. "There is only one of him and many of you!"

Miles warned them to be careful. "You remember me from the old days," he said. "I have not changed. Attack me and you will find out." The servants stood frozen.

Hugh shouted, "Go arm yourselves and guard the doors!" Then he turned to Miles and said, "You will find that you cannot escape."

"Escape?" said Miles. "I am master of Hendon Hall and all its lands. I will remain here, where I belong."

E COMPREHENSION

Write the answers.
1. Why did the police officer agree to let Edward escape?
2. Do you think Edward was impressed with the size of Hendon Hall? Why or why not?
3. Do you think Hugh is telling the truth about not recognizing Miles? Explain your answer.
4. Do you think Edith is telling the truth about not recognizing Miles? Explain your answer.
5. What do you think Miles should do to prove who he really is?

F WRITING

Pretend that Miles really has died in battle. Also pretend that you are the officer who has to write a letter to Miles's family explaining what happened.

Write the letter and try to answer the following questions:
- How do you feel about Miles's death?
- What do you know about Miles?
- How did Miles die?
- What courage or other qualities did Miles show during the battle?
- What can you do to help Miles's family?

A WORD LISTS

1

Word Endings
1. overpowered
2. tormented
3. parted
4. remembered
5. horrified
6. treated

2

Vocabulary Preview
1. prison cell
2. smuggle
3. deny
4. daily
5. deathbed
6. gossip
7. coronation
8. stocks

B VOCABULARY DEFINITIONS

1. **prison cell**—A *prison cell* is a small room that prisoners live in.
   • What's a *prison cell*?
2. **smuggle**—When you *smuggle* something, you hide it and take it to some place. If a man hides some money and takes it into a prison cell, he *smuggles* the money into the cell.
   • What do you do when you *smuggle* something?
3. **deny**—When you say that something is not true, you *deny* that thing. When you say that you do not know a person, you *deny* knowing that person.
   • When you say you did not see something, you ■■■■.
4. **daily**—If you do something every day, you do it *daily.*
   • What's another way of saying *He ate every day*?

5. **deathbed**—People who are on their *deathbeds* are dying.
   • What's another way of saying *The man was dying*?
6. **gossip**—When you *gossip* about something, you spread rumors about that thing.
   • What are you doing when you spread rumors?
7. **coronation**—A *coronation* is an important event in which a crown is placed on the head of a new king. A king is not officially a king until after the *coronation.*
   • What is a *coronation*?
8. **stocks**—The *stocks* is a device used for torturing prisoners. It consists of a wooden frame that is locked over the prisoners' arms and legs. The picture on page 262 shows a *stocks.*
   • What is a *stocks*?

C VOCABULARY REVIEW

slumber
innocent
penalty
mistreat
armed
betray
bound
duties
reel

1. The punishment somebody receives for breaking the rules is the ▮▮▮.
2. Another word for *stagger* is ▮▮▮.
3. If a person staggers from a blow, that person ▮▮▮.
4. Another word for sleep is ▮▮▮.
5. What's another way of saying *She slept for hours*?
6. Somebody who has a weapon is ▮▮▮.
7. The things that you should do are your ▮▮▮.
8. If a person should be at school on time, that person has a ▮▮▮
9. If you tied somebody up, you ▮▮▮ that person.

D READING

Chapter 21
In Prison

Hugh and the servants left the room. Edward sat thoughtfully for a few moments, then observed, "It is strange that there are no soldiers out looking for me."

Miles said to himself, "His mind is still ruined."

Edward then announced a plan. "I will write a letter in three languages—English, Latin, and Greek," he said to Miles. "Take that letter to the palace and deliver it to one person—Hertford. When he reads it, he will know it comes from the real king."

Miles said, "Wouldn't it be better for us to wait here until I prove who I really am?"

Edward began to scold Miles for worrying about such small matters, but just then Lady Edith entered. She was very pale. Miles sprang forward, but she stopped him with a gesture. She sat down and asked him to do the same. Then she said, "I have come to warn you. If I can't persuade you to forget your mad dream, then I will try to persuade you to save yourself. You are in great danger." She stared steadily at Miles. Slowly, she continued, "I know my husband. Hugh will deny you, and he will see that you are destroyed."

Miles tried to explain that he was Miles Hendon, but she stopped him with a gesture and said, "Arthur and his father are free from the terror of Hugh because they are dead. If you stay here, you will suffer the same fate they suffered. So, please go and do not hesitate. Take this purse of gold and leave at once, while you still can."

Miles did not accept the purse. Instead, he rose and stood before Edith, saying, "Look me in the eyes and tell me if I am Miles Hendon."

"I do not know you," she replied in a steady voice. "Now leave, while you can."

At that moment, four officers burst into the room, and a terrible struggle began. Miles and Edward were soon overpowered and dragged away to prison. ♦

• • •

The cells inside the prison were crowded, so the two friends were chained together in a large room. There were over twenty other prisoners—both men and women—in this room. All the prisoners were chained together in pairs. Edward complained loudly about how he had been treated, but nobody paid much attention to him. Miles became solemn. After being so joyful at the thought of coming home, he felt like somebody who has stepped outside to see a beautiful rainbow and been struck by lightning.

Gradually his tormented thoughts settled, and then his mind focused on Edith. He couldn't understand why she wouldn't remember him.

The days in prison went by slowly. There was little to do except think. A week after Miles and Edward had entered the prison, a guard brought an old man into the room, saying, "The person who claims to be Miles Hendon is in this room. Look around and see if you can identify that person."

Miles looked at the old man and recognized him instantly. He was Blake An-drews, a servant who had spent all his life at Hendon Hall. At first, Miles experienced a spark of hope, but then he concluded that Blake would lie the same way the others had lied.

Blake gazed around the room, glanced at each face, and then said, "I don't see him in this motley bunch. Which one claims to be Miles Hendon?"

The prison guard laughed, "Here," he said, pointing to Miles. "This big animal is the one."

The old man approached Miles, examined him, then shook his head and said, "This man is not Miles Hendon and has never been Miles Hendon."

The guard laughed and left the room. As soon as he was out of sight, Blake dropped to his knees and whispered, "I am thankful you have come back, my master. I denied it was you, but if you say the word, I will tell the truth, even though I will be hanged for it."

"No," said Miles. "There is no need for that. I am grateful enough that you are still true to me."

In the following days, Blake became quite valuable to Miles and Edward. He visited them every day and smuggled in things for them to eat. He also brought them news. Through these daily visits, Miles learned the true story of his family.

Miles's brother Arthur had died six years ago. After Arthur's death, Miles's father became ill and believed he was going to die as well. He wanted to see Hugh and Edith married before he died, but Edith begged for a delay in the marriage, hoping that Miles would return. Then the letter about Miles's death came. The letter shocked Edith, who finally agreed to marry Hugh when Miles's father was on his deathbed. ★

It was not a happy marriage. According to rumors, Edith had discovered that the letter about Miles's death had been written by Hugh. Other rumors told of Hugh's cruelty to Edith. After the death of his father, Hugh got rid of the servants who had been faithful to his father and replaced them with servants who would be loyal to him.

One bit of gossip that Blake delivered interested Edward greatly. Blake reported that people in London were saying that the king was mad. Edward objected loudly to that comment, pointing out that he was not even slightly mad. After Miles managed to quiet Edward, the old servant said that Hugh was planning to go to the coronation of the new king.

Blake explained that although the new king was supposed to be mad, he had done some good things, and everybody was talking about how intelligent he was. The old servant concluded by saying, "The king is now working on changing the cruel laws that threaten the people."

This news amazed and saddened Edward. When he was feeling his gloomiest, a guard entered the room and announced that the prisoners were going into the prison yard for a little while. That announcement raised Edward's spirits, and he tried to hurry the other prisoners so that he could get outside quickly and again look at the sky, rather than the dark walls of his prison room.

Once outside, however, Edward was horrified to learn the real reason for their visit to the yard. The prison guards grabbed Miles and led him to the stocks, with a mob of cackling prisoners following.

The guards placed Miles in the device, and the mob then proceeded to throw things at him and hurl insults.

"What is the meaning of this?" Edward demanded as he pushed through the mob.

One of the prisoners explained, "That's his punishment for pretending to be Miles Hendon."

Edward rushed forward and announced angrily to a guard, "Take him out of those stocks immediately. He is my servant, and you shall not treat him this way!"

"Who do you think you're talking to?" the guard said as he grabbed Edward. "You will talk differently after you have felt the sting of my whip."

At that moment, Hugh Hendon rode up on a fine horse, and the mob parted to let him through. "Yes," Hugh said with a smile, "I think the boy should be flogged so he will learn some manners."

E COMPREHENSION

Write the answers.
1. Do you think Edward's letter would have convinced Hertford that Edward is really the king? Explain your answer.
2. Why did Edith want Miles to leave Hendon Hall?
3. The book says that Miles "felt like somebody who has stepped outside to see a beautiful rainbow and been struck by lightning." Explain what that sentence means.
4. Why did Edward object to Blake's comments about the new king?
5. How might Miles come to Edward's rescue, even though Miles is in the stocks?

F WRITING

Pretend you are Edward.

Write a letter to Hertford to prove that you are the real king. Try to answer the following questions:
- Why are you no longer in the palace?
- Why has Tom Canty taken your place?
- How can you prove that you're really Edward Tudor?
- What do you want Hertford to do?

A WORD LISTS

1	2	3	4
Hard Words	*Word Endings*	*Word Practice*	*Vocabulary Preview*
1. ceremony	1. imagination	1. deafen	1. riot
2. procession	2. coronation	2. broken	2. procession
3. riot	3. concentration	3. brokenhearted	3. ceremony
4. imposter	4. expression	4. deafening	
5. aisle	5. hesitation	5. cannon	
	6. procession		

B VOCABULARY DEFINITIONS

1. **riot**—A *riot* is a large fight that involves a mob.
   • What do we call a large fight that involves a mob?

2. **procession**—A *procession* is a line of people that moves from one place to another. A line of people going through the lunchroom is a *procession* of people going through the lunchroom.
   • A line of people going on a fire drill is a ▬▬▬.

3. **ceremony**—A *ceremony* is an important event—such as a graduation or a coronation—that always takes place in the same way.
   • What's a *ceremony*?

C VOCABULARY REVIEW

gossip
reel
stocks
deathbeds
coronation
smuggle
penalty
armed
prison cell
deny
daily

1. When you hide something and take it to some place, you ▬▬ that thing.
2. What's another way of saying *She visited her grandmother every day*?
3. People who are dying are on their ▬▬.
4. A small room that prisoners live in is a ▬▬.
5. An important event in which the crown is officially placed on the head of a new king is a ▬▬.
6. When you say that something is not true, you ▬▬ that thing.
7. When you spread rumors about something, you ▬▬ about that thing.

D READING

Chapter 22
To London

The guard was holding Edward as Hugh Hendon smiled from his horse. Just as the guard was ready to strip off the boy's shirt, Miles said, "No, do not strike that boy. He is mad, and he does not know what he says. I will take his punishment."

Hugh's smile grew larger. "Indeed," he exclaimed. "Then let that man take the boy's punishment. And make the punishment something he will remember."

Edward watched with empty horror as the guards removed Miles from the stocks, stripped off his shirt, and struck him with the terrible whip.

Miles did not cry out. His face kept the same hard expression. When the beating was finished, Hugh turned his horse around, and the crowd quickly parted to let him leave. The guards again placed Miles in the stocks, and soon the crowd left.

Edward slowly approached Miles and knelt down beside him. He picked up a small stick from the ground. "You are very brave," the little king said as he touched Miles lightly on his bleeding shoulder with the stick. "I, the king of England, make you an earl. You are now Earl Miles Hendon."

Poor Miles didn't know whether to

laugh or cry. He felt tears forming in his eyes, but he couldn't tell whether they came from his terrible pain or from the terrible humor of being a prisoner who is both a knight and an earl.

Miles was kept in the stocks all day and all the following day. On the morning of the next day, the guards released him and gave him back his donkeys and his sword. Then they announced that he and Edward were free to leave but could never come back to Hendon Hall or the village. ♦

Once outside the prison walls, Miles wondered where he should go. He remembered what Blake had said about the new king, so perhaps he should go to this intelligent boy and tell him what had happened at Hendon Hall. But then he wondered how someone who looked like a vagrant could ever get inside the palace to talk to the king.

At a loss for an answer, Miles turned to Edward and asked where they should go.

"To London!" said Edward. "I must reclaim the throne before the coronation!"

Miles felt pity for the poor boy's continuing madness, but he agreed that London was their only hope.

The two rode on their donkeys for several days without any trouble. At last, they reached London Bridge around ten o'clock at night. The bridge was swarming with a mob of howling people. They were celebrating the coronation, which would take place the very next day.

Just then, a fight started among some men on the bridge. One person tripped and fell into another person, who fell into another, and another. In a few moments, the fight spread until it became a riot. As the riot spread around the two companions, Edward's donkey reared up and threw him to the street.

Miles and Edward were soon hope-

lessly separated from each other and lost in the roaring mob. And that is where we leave them.

• • •

When we left Tom Canty, he was beginning to enjoy playing the part of a king. As time passed, he enjoyed it even more. His fears faded and died. His embarrassment left him and was replaced with quiet confidence. He loved hearing the horns sound as he approached and the distant voices announcing, "Make way for the king!"

From time to time, Tom was troubled when he thought about the real king and what might have happened to him. But as weeks passed and Edward did not return, Tom thought less about him. He thought more about his own new experiences, until thoughts of Edward nearly vanished from his mind.

Tom's feelings about his mother, his sisters, and his grandmother changed in the same way. At first, he missed them greatly, but later he began to hope that he would never see them again. He was afraid he would have to return to Pudding Lane and the life he had known before he was king.

Sometimes, when Tom thought about his family in this way, he hated himself for being so heartless. He would picture their poor faces, and they made him feel lower than the worms that wriggle along the ground. Even these feelings, however, were beginning to vanish from his mind.

While the real king fought his way through the riot in search of Miles, Tom lay on silk sheets feeling very satisfied. Tomorrow was coronation day—the day that he would become the official king of England. ★

When Tom awoke the next morning, he could hear the voices of thousands of people in the distance. They lined the Thames River, waiting for the king to enter his royal barge and move down the river to the Tower of London. Once at the tower, Tom would ride a horse through the streets of London to a splendid church called Westminster Abbey, where the coronation ceremony would be held.

Within an hour, Tom and the royal party were floating down the river. When Tom arrived at the Tower of London, cannons shot out hot tongues of flame and white clouds of smoke, followed by deafening explosions that made the ground tremble. The cannons fired again and again until the tower disappeared in a great cloud of smoke.

Tom was dressed in splendid clothes. He mounted a magnificent war horse that pranced nervously. Next to Tom was Hertford, riding a horse like Tom's. Behind Tom and Hertford followed a line of lords, including the Mayor of London. It was a splendid sight, and as the troop moved slowly down the streets, people bowed and cheered and cried out encouragement for the new king. Tom responded by holding his head high and smiling.

Just as Tom was at the height of enjoyment, he caught sight of a pale, puzzled face straining forward from the second row of the crowd. The eyes of that face were fixed on Tom, who felt suddenly sick as he recognized who it was. It was his mother!

Without thinking, Tom waved to her. An instant later, she tore through the crowd of people, pushed her way past the guards, and stood at Tom's side. She embraced his leg and covered it with kisses as she cried, "Oh, my child, my darling!" Her expression showed pure joy.

An instant later, an officer of the king's guard snatched her away and sent her reeling back into the crowd. Tom heard himself saying, "I do not know you, woman!"

As the procession moved on, Tom looked backward to get another glimpse of his mother. She looked brokenhearted, and he was ashamed. He wondered why he had betrayed her for the worthless robes and empty life of a king. He rode with his head down and kept hearing the words that he had said: "I do not know you, woman."

Hertford quickly noticed the change in the young king. He reminded Tom that everybody was looking at him and that he should smile. Then Hertford added, "We should punish that pauper. She was the one who disturbed you."

The handsome figure of the king turned his eyes to Hertford and said, in a dead voice, "She is my mother."

"Oh, no!" Hertford exclaimed. "He's gone mad again!"

E COMPREHENSION

Write the answers.
1. Why do you think Miles took Edward's punishment?
2. Why was Tom growing to like being a king?
3. While he was king, how did Tom's feelings about his family change?
4. Why did Tom pretend he didn't know his mother?
5. Why did Hertford think Tom had gone mad again?

F WRITING

When Tom's mother ran up to him, he pretended not to know her, but he could have welcomed her with open arms.

Write a conversation between Tom, his mother, and Hertford as the procession moves toward Westminster Abbey. Begin the conversation by having Tom welcome his mother. Then show what happens next. What does Tom's mother say? What does Hertford say? What does Tom decide to do?

A WORD LISTS

1 *Word Endings*	2 *Word Practice*	3 *Vocabulary Preview*
1. worthless	1. form	1. under arrest
2. heartless	2. platform	2. imposter
3. hopeless	3. loud	
4. motionless	4. aloud	
5. speechless	5. suspicious	
	6. suspicion	

B VOCABULARY DEFINITIONS

1. **under arrest**—When a person is *under arrest,* that person is held by the police or other officers of the law.
   • What happens to someone who is *under arrest*?

2. **imposter**—Someone who pretends to be somebody else is an *imposter.*
   • What do we call someone who pretends to be somebody else?

C VOCABULARY REVIEW

deny
ceremony
daily
procession
riot

1. A line of people that moves from one place to another is a ▨▨▨▨.
2. A line of people going on a fire drill is a ▨▨▨▨.
3. An important event that always takes place in the same way is a ▨▨▨▨.
4. A large fight that involves a mob is a ▨▨▨▨.

Chapter 23
Coronation Day

At last the procession reached Westminster Abbey, the towering church where the coronation ceremony would take place. A long line of dukes, earls, counts, lords and ladies filed inside and took their seats. Next came the king's sisters, Elizabeth and Mary, accompanied by Lady Jane Grey. At last, the horns sounded to announce the king.

The crowd rose to its feet and stood motionless as Tom Canty walked slowly toward the throne, which sat on a platform at the front of the church. With each step toward the throne, Tom's face grew more pale. He was confused and ashamed.

Tom climbed up the platform and sat on the throne at last. Silent moments passed as a mighty lord walked toward Tom, holding the crown that could be worn only by the king of England. Once that crown was placed on Tom's head, he would be the official king. ♦

Just as the lord was lowering the crown onto Tom's head, the ceremony was interrupted by an incredible sight. A young boy wearing an old suit was standing in the middle aisle of the church. He raised his hand and announced loudly, "Do not place the crown on that imposter, for I am the real king of England!"

In an instant, guards grabbed the boy, but in that same instant, Tom jumped from the throne and cried out in a ringing voice, "Take your hands off him! He is the king!"

The huge audience was shocked. People wondered whether they were awake or having some sort of terrible dream. Hertford stepped forward and said above the mumbling of the crowd, "Grab that pauper! The king has gone mad!"

Before anybody had a chance to obey Hertford, Tom stamped his foot again and cried out, "I told you not to touch him! He is the real king!"

The hands that held Edward let go, and the audience fell into deep silence. The true king walked forward with confidence and stepped up on the platform. The mock king ran with a glad face to meet him. Tom fell to his knees and said, "Oh, my king, put on the crown and take your place as king of England."

Hertford turned his sharp eyes toward the shabbily dressed boy who stood in front of the kneeling king. His eyes quickly softened and gave way to an expression of wondering surprise. The boys were identical! Hertford approached Edward and said in a gentle voice, "Excuse me, sir, would you mind if I asked you a few questions?"

"I will gladly answer them, my lord."

Hertford asked many questions about the king's duties and the country's laws. The boy answered every question correctly without the slightest hesitation. He described the rooms in the palace, including the king's apartment. All who listened were amazed. People turned to each other and said, "Perhaps he is the real king."

Tom Canty smiled broadly. But Hertford slowly shook his head and said to Edward, "You have shown great knowledge, but your knowledge is no greater than that of the king you see robed before you. He can also answer the questions I have asked you." This statement saddened Tom, and he felt his hopes fall.

There was a sudden shift in the crowd as people began to repeat what Hertford had just said. "Yes," they said, "his answers to the questions don't prove that he is the true king."

"This situation is dangerous," Hertford said. "We cannot have any doubt about who the real king is. Such doubt could divide the country and ruin it."

Just then, Hertford's face lit up, and he said to the shabbily dressed boy, "I have one more question for you. If you answer it correctly, you will prove that you are indeed the king of England."

"I will answer it," Edward said. ★

"Ever since Henry's death, we have been unable to find the royal seal. As far as we know, the last person to have this seal was the real prince. If you can tell me where the seal is, you will tell us something that only the true king of England could know."

This question was such a good one that the lords and ladies applauded Hertford and nodded at each other with approving smiles. They were saying to themselves, "Yes, this young man has been carefully taught about the palace, but an imposter could not possibly know where the seal is."

Hertford expected Edward to be speechless and confused. But nothing like that happened. Instead, the lad answered promptly in a confident voice, "This puzzle is not difficult."

He turned to Lord Saint John and spoke in the manner of a person used to giving commands. "Go to the private cabinet in my apartment," he commanded. "You will find a button just above the bottom shelf. Press the button, and a secret door will open. The royal seal is in a cabinet behind the door."

The entire company was struck with wonder over this speech. Lord Saint John started to carry out the command and then stopped with embarrassment as he realized that he was taking orders from a young vagrant. Seeing that he had stopped, Tom said sharply, "What are you waiting for? Didn't you hear the king's command? Go!"

An instant later, Lord Saint John was hurrying toward the king's apartment. As the group waited for his return, a strange change came over the lords who stood on the platform. One by one they moved toward Edward, staring at him with wonder, until Tom Canty stood alone on one side of the platform, outside the thick ring of people that surrounded the true king.

Soon, Lord Saint John returned. As he moved down the middle aisle of the church, the interest was so great that the low murmurings of the crowd died out and were followed by a deep silence. Every eye was fixed on him. At last, he reached the platform, paused a moment, and then moved toward Tom Canty. Quietly, he announced, "Your Highness, the seal is not there."

Immediately, the crowd that had circled Edward melted, and he stood alone, without friend or supporter. The eyes that had looked at him with wonder now stared with anger. Hertford called out, "Place this beggar under arrest!"

Guards sprang forward to grab Edward, but Tom waved them off. "Get back!" he commanded. "Any person who touches him will be punished."

Hertford was angry and confused. He turned to Lord Saint John and asked, "Did you search the cabinet carefully?"

Lord Saint John nodded. "Yes, very carefully. And it is not . . . "

Tom interrupted by springing forward and shouting, "Can you describe this thing you are looking for—this royal seal?"

Hertford and Lord Saint John looked at each other and blinked. Then Hertford turned to Tom and said, "Of course."

E COMPREHENSION

Write the answers.
1. Why was Tom so ashamed as he approached the throne?
2. Why wasn't Hertford satisfied with Edward's answers to his questions?
3. Why did Hertford ask Edward about the royal seal?
4. Why did the lords gather around Edward while Lord Saint John looked for the seal?
5. Where do you think the royal seal is? Explain your answer.

F WRITING

Write your own ending for *The Prince and the Pauper,* beginning with the end of this chapter. Try to answer the following questions:
- What information does Tom have about the royal seal?
- What does Edward do with Tom's information?
- What do Hertford and the other lords do?
- What happens to Miles Hendon?

A WORD LISTS

1
Word Endings
1. incredible
2. impossible
3. terrible
4. horrible

2
Word Practice
1. product
2. produce
3. giant
4. garage
5. garbage

B VOCABULARY REVIEW

riot
ceremony
under arrest
procession
imposter

1. Someone who pretends to be somebody else is an ███████ .
2. When a police officer holds a person, the officer places that person ███████ .

Chapter 24
The Royal Seal

Tom Canty asked eager questions about the royal seal: "Is it large and round? Is it very heavy? Does it have letters on it?"

After the questions were answered, Tom said, "So that thing is the royal seal. If you had described it to me earlier, you could have had it three weeks ago. I know where the royal seal is, but I was not the one who put it there."

Tom pointed to Edward and continued, "The true king put it there, and he will tell you where it is. Then you will believe him."

Tom now spoke quietly to Edward. "Think about the day we met. Remember that you rushed out to scold the soldier when you were dressed in my rags. Now think carefully about the last thing you did before you rushed from the room. You did something with the royal seal."

A silence followed. During the silence nobody moved or whispered, and all eyes were fixed on Edward, who was frowning as he groped through his memories to recall the event. One small event, but an event so important that it could make a difference about who sat on the throne of England.

Moment after moment passed, and the moments became minutes. Still Edward struggled silently and gave no sign of remembering what had happened. At last, he said in a trembling voice, "I can remember the scene, but I can't remember anything about the seal." He paused and then continued calmly, "I cannot recall the event, so I cannot regain the throne." ♦

"Think harder!" cried Tom, looking sternly at Edward. "Do not give up!"

Suddenly, Tom had an idea. "I will describe some of the things that happened," he said to Edward. "Listen carefully to what I say, and I'm sure your memory will return. When we were in your apartment, I told you about where I lived, about my family, and about the games that my friends and I played. Do you remember?" Edward nodded his head.

Tom paused before continuing. "Now remember what happened next. You gave me something to eat and drink. You sent the servant out of the room so I would not be embarrassed over my poor manners. Do you remember that?"

Edward nodded. Tom continued with his questions as the lords and ladies listened with amazement. The story sounded true to them, but it was so impossible that they could not bring themselves to believe it. Then Tom asked Edward, "Do you remember that I had a wish to dress like a prince, and you had a dream of being as free as the other lads from Pudding Lane? So, we exchanged clothes."

Edward nodded again. "Then," Tom said, "as we stood in front of the mirror,

wearing each other's clothes, we noticed that we looked so much like each other that it was almost impossible to tell that we had switched places. You noticed the only difference—a bruise that I had received from the soldier at the gate."

"Yes, I remember," Edward replied.

"You became angry over the bruise and started toward the door of the room. You passed the table, and the seal was on that table. You picked it up and looked nervously around the room, as if you were trying to think of where to hide it. Your eye suddenly caught sight of . . . "

"That's enough, thank you," Edward said with a confident voice. He turned to Lord Saint John and said, "Inside my apartment is a suit of armor, standing next to the door. If you look inside the helmet, you will find the royal seal."

"Right, my king!" Tom exclaimed. "Now everybody will know who the true king is. Go, Lord Saint John! Go as if you had wings on your feet!"

Everybody in Westminster Abbey was standing, struck dumb with confusion. This confusion burst into a sudden, deafening buzz of conversation, which grew louder and louder until Lord Saint John returned. Then a hush fell over the crowd. Lord Saint John moved to the platform and without saying anything held the royal seal over his head. Immediately, a deafening shout went up from the audience, "Long live the true king!"

The chant went on for about five minutes. During this time, all the lords and ladies on the platform knelt in front of Edward, who was smiling broadly. At last, Tom approached the true king and said, "Now these splendid clothes belong to you."

No sooner were the words out of Tom's mouth than Hertford pointed to him and said, "Strip the clothes from that imposter and throw him in prison."

Edward said, "No! If it weren't for him I would not be recognized as the true king." Then Edward turned to Tom and asked, "Why were you able to remember where the seal was, when I couldn't remember it myself?" ★

"That was easy. I have used it on many occasions."

"Used it? How could you use it if you didn't know how it was supposed to be used?"

Tom replied, "I did not use it to mark letters."

"Then how did you use it?"

Tom blushed and looked down. Edward repeated the question. At last, Tom looked up and managed to say, "I used the seal to crack nuts."

The audience broke into thunderous laughter.

The royal robe was removed from Tom's shoulders and placed on Edward's. Then the coronation ceremony continued. While cannons thundered to announce the coronation, the crown was placed upon the new king's head, and the entire city of London rocked with applause.

• • •

We left Miles Hendon on London Bridge the night before the coronation. After escaping the riot, Miles searched for Edward. He had lost his donkey, so he had to walk through dark alleys and empty streets. But he could not find a trace of the boy. He continued his search all night and until noon the next day.

Miles threaded his way through the large crowds that were lining the streets, waiting for the coronation procession. He drifted here and there, hoping to find a sign of the boy. At last, he gave up and wandered from the city to a quiet place where he could make better plans for finding his strange, brave friend.

When Miles finally stopped to rest, he was far from the city. He stretched out on the cool ground and listened to the distant cannons that announced the crowning of the new king.

In a few moments, Miles fell asleep. When he awoke the next morning, he was stiff and cold. He washed his face in a river, drank some water, and formed a plan. He knew a lord who lived in Westminster Palace—Sir Humphry Marlow. Perhaps he could help.

Miles walked back to the gates of the palace and stood outside, hoping to find the friendly face of somebody who could carry a message to Sir Humphry. As Miles stood there, Humphry, the whipping boy, left the palace grounds. He stopped to look at Miles and said to himself, "That man looks exactly like the one King Edward has described."

Miles walked up to Humphry and asked, "Do you work inside the palace?"

"Yes, I do."

"Do you know Sir Humphry Marlow?"

Humphry knew him very well because Sir Humphry Marlow was the boy's dead father. "I know him," Humphry said.

"Is he inside?" Miles asked.

"Yes he is," Humphry replied, and then said to himself, "inside his grave."

Miles asked the boy to tell Sir Humphry Marlow that Miles Hendon wanted to see him, if that was possible. The boy agreed, and he returned to the palace at once—but not to fetch his dead father. Instead, he planned to describe Miles to Edward and find out what the king wanted to do.

D COMPREHENSION

Write the answers.

1. When Hertford was looking for the royal seal after Henry died, why hadn't Tom told him where it was?
2. When Tom was talking to Edward, why did he describe their first meeting in such detail?
3. Why did everybody laugh when Tom explained what he had used the seal for?
4. Why did Miles come to the palace?
5. How do you think Miles will feel if he sees Edward?

E WRITING

Pretend you are a newspaper reporter.

Write a story about the coronation of King Edward. Try to answer the following questions in your story:

- What was the most important thing that happened during the coronation ceremony?
- What other events happened during the ceremony?
- Where and when did the ceremony take place?
- What comments did people make about the coronation?
- Who is ruling England now?

A WORD LISTS

1
Word Endings
1. delicious
2. suspicious
3. prosperous
4. dangerous

2
Word Practice
1. gaze
2. glaze
3. desolate
4. poverty
5. ridicule
6. ridiculous

B READING

Chapter 25
Edward as King

After Humphry left, Miles sat down on a stone bench to await the boy's return. Time passed slowly, but then a group of guards approached Miles. The head guard bowed to Miles and said, "Would you please follow me inside, sir?"

Miles couldn't figure out why the guard was being so polite, but he followed him through the gates, across the great lawn, up the steps, and into the palace. Along the way, they passed splendidly dressed men and women. Miles could hear them laughing at his shabby clothes.

The guard delivered Miles to another guard, who was dressed in a bright uniform. This guard took Miles up a broad stairway, past more groups of richly dressed people, and into a huge, crowded room. Then he left Miles standing in the middle of this room.

Miles was completely confused. In front of him was the throne of England, and on the throne sat the young king, who had turned away to speak with a lord. After a few moments, the king turned his face toward Miles. The sight nearly took Miles's breath away. He stood in stunned silence, gazing at the fair young face. Without thinking, he said aloud, "He is the lord of the kingdom of dreams!" ◆

Miles quickly looked around the mag-

nificent room. "Is this a dream?" he asked himself. To test whether it was a dream, he walked to the wall, picked up a chair, brought it back, placed it on the floor in front of the king, and sat down.

Two guards shot forward and grabbed Miles, saying, "How dare you sit in the presence of the king!"

The king's face sparkled with delight. Then he raised his hand and said, "Don't touch him. He has the right to sit in my presence."

The audience became silent as Edward continued: "This man is my trusted servant, Miles Hendon. He saved my life, and for his bravery, I made him a knight. He took punishment for me in prison, and for that brave act, I made him an earl. He will have all the land and all the riches of an earl, and he may sit in my presence for the rest of his life."

The people in the audience looked with puzzled eyes—first at the king, then at this ragged figure standing before him, then back to the king. Miles shook his head and muttered to himself, "This is the boy I tried to impress with the seventy rooms of Hendon Hall."

Miles shook his head in embarrassment. "I should hide my head in a bag," he thought. A moment later, however, his manners returned to him. He rose from the chair, approached the king, and dropped to one knee before him, saying, "I am your humble servant, my king."

Then Miles rose, stepped to the side of the throne, and turned toward the audience. As he looked around, his eyes settled on two people near the back of the room: Sir Hugh Hendon and Lady Edith.

Miles pointed out the couple to the king, who instantly said, "Strip that robber of Hendon Hall and of all the other things that he has stolen! Then lock him up inside the palace until I have time to deal with him." ★

As the guards led Hugh away, Tom Canty entered the room wearing a rich outfit. He knelt before the king, and Edward said, "I have learned the story of these past weeks, and I am very pleased with you. You have ruled with intelligence and kindness, and for the rest of your life, you will be recognized as one who has been king. You will wear a special costume that nobody can copy. You will live with your mother, grandmother, and sisters in a fine cottage. And you will have the title of King's Ward. Thank you."

The proud and happy Tom rose and kissed Edward's hand. After he was led from the throne room, he wasted no time in finding his mother, grandmother, and sisters and telling them about their good fortune.

It took days for all the mysteries to be cleared up. Within a few hours, however, Miles and the king discovered why Edith had denied knowing Miles. When she had caught a glimpse of him in Hendon Hall, she had known instantly who he was. At first, she had refused to lie about not knowing Miles. But Hugh had told her that if she didn't lie, he would have Miles killed, so she pretended not to know Miles.

Hugh was sent to prison for his terrible crimes, and he died soon afterward. Then Miles married Edith and returned to Hendon Hall, where there was great rejoicing.

Tom Canty's father was never heard of again.

The king later found Yokel, the poor farmer who had been branded and sold as a slave. He gave Yokel a small farm. He also rewarded the judge who had kept him from hanging for the stolen ham, and he sent gifts to the widow and the two girls who had made breakfast for him. Finally, he sent a gift to the woman who had lost her ham.

King Edward the Sixth died when he was only fifteen, but he spent his years well. He changed many of his father's harsh laws so the poor would not suffer as much. More than once, lords tried to tell him that he was too kind and that he should keep the laws. But young Edward would answer, "What do you know about suffering? I know, and the people of England know, for I have lived among them."

D COMPREHENSION

Write the answers.
1. Why did Miles think he was dreaming when he stood in the throne room?
2. Why did Miles decide to sit in Edward's presence?
3. Why had Edith pretended not to know Miles?
4. When he was king, how did Edward help poor people in England?
5. Why did Edward know about suffering?

E WRITING

You have now read all the stories, novels, poems, articles, and other selections in your textbooks.

Study the tables of contents, then write an essay that explains which selection you liked the most. Try to answer the following questions:
- Which selection did you like the most?
- Why did you like that selection?
- Why did you prefer it to other selections?
- Which other selections did you like?
- Which selection did you dislike?

Glossary

A

abandon When you stop an activity that you started, you *abandon* that activity.

ability If you have the *ability* to do something, you are able to do that thing.

abundant If there is a lot of something, that thing is *abundant*.

agile *Agile* is another word for *nimble*.

alas *Alas* is a word you use to show you're unhappy or concerned.

alley An *alley* is a narrow street that runs behind houses.

aloft *Aloft* means "in the air."

appetite Your *appetite* is your desire for food.

armed Somebody who has a weapon is *armed*.

article of clothing An *article of clothing* is a piece of clothing.

assist When you help somebody, you *assist* that person.

astonishment *Astonishment* is another word for *amazement*.

athlete An *athlete* is a person who competes in sporting events.

B

balk After a baseball pitcher winds up, the pitcher is supposed to throw the ball to the catcher. If the pitcher does anything else, the pitcher *balks*, and all players who are on base can advance one base.

band *Band* is another word for *group*.

bankrupt When you lose all your money, you are *bankrupt*.

barge A *barge* is a large, flat boat that travels on rivers.

betray You *betray* somebody by pretending to be that person's friend and then tricking that person.

biography The true story of somebody's life is called a *biography*.

blurred Things that do not look clear are *blurred*.

bold When you are *bold*, you are confident.

bound When a person is *bound*, that person is tied up.

brand When you *brand* an animal, you make a mark on the animal with a hot piece of iron.

brawl A *brawl* is a rough fight.

burly *Burly* is another way of saying *stout and strong*.

butler A *butler* is a male servant who is in charge of other servants.

C

calculate When you *calculate*, you figure out.

calf A *calf* is a cow or a bull that is not full-grown.

capable If you are able to do something, you are *capable* of doing that thing.

career A person's *career* is that person's main job.

carve When you *carve* wood, you shape the wood by cutting it.

cattle Cows and bulls are *cattle*.

ceremony A *ceremony* is an important event that always takes place in the same way.

chandelier A *chandelier* is a fancy light with many ornaments.

chant When you say the same thing over and over, you *chant* that thing.

chariot A *chariot* is a two-wheeled cart drawn by horses.

charred Wood that is badly burned is *charred* wood.

clothesline A *clothesline* is a thin rope you hang wet clothes on to dry.

complain When you *complain*, you say you don't like something.

conceal When you *conceal* something, you hide it.

conduct When you *conduct*, you lead.

confess When people *confess*, they tell the truth about a secret.

confine When you are *confined* to a place, you cannot leave that place.

conquer When you *conquer* something, you gain control over it.

contract A *contract* is a written agreement.

convince When you make somebody believe something, you *convince* the person that what you're saying is true.

coronation A *coronation* is an important event in which the crown is placed on the head of a new king or queen.

cousin The child of your aunt or your uncle is your *cousin*.

craft *Craft* is another word for *boat*.

cultivate When you *cultivate* a field, you get rid of the weeds and break up the soil so you can plant crops.

daily If you do something every day, you do it *daily*.

daring When you are *daring*, you take chances.

deathbed People who are on their *deathbeds* are dying.

decent Another word for *good* is *decent*.

defeat When you *defeat* somebody, you win a victory over that person.

deity A *deity* is a god or a goddess.

deny When you say that something is not true, you *deny* that thing.

deserve When you *deserve* something, you are worthy of that thing.

desolate Something that is *desolate* is barren, gloomy, and uninhabited.

despair When you feel no hope, you feel *despair*.

despite *Despite* means "in spite of."

diaper *Diaper* is a soft fabric that is used for napkins and towels.

dignity When somebody acts with confidence and good manners, that person acts with *dignity*.

dimple A *dimple* is a little dent in a person's cheek or chin.

disagreeable *Disagreeable* is the opposite of *agreeable*.

discontented When you are *discontented*, you are dissatisfied.

dismiss When you *dismiss* somebody, you tell that person to leave.

distressed *Distressed* is another word for *troubled*.

draped Something that is *draped* hangs down from something else.

dread When you *dread* doing something, you don't look forward to doing it.

drowsy *Drowsy* is another word for *sleepy.*

dugout The *dugout* is the place where baseball players sit when they wait for their turn at bat.

duties Your *duties* are the things you must do.

E

envy When you *envy* people, you wish you had something they have.

evidence Facts that make you conclude something are *evidence.*

eye When you *eye* something, you study it with your eyes.

F

fascinated When you are *fascinated* with something, you are interested and delighted by that thing.

fathom A *fathom* is a unit of length that equals six feet.

fertile *Fertile* land is land that is capable of growing good crops.

file A *file* is a line.

filth *Filth* is another way of saying *garbage and dirt.*

fined When you are *fined* for breaking the law, you must pay a certain amount of money.

flogged When somebody is beaten with a whip, that person is *flogged.*

foreman A *foreman* is a boss.

foul *Foul* is another way of saying *very bad.*

fragrance A pleasant smell is a *fragrance.*

frenzy When you do things in a *frenzy,* you do them in a hurried and excited way.

G

gagged When a person is *gagged,* the person's mouth is covered and he or she cannot talk.

garment *Garment* is another way of saying *article of clothing.*

gasp When you catch your breath loudly, you *gasp.*

gifted Somebody who has a lot of ability is *gifted.*

gleam *Gleam* is another word for *shine.*

glossy When something is *glossy,* it is smooth and shiny.

gossip When you *gossip* about something, you spread rumors about that thing.

grave One meaning of *grave* is serious.

greedy When you are *greedy,* you are never satisfied with how much you have.

grief *Grief* is another way of saying *great sorrow.*

grope When you feel your way in the dark, you *grope.*

H

harbor A *harbor* is a place where ships tie up.

hardware Hammers, nails, knives, and other objects made of metal are called *hardware.*

hasty *Hasty* is another word for *quick.*

hither *Hither* means "to this place."

honor An *honor* is an award you receive for good work.

hospitable When you treat guests kindly, you are *hospitable* to them.

hospitality When you show *hospitality* to somebody, you are very kind to that person.

hue *Hue* is another word for *color.*

humble *Humble* is the opposite of *proud and conceited.*

humorous *Humorous* is another word for *funny.*

hustle When you *hustle,* you move very fast.

identical Things that are *identical* are the same in every way.

ignorant If a person is *ignorant,* that person does not understand things.

imposter Someone who pretends to be somebody else is an *imposter.*

in disguise When you are *in disguise,* you are dressed so that nobody can recognize you.

infant An *infant* is a newborn child.

inform When you give people information about something, you *inform* them about that thing.

inhabitant Somebody who lives in a place is an *inhabitant* of that place.

inhale When you *inhale,* you breathe in.

inn An *inn* is a small hotel that serves meals and has rooms where people stay.

innocent Someone who is not guilty of doing something wrong is *innocent.*

insane *Insane* is another word for *crazy.*

inspect When you *inspect* something, you look at it closely.

insult An *insult* is a name or a gesture that is supposed to make you mad.

intend If you plan to do something, you *intend* to do that thing.

interview When a reporter conducts an *interview,* the reporter asks somebody questions.

invest When you *invest* in a deal, you put money into the deal and try to make a profit.

irritable When you are *irritable,* you are grouchy.

lash *Lash* is another word for *whip.*

lecture When somebody gives a *lecture,* he or she talks to a group of people about a particular subject.

limb A *limb* is an arm or a leg.

linen *Linen* is an expensive cloth that some sheets and clothes are made of.

long for When you *long for* something, you really want that thing.

long jump When athletes compete in a *long jump,* they run up to a line and then jump as far as they can.

lumbering When you walk with heavy steps, you are *lumbering.*

mad *Mad* is another word for *insane.*

major leagues The *major leagues* are the professional baseball leagues with the best players.

mechanic A *mechanic* is a person who fixes automobiles and other machines.

merciful The opposite of *cruel* is *merciful.*

miraculous When something is *miraculous,* it is like a miracle.

misplaced If you don't remember where you put something, you have *misplaced* that thing.

mistreat When something is treated poorly, that thing is *mistreated*.

motley Something that is made up of many different types of things is called *motley*.

mourn When you *mourn* the death of a person, you show that you are sad about the person's death.

N

narrator A person who tells a story is called a *narrator*.

National League pennant Each year, the National League baseball team that wins the playoffs wins the *National League pennant*.

nimble *Nimble* is the opposite of *awkward*.

O

occupied When you are *occupied* with something, you are busy with that thing.

officer An *officer* in the military is a person who is in charge of soldiers.

official When something is *official*, it is the real thing.

opportunity When you have a chance to do something, you have an *opportunity* to do that thing.

oppose When you're against an idea, you *oppose* that idea.

optimistic When you are *optimistic*, you look on the good side of things.

ordeal An *ordeal* is an extremely difficult experience.

organization Another word for *business* is *organization*.

original If something is not a copy of anything else, it is an *original*.

overcast When the sky is gray and cloudy, the sky is *overcast*.

P

page A *page* is a young boy who serves a royal person.

pantry A *pantry* is a room where food is stored.

parlor A *parlor* is a living room or a small sitting room.

patrician A *patrician* is a lord, a lady, or a member of the Royal Family.

pauper *Paupers* are people who have no money.

pearly When something is *pearly*, it is like a pearl.

peddler A *peddler* is a person who goes down the street with something to sell.

penalty A *penalty* is the punishment somebody receives for breaking the rules.

persuade *Persuade* is another word for *convince*.

pester *Pester* is another word for *annoy*.

pity *Pity* is another word for *sorrow*.

plant Another word for *factory* is *plant*.

plumbing The pipes and fixtures that bring water into a building are called *plumbing*.

plump When something is *plump*, it is a little bit fat and round.

portrait A painting of somebody is a *portrait* of that person.

pose When you *pose*, you try to look very attractive.

poverty *Poverty* is the state of being poor.

priest A *priest* is an important man who works in a church.

prince A *prince* is the son of a king or a queen.

prison cell A *prison cell* is a small room that prisoners live in.

procession A *procession* is a line of people that moves from one place to another.

profit A *profit* is the extra money you make from a business.

promoted When you are *promoted*, you get a more important job.

properly When you do things *properly*, you do them in the right way.

prosper When you *prosper*, you earn money and do well.

Q

quarterback A *quarterback* is the player who directs a football team when the team has the football.

R

rattled A person who is *rattled* feels nervous.

reel *Reel* is another word for *stagger*.

refuse When you *refuse* an offer, you say "no" to the offer.

regain your senses When you *regain your senses*, you regain the power to think clearly.

regret When you are sorry about something that happened, you *regret* that thing.

resident A *resident* is a person who lives in a place.

restricted to *Restricted to* means "limited to."

retire When you have worked a long time and then stop working, you *retire* from work.

retreat When you *retreat*, you move backwards.

riot A *riot* is a large fight that involves a mob.

rookie A baseball player who is playing in his or her first year is called a *rookie*.

rose water *Rose water* is a kind of perfume made with water and roses.

rude The opposite of *polite* is *rude*.

ruffian A *ruffian* is a rude and rough person.

ruler A *ruler* is a person who is in charge of a country.

run a risk When you take a chance that may be dangerous, you *run a risk*.

S

salute When you *salute*, you make a gesture that shows respect.

saucer A *saucer* is a little plate that is placed under a cup.

schedule When you *schedule* something, you figure out where and when it will be.

scout A *scout* for a baseball team goes to colleges and other places to find players the team might hire.

scurry *Scurry* is another word for *scamper*.

seal A *seal* is a tool that puts a special mark on a piece of paper.

seaman A *seaman* is a sailor.

secure *Secure* is another word for *safe*.

selfish *Selfish* people are only concerned about themselves.

shattered When something is broken into many pieces, it is *shattered*.

shawl A *shawl* is piece of cloth you hang over your shoulders.

shrewd *Shrewd* is another word for *smart*.

shudder *Shudder* is another word for *shiver*.

sift *Sift* is another word for *fall through*.

sling A *sling* is a loop of cloth you put your arm in when it's injured.

slum A *slum* is a poor, crowded neighborhood with run-down houses and buildings.

slumber *Slumber* is another word for *sleep*.

smuggle When you *smuggle* something, you hide it and take it to some place.

sole A *sole* is the bottom part of your feet or of your shoes.

soothe *Soothe* is another word for *relax*.

spacious Something that has a lot of space in it is *spacious*.

spectacular When something is *spectacular*, it is very impressive.

spell A *spell* is a magic charm.

staff A *staff* is a long stick that you carry.

steal a base When a baseball player *steals a base*, the player runs to the next base before the batter hits the ball.

stocks The *stocks* is a device used for torturing prisoners.

stout Something that is thick and sturdy is *stout*.

stricken When you are struck by a powerful emotion, you are *stricken* by that emotion.

stubborn When you are *stubborn*, you do not change your behavior, no matter what happens.

subtle Something that is *subtle* is hard to see or understand.

suburbs The *suburbs* are the small cities and towns that surround a large city.

supervisor A *supervisor* is a boss.

suspicious When you are *suspicious* about something, you don't really believe that it is true.

sympathy When you show *sympathy* toward somebody, you share that person's feelings.

T

take advantage When a person is helpless and you make them do what you want, you *take advantage* of that person.

talented If a person has a lot of skill, that person is *talented*.

tattered When something is *tattered*, it is torn and shredded.

terrify *Terrify* is another way of saying *greatly frighten*.

toil When you *toil*, you work very hard.

toils A *toils* is a trap.

torment When you *torment* someone, you tease and annoy that person.

trace of When there is no *trace of* a person, there is no clue that the person is around.

trade When you *trade* with someone, you give them something and they give you something.

tragic Something that is very sad is *tragic*.

trance When you have a daydream or get lost in thought, you go into a *trance*.

trust appearances When you *trust appearances*, you believe in the way that things look, not in the way they are.

U

under arrest When a person is *under arrest*, that person is held by the police or other officers of the law.

unleash When you *unleash* something, you let it run free.

V

vagrant A *vagrant* is a person who does not have a place to live and has no job.

vast Something that is very large is *vast*.

victim A *victim* is somebody who is harmed.

W

wages The money that you earn when you work for somebody is called your *wages*.

wand A *wand* is a small staff that is decorated.

ward Some cities are divided into sections called *wards*.

weary When you are *weary*, you are very tired.

widow A *widow* is a woman whose husband is dead.

wisdom Great knowledge is *wisdom*.

withdraw When you take something back, you *withdraw* that thing.

witty *Witty* is another word for *funny*.

LESSON 66

2. a. Lion
   b. Dorothy
3. a. Gold
   b. Yukon River
4. a. Factual
   b. Fictional
5. a. Carrying things
   b. Food

6. a. Scarlet tanager
   b. Salmon
7. a. Buck
   b. Toto
8. a. Steeplechase
   b. Liverpool
9. a. Wild
   b. Domestic

10. a. Tiger
    b. Galápagos tortoise
11. a. Land of the North
    b. Land of the South
12. a. Jackie Robinson
    b. Brooklyn Dodgers